I0804720

Certifying China

Earth System Governance

Frank Biermann and Oran R. Young, series editors

Oran R. Young, *Institutional Dynamics: Emergent Patterns in International Environmental Governance*

Frank Biermann and Philipp Pattberg, eds., *Global Environmental Governance Reconsidered*

Olav Schram Stokke, *Disaggregating International Regimes: A New Approach to Evaluation and Comparison*

Aarti Gupta and Michael Mason, eds., *Transparency in Global Environmental Governance: Critical Perspectives*

Sikina Jinnah, *Post-Treaty Politics: Secretariat Influence in Global Environmental Governance*

Frank Biermann, *Earth System Governance: World Politics in the Anthropocene*

Walter F. Baber and Robert B. Bartlett, *Consensus in Global Environmental Governance: Deliberative Democracy in Nature's Regime*

Diarmuid Torney, *European Climate Leadership in Question: Policies toward China and India*

David Ciplet, J. Timmons Roberts, and Mizan R. Khan, *Power in a Warming World: The New Global Politics of Climate Change and the Remaking of Environmental Inequality*

Simon Nicholson and Sikina Jinnah, eds., *New Earth Politics: Essays from the Anthropocene*

Norichika Kanie and Frank Biermann, eds., *Governing through Goals: Sustainable Development Goals as Governance Innovation*

Oran R. Young, *Governing Complex Systems: Social Capital for the Anthropocene*

Susan Park and Teresa Kramarz, eds., *Global Environmental Governance and the Accountability Trap*

Teresa Kramarz, *Forgotten Values: The World Bank and Its Partnerships for the Environment*

Lena Partzsch, *Alternatives to Multilateralism: New Forms of Social and Environmental Governance*

Katharina Rietig, *Learning in Governance: Climate Policy Integration in the European Union*

Yixian Sun, *Certifying China: The Rise and Limits of Transnational Sustainability Governance in Emerging Economies*

Related books from Institutional Dimensions of Global Environmental Change: A Core Research Project of the International Human Dimensions Programme on Global Environmental Change

Oran R. Young, Leslie A. King, and Heike Schroeder, eds., *Institutions and Environmental Change: Principal Findings, Applications, and Research Frontiers*

Frank Biermann and Bernd Siebenhüner, eds., *Managers of Global Change: The Influence of International Environmental Bureaucracies*

Sebastian Oberthür and Olav Schram Stokke, eds., *Managing Institutional Complexity: Regime Interplay and Global Environmental Change*

Certifying China

The Rise and Limits of Transnational Sustainability Governance in Emerging Economies

Yixian Sun

The MIT Press
Cambridge, Massachusetts
London, England

Published with the support of the Swiss National Science Foundation.

The MIT Press would like to thank the anonymous peer reviewers who provided comments on drafts of this book. The generous work of academic experts is essential for establishing the authority and quality of our publications. We acknowledge with gratitude the contributions of these otherwise uncredited readers.

This book was set in Stone Serif and Stone Sans by Westchester Publishing Services. Printed and bound in the United States of America.

Library of Congress Cataloging-in-Publication Data

Names: Sun, Yixian (Lecturer in international development), author.
Title: Certifying China : the rise and limits of transnational sustainability governance in emerging economies / Yixian Sun.
Description: Cambridge, Massachusetts : The MIT Press, [2022] | Series: Earth system governance | Includes bibliographical references and index.
Identifiers: LCCN 2021023061 | ISBN 9780262543699 (paperback)
Subjects: LCSH: Agricultural industries—Certification—China. | Agricultural industries—Environmental aspects—China. | Sustainable agriculture—Certification—China. | Business logistics—Environmental aspects—China. | Social responsibility of business—China. | Transnationalism.
Classification: LCC HD9016.C62 S7997 2022 | DDC 338.1/85151—dc23
LC record available at https://lccn.loc.gov/2021023061

10 9 8 7 6 5 4 3 2 1

To my beloved Guang
this be given

Contents

Series Foreword

Humans now influence all biological and physical systems of the planet. Almost no species, land area, or part of the oceans has remained unaffected by the expansion of the human species. Recent scientific findings suggest that the entire Earth system now operates outside the normal state exhibited over at least the past 500,000 years. Yet at the same time, it is apparent that the institutions, organizations, and mechanisms by which humans govern their relationship with the natural environment and global biogeochemical systems are utterly insufficient—and poorly understood. More fundamental and applied research is needed.

Such research is no easy undertaking. It must span the entire globe, because only integrated global solutions can ensure a sustainable coevolution of biophysical and socioeconomic systems. But it must also draw on local experiences and insights. Research on Earth system governance must be about places in all their diversity, yet seek to integrate place-based research within a global understanding of the myriad human interactions with the Earth system. Eventually, the task is to develop integrated systems of governance, from the local to the global level, that ensure the sustainable development of the coupled socioecological system that the Earth has become.

The series Earth System Governance is designed to address this research challenge. Books in this series will pursue this challenge from a variety of disciplinary perspectives, at different levels of governance, and with a range of methods. Yet all will further one common aim: analyzing current systems of Earth system governance with a view to increased understanding and possible improvements and reform. Books in this series will be of interest to the academic community but will also inform practitioners and at times contribute to policy debates.

This series is related to the long-term international research program "Earth System Governance Project."

Frank Biermann, Copernicus Institute of Sustainable Development, Utrecht University

Oran R. Young, Bren School, University of California, Santa Barbara
Earth System Governance Series Editors

Acknowledgments

Since I left China for graduate school 10 years ago to study international relations, I keep pondering how the world understands my home country and how China can contribute to global common goods. Hence, my initial motivation for this research is to understand China's interaction with the rest of the world. From the very beginning, I decided to focus on environmental sustainability, as I believe this is the most critical challenge that our world faces in the twenty-first century. I have found a strong interest in governance at the transnational level gradually building, in which China's involvement should be important but has yet to receive sufficient scholarly attention.

But finishing this book has been a long journey filled with joy and frustration. I am lucky to have not been alone in this effort. I am tremendously indebted to several mentors who have guided me through this intellectual adventure. Liliana Andonova, my doctoral supervisor and the person who brought me to the field of environmental politics and transnational governance, deserves special thanks for her advice and long-standing support during and after my PhD. She consistently encourages me to think broadly and analyze rigorously. I cannot describe in words how much I have gained from her mentorship. I also owe a debt of gratitude to Thomas Hale for serving as my thesis co-supervisor and having provided critical comments. Tom always reminds me to think about the big picture question on China's role in this changing world, and his comments helped me significantly improve this work. Ben Cashore is another mentor that I thank for his support of this project and suggestions on how to refine my argument. It was my honor to be Ben's postdoc, although for a relatively short time, and to learn from him how to become an outstanding and generous scholar.

This work would also be not possible without the suggestions and help of many other great scholars. My gratitude goes first to the Earth System Governance Series editors Frank Biermann and Oran Young. Their encouragement and support have been indispensable for me to turn my doctoral thesis into a book. I am also thankful to Stacy VanDeveer, D. G. Webster, and Peter Haas for their participation in my book workshop in New Haven and their very helpful comments on an early version of the manuscript. The book would not be in its current form without those comments. During my PhD, Graeme Auld and Jonas Pontusson gave kind suggestions on the design of this project, and James Hollway and Jörg Balsiger as my committee members also provided useful comments. This work has greatly benefited from conversations and exchanges with several collaborators and also friends, who not only generously shared their thoughts and experiences but also gave important moral support to me to carry on this project. They include Michael Bloomfield, Lukas Fesenfeld, Janina Grabs, Philip Schleifer, and Hamish van der Ven. Hamish and Michael also provided with me useful tips on book writing and publication.

Moreover, I thank the Swiss National Science Foundation for their generous financial support for the research of this book through the Doc.CH grant as well as their Early Postdoc.Mobility fellowship for giving me a peaceful time to prepare the manuscript. I have finished the research for this book while being affiliated with the Centre for International Environmental Studies (CIES) at the Graduate Institute of International and Development Studies. I benefited from the interdisciplinary environment at CIES and from inspiring discussions with its staff and associates. During my postdoc at Yale, this project received additional support from the Governance, Environment, and Markets Initiative (GEM) in the erstwhile School of Forestry and Environmental Studies. I am especially grateful to Nora Moraga-Lewy and Evelin Toth for their research assistance. I finished the final revisions of the manuscript at the University of Bath, where I have found a new home in the Department of Social and Policy Sciences and the International Development group. My colleagues at Bath have given me the warmest welcome. My head of department Joe Devine and my mentor Roy Maconachie have helped me complete a smooth transition to a tenure-track position.

At several points, I found this research project to be an impossible mission. Fortunately, it turned out to be possible with the kind support of many people I met during my fieldwork. I am tremendously grateful to all practitioners who accepted my interview requests. Many of them, especially those working for Chinese organizations, had little knowledge about or experience with academic research, but they all spent precious time to help me as much as they could. Special thanks to Xiao Qiang at the Tea Research Institute of Chinese Academy of Agricultural Sciences, who introduced me to a range of stakeholders in China's tea industry, and also thanks to Sophia Lin and James Gu for sharing their contacts for stakeholders in China's seafood and palm oil sectors. I also appreciate my friends Tim Fang and Zhengxiang Jiang for having hosted me during my research stays in Beijing.

This journey does not only consist of research efforts, but also of life experiences in the past 7 years in four countries and three continents. Therefore, I thank many friends that I have made in Geneva, New Haven, Bath, and China as well as through the *Earth Negotiations Bulletin* for sharing happiness and anxieties in life, work, and hobbies. I cannot list all names here, but I express my sincere gratitude for your company in the past. Carse Ramos deserves special thanks for reading much of my work and providing careful editorial suggestions.

I have been very pleased to work with Beth Clevenger at the MIT Press. I thank Beth for her continuous support and patience. Two anonymous reviewers provided kind and thoughtful suggestions, which helped me improve the final manuscript.

This book is dedicated to my family. I thank my mom for always being supportive in every way of my intellectual endeavors. I am indebted to my maternal grandparents with whom I grew up, as they allowed me to be extremely curious and helped me develop critical thinking skills from the beginning. I am also thankful to my parents-in-law for their understanding.

My progress in this journey would have been impossible without the support of my love, Guang Yang. As my partner and my best friend, she always challenges me to think more critically and encourages me to step out of my comfort zone. She has the magical power to make our life beautiful. I feel blessed for having my beloved Guang accompany me on this journey.

This journey has made me realize that all human endeavors for understanding and changing our world are endless. So, this is not the end but just a new beginning.

List of Abbreviations

ACFSMC	All-China Federation of Supply and Marketing Cooperatives
ASC	Aquaculture Stewardship Council
BAP	Best Aquaculture Practices
CAPPMA	China Aquatic Products Processing and Marketing Alliance
CCFA	China Chain Store and Franchise Association
CFNA	China Chamber of Commerce for Import and Export of Foodstuffs, Native Produce and Animal By-Products
CIED	Chinese Industrial Enterprise Database
CNCA	Certification and Accreditation Administration of the People's Republic of China
COFCO	China National Cereals, Oils and Foodstuffs Corporation
CSR	Corporate social responsibility
CTMA	China Tea Marketing Association
DFID	Department for International Development of the United Kingdom
FAO	Food and Agriculture Organization of the United Nations
FOS	Friend of the Sea
FSC	Forest Stewardship Council
GAA	Global Aquaculture Alliance
GAP	Good Agricultural Practices
ISO	International Organization for Standardization
MOFCOM	Ministry of Commerce of the People's Republic of China
MoU	Memorandum of Understanding
MSC	Marine Stewardship Council
NGO	Nongovernment organization
NSMD	Non-state market-driven

OTPS	Organic Tea Producer Survey
RA	Rainforest Alliance
RSPO	Roundtable on Sustainable Palm Oil
RTRS	Roundtable on Responsible Soy
SOE	State-owned enterprise
WWF	World Wide Fund for Nature

1 Introduction: Eco-Certification and Emerging Economies

In the early 1990s, Mr. H, who was in his thirties at that time, was already the general manager of a state-owned tea company in the Jiangxi province of China. However, he was struggling to find customers for tea produced in his county, Wuyuan—which had been famous for its green tea for more than 1,000 years—in a free and open market after the government had ceased to control the product price and distribution. He had tried a variety of strategies, including building connections with retailers in Shanghai and Beijing, developing different types of tea products, and applying for a government award of green food. Unfortunately, even after several years, all such efforts did not increase his sales. Finally, with the support of the China Green Food Development Center, affiliated with the Chinese Ministry of Agriculture, he participated in an international expo and met representatives from a German trading company. These German merchants indicated that they would be interested in Mr. H's products if his tea had the organic certification recognized by the European market. Mr. H soon sensed opportunities through this encounter and invited the German company for a visit to Wuyuan. In August 1997, the company and its partner certifier visited the tea farms supplying Mr. H and were satisfied by the conditions they found there. After conducting an evaluation, the auditors believed that these farms met the relevant organic standards, so the German company decided to place an order for 200 kilograms of tea with Mr. H.

Twenty years later, in 2017, when telling me about his first experience with certification, Mr. H proudly stated that by selling only organic and Fairtrade tea certified according to international standards, his company has been able to export more than 1,000 metric tons of products per year, which represents more than half of China's organic tea exports to Europe. He emphasized that organic and Fairtrade certifications have completely changed his business trajectory and that he is personally so committed to the vision of sustainable production championed by these certification programs that he continues this practice even though this is costly.

The story of Mr. H is a telling example of how eco-certification has been taken up and understood by Chinese businesses.[1] Yet his experience may sound unusual to many of his peer companies, who barely recognize various certification programs and do not understand their required standards. In fact, sustainability certification and labels remain new to the Chinese market. About 10 years ago, when I left China to study in Switzerland, I heard the term "certified sustainable timber" for the first time and saw the "tick tree" logo of the Forest Stewardship Council, which was a common sight in European supermarkets for anyone paying attention to product packaging. Since then, every time that I go back to my hometown, Nanjing, I have tried to find the ecolabels that I had seen in Europe while grocery shopping. In the beginning, I was quite disappointed and wondered why these labels "disappeared" in China. But after a few years, I was finally able to find some familiar logos in supermarkets, coffee shops, and even on e-commerce platforms. Obviously, not all companies operating in China have embraced these programs initiated and managed by non-state actors, and certified products are likely to be more common in certain sectors than in others. But there is no doubt that some changes have happened in China regarding this novel mode of governance.[2] This book seeks to explain how such changes happened in China and the variation across different sectors and companies in their support for eco-certification. By showing the conditions under which transnational eco-certification arise in the unique context of China, the book will shed light on the potential and limits of this new governance mode in driving the world's most populous country toward sustainable production and consumption.

* * *

Over the past two decades, non-state actors, including both businesses and civil society organizations, have launched various initiatives operating across national borders to address urgent sustainability challenges, such as environmental degradation, climate change, and labor rights violations (Auld, Bernstein, and Cashore 2008; Dauvergne and Lister 2013; Bulkeley et al. 2014). Being conceptualized as "transnational governance," this phenomenon denotes "the processes in which non-state actors adopt rules that seek to move behavior toward a shared, public goal in at least two states"

(Roger and Dauvergne 2016: 416).[3] Among many transnational governance initiatives, eco-certification has been seen as one of the most prominent modes for embedding environmental and social norms in global markets (Raynolds 2000; Bernstein and Cashore 2007). Its potential lies in the assumption that demand along the supply chain can drive businesses to adopt good practices for social, environmental, and economic sustainability. In fact, with the rise of global value chains where the full range of activities that bring a product from its conception to its end use are carried out on a global scale, individual states face enormous challenges in regulating sustainability impacts of many economic activities (Gereffi, Humphrey, and Sturgeon 2005; Gibbon, Bair, and Ponte 2008). Therefore, by incentivizing firms' compliance, eco-certification holds the promise to significantly improve governance in global value chains. Based on this premise, certification has been applied quickly in various sectors and also widely studied in the literature on environmental governance and sustainable development.

Our generation has witnessed a dramatic rise of eco-certification in global sustainability governance. For commodities like coffee, cocoa, and even tea, eco-certification now regulates more than 20% of the global production volume, and therefore, no longer seems like a new phenomenon in niche markets (Willer et al. 2019). Today, consumers in Europe and North America can easily find labels indicating that products are from organic farms, sustainable forests and fisheries, or fair trade cooperatives. Moreover, although most of the existing certification programs originate from developed countries, over the past decade, many have expanded their geographic reach, trying to promote sustainable production and consumption in developing countries and emerging economies. For instance, as of 2015, Rainforest Alliance, a leading certification program for sustainable agriculture, had been introduced to tea farmers in 18 countries, and the tea produced on its certified farms was sold in 125 countries (Milder and Newsom 2015). Similarly, as of March 2017, the Marine Stewardship Council's standards had been adopted by over 300 fisheries in 34 countries and by processors and retailers in 94 countries (MSC 2017b).

However, despite efforts made by certification programs to increase their global presence, in many sectors, progress on the market uptake of certified products remains slow. To date, only 1.5% of the area on which soybeans are planted globally is compliant with at least one certification standard, and the percentages are estimated to be less than 10% for bananas, farmed fish, and sugarcane (Potts et al. 2016; Willer et al. 2019). Meanwhile, the growth of eco-certification is uneven across regions such that sustainable production practices may not be adopted in the places where they are most needed. As an example, most of the farmed fish in the world is produced and consumed in developing countries with weak regulations on environmental and social issues; yet sustainable seafood standards have been rarely used in these countries (Bailey et al. 2018; Belton, Bush, and Little 2018).

The limited use of eco-certification around the world poses a key challenge to this new mode of sustainability governance. With insufficient market share, eco-certification is incapable of generating considerable environmental and social benefits. The assumption here is that if certification programs set credible and rigorous standards, the widespread adoption of their standards is likely to drive dramatic change in business practices throughout global supply chains, which could contribute to maintaining sustainability of the Earth system.[4] Hence, to make this new governance mode more effective, we must investigate the challenges it faces in gaining market share around the world.

Why, despite more than 10 years of growth, have many eco-certification programs still not become mainstream in their markets? Many researchers have addressed this question by uncovering the barriers preventing actors in the Global South from adopting relevant standards, which include the difficulty of Southern producers—especially smallholders—to change practices (Klooster 2006; Marschke and Wilkings 2014; Brandi et al. 2015), insufficient financial incentives and technical support (Cashore et al. 2006; Loconto and Dankers 2014), and domestic rules, institutions, and even political cultures that run counter to transnational governance (Bartley 2010; Andonova 2014; Peña 2016). Moreover, rising consumption in the Global South over the past decade or so has further increased concerns about the prospects of eco-certification to lead sustainability transformations in global markets (Mayer and Gereffi 2010; Nadvi 2014). In fact, some preliminary evidence shows that large emerging economies, such as China and India, have become major end markets for many commodities but still lack consumer demand for sustainable products (Kaplinsky, Terheggen, and Tijaja 2011; Schleifer 2016). Thus, the extent to which these countries embrace sustainability governance in global value chains seems to determine the overall impact of the relevant programs. In other words, to become an effective governance mode to support the sustainable development of human society, eco-certification needs to gain enough traction in large emerging economies (ISEAL Alliance 2015).[5]

While emerging economies have become increasingly important for almost all eco-certification programs, the literature on sustainability governance has paid insufficient attention to the dynamics in this part of the world. This may be because early studies tend to explore why nonstate actors developed governance systems without state enforcement and because most certification programs were created first in the Global North or by Northern-based stakeholders (Vogel 2008; Hale 2020). As a result, to date, we still know little about whether and through which mechanisms transnational governance is taken up in emerging economies.

This research gap is especially astonishing in the case of China, a country that is now at the center of global value chains by being the world's largest producer and consumer of many products (Gereffi 2014). Table 1.1 lists China's position in the global supply chains of several commodities that are targeted by eco-certification. The figures are significant: in 2015, China produced, by volume, over 62% of the aquaculture and 40% of the tea in the world; it was also the world's largest consumer of soybeans (29%) and third largest consumer of palm oil (10%).[6] These numbers suggest that production and consumption in China have significant impacts on the environment and people, both inside and outside of the country, causing deforestation, depletion of fisheries, soil and water pollution, and antibiotics resistance (Liu and Diamond 2005; Hao et al. 2016; He et al. 2018). Therefore, the choices that government officials, businesses, and consumers in China are making on sustainability issues not only influence the health and well-being of the country but also "the very future of the planet" (Shapiro 2016: 2). If certification programs thrive in China with standards that are carefully designed and implemented, they could help the world's most populous country continue its development without harming the ecosystems on Earth.

When considering China's engagement with global sustainability governance, researchers have pointed out both challenges and progress. On one hand, many have worried that China's rapid development poses significant challenges to protecting our planet (e.g., Liu and Raven 2010; Economy and Levi 2014). For a very long time, the country has prioritized economic growth over environmental protection and social equity; more recently, its expanding resource quest around the world has generated many negative

Table 1.1
China in global commodity chains and the relevant eco-certification programs

Commodity	China's position in global supply chains	Leading transnational governance programs	Year certification started in China
Banana	Second largest producer (9%); second largest consumer (13%); fourth largest importer (6%)	Rainforest Alliance Fairtrade International	Not yet Not yet
Cotton	Second largest producer (23%); largest consumer (31%); third largest importer (13%)	Better Cotton Initiative	2011
Palm oil	Third largest consumer (10%); second largest importer (13%)	Roundtable on Sustainable Palm Oil	2011
Roundwood	Third largest producer (9%); second largest consumer (11%); largest importer (37%)	Forest Stewardship Council Programme for the Endorsement of Forest Certification	2001 2007
Seafood	Largest producer (18% for wild catch and 62% for aquaculture); largest consumer (37%); largest exporter (14%); largest importer (6%)	Marine Stewardship Council Global Aquaculture Alliance's Best Aquaculture Practices Aquaculture Stewardship Council Friend of the Sea	2005 for processors and 2014 for fisheries 2006 2015 Not yet
Soybean	Fourth largest producer (4%); largest consumer (29%) and the largest importer (62%)	Roundtable on Responsible Soy	2013
Sugarcane	Fourth largest producer (6%); second largest consumer (9%); largest importer (10%)	Bonsucro	Not yet
Tea	Largest producer (38%); largest consumer (33%); second largest exporter (19%)	Rainforest Alliance UTZ Fairtrade International	2007 2014 2001

Notes: Percentages in parentheses indicate the proportion of China's production, consumption, or trade volume over the global total as of 2015. The European Union does not count as a single economy. Organic certification is excluded from the table, as different countries or regions have their own schemes subject to public regulation.
Data sources: FAO 2018a, 2018b, 2018c.

impacts on the global environment. Researchers with this concern often attribute the limits of environmental governance in China to the country's decentralized, authoritarian political system, arguing that it causes a lack of transparency, official accountability, and rule of law in the relevant policy processes (Economy 2010, 2014). One of the most frequently cited issues in this respect is the Chinese state's control over civil society, which has prevented citizens from actively participating in sustainability governance. This institutional feature may have huge implications for eco-certification programs, as many of them were developed by NGOs and became prominent in their markets through activist campaigns targeting businesses (Bartley 2003; Sasser et al. 2006; Bloomfield 2017a). From this perspective, the permissive socio-political environment for the rise of private governance in the West may simply not exist in China. If this is the case, eco-certification programs led by non-state actors will be limited in their ability to operate in China and gain support of local stakeholders.

On the other hand, scholars of environmental politics have suggested that China has been gradually transforming into a global leader in the fight to save the planet by driving a global clean energy revolution, phasing out coal consumption, controlling pollution, and developing a system of green finance (Finamore 2018). In fact, over the past decade, Beijing has taken many strong steps toward protecting the environment and promoting sustainable development. Progress has been especially noticeable in the development of the clean energy industry (Lewis 2013; Gallagher 2014). In 2014, the central government launched a "war on pollution" by leveraging a range of policy tools throughout the country, including administrative controls, strict regulations, economic incentives, and public campaigns (Wong and Karplus 2017). More fundamentally, the concept of "ecological civilization" has been strongly endorsed by Xi Jinping since his accession to power in 2012, and by adding the concept to China's five-year plan and constitution, the government identified establishing an ecological civilization as a long-term task critical to the future of China (Hansen, Li, and Svarverud 2018). Hence, given the emphasis on environmental governance by the Chinese state, we may also expect that eco-certification programs can find a footing in the country to disseminate their standards, especially if the government finds this new governance mode useful in addressing some sustainability problems.

Bearing in mind both the pessimism and optimism about China's sustainability governance, I began my research on the rise and spread of eco-certification in the world's largest emerging economy. After obtaining access to various data and speaking to many practitioners working for different stakeholders, I realized that the picture is much more nuanced than what was expected by many other researchers. Over the past two decades, the role of transnational certification programs has evolved quickly in China's governance landscape, yet the same governance mode has grown unevenly across different supply chains. Therefore, researchers and practitioners should not infer the potential of transnational sustainability governance in China based on the country's sociopolitical system. Instead, the specific ways in which transnational and domestic stakeholders interact with one another often determine to what extent this new governance mode can thrive in the world's largest emerging economy.

More specifically, I find that transnational governance programs can be quickly adopted in China's commodity chains when they have support from actors in the Chinese state bureaucracy. In other words, some Chinese state actors, including those in extrabureaucracies (or *shiye danwei*), especially state-sponsored industry associations, are willing to leverage private rules set by transnational certification programs to achieve their own development goals. Unlike the conventional expectation that the Chinese state has little interest in or is unwilling to accept transnational governance, by identifying interests of different actors in the "state," my research shows that national industry associations can be important allies of transnational programs to promote sustainability governance. Due to their influence and networks in the country, these domestic actors could effectively nudge local businesses to adopt sustainability standards, although environmental conservation may not be their primary goal. In many instances, such support is a more important driving force than market mechanisms for the rise of transnational sustainability governance in China.

I substantiate this argument by comparing the dynamics of transnational certifications in three of China's agricultural supply chains. Before introducing my analytical framework and empirical cases, it is necessary to consider, in the rest of this chapter, the emergence of non-state actors and institutions in global environmental politics and the influence that China may have in the new phenomenon of transnational governance. After a brief explanation of my research approach, the chapter ends with an outline of the book.

1.1 Transnational Sustainability Governance in a Globalized World

Since the 1990s, the global governance system has undergone a major transformation from a largely state-led process into a multi-actor system to produce global public goods (Ruggie 2004). This transformation of "transnationalism" is especially significant in environmental politics due to the scale of many environmental issues, economic globalization, and expansion of social movements (Andonova and Mitchell 2010; Newell, Pattberg, and Schroeder 2012; Hale 2020). A key manifestation of it is the rise of governance initiatives led by non-state actors, operating across national borders, through which rules are created, compliance is elicited, and goods are provided in pursuit of collective goals (Cutler, Haufler, and Porter 1999; Hall and Biersteker 2002; Djelic and Sahlin-Andersson 2006; Hale and Held 2011). As a new governance mode, these initiatives attempt to provide a response to the global environmental crisis.

A rich literature attempts to conceptualize this phenomenon of transnational governance and explain why and how it has occurred in the field of sustainable development. One of the most influential conceptualizations is non-state market-driven (NSMD) governance, which refers to institutions using global supply chains to recognize, track, and label products and services from environmentally and socially responsible businesses (Cashore 2002; Bernstein and Cashore 2007). Relatedly, research has focused on the governance strategy of disclosing information to consumers (Bullock 2017). Another important lens of conceptualization sees such institutions as "voluntary clubs" that provide excludable but nonrivalrous public goods (Prakash and Potoski 2006a).

Overall, different conceptual strands weave together to suggest three key features of transnational governance.[7] First, there is no use of states' sovereign authority to make and enforce rules. This does not exclude the possibility that states remain influential stakeholders. But transnational governance programs do not derive their governing authority from states, nor are they accountable to states. Second, governance is achieved by reconfiguring global markets. To do this, programs draw on various policy tools, including price premium, information disclosure, and moral pressure, to change the costs to or benefits for their targets. Third, there are some mechanisms to verify compliance. In this respect, third-party auditing is often deemed as trustworthy in making private rules prescriptive. Therefore, eco-certification programs created by firms and NGOs that operate across borders are a subtype of transnational governance. These programs set standards for production processes to ameliorate sustainability issues associated with relevant supply chains, such as environmental degradation and labor rights violation.

To identify the forces driving the emergence of transnational governance, many scholars have underscored the limits of state-based regulation in reducing the environmental and social impacts of increasingly globalized production systems (Knill and Lehmkuhl, 2002; Falkner 2003; Vogel 2008). From this perspective, transnational governance is understood as a functional response to serious sustainability challenges, which often transcends national boundaries. This functionalist explanation could be attributed to broader changes in the economic and social structures of world politics, including the growing power of multinational companies (Gereffi, Humphrey, and Sturgeon 2005; Clapp and Fuchs 2009), the rise of transnational activist groups (Wapner 1995; Bartley 2003), and even an ideological shift toward neoliberalism (Bernstein 2002; Busch 2014).

Following this functionalist logic, a large body of scholarship considers the role played by different stakeholders in making and supporting transnational institutions and uncovers the strategic behaviors employed by relevant actors (Mattli and Woods 2009). From the perspective of businesses, this strand of research has highlighted the function of transnational institutions in promoting collective action in the market in order to protect firms' reputations, build competitive advantage, and preempt government regulation (Haufler 2001; King, Lenox, and Terlaak 2005; Esty and Winston 2006). For example, studies drawing on club theory suggest that firms have self-interest in adopting transnational rules that produce positive social externalities, because their memberships in relevant governance programs bring them rewards from stakeholders (Prakash and Potoski 2007b; Potoski and Prakash 2009). Another strand of research focuses on civil society and social movements, suggesting that NGOs leverage their moral authority and expertise to initiate transnational governance as institutional arrangements to fill the regulatory void left by states, especially in the developing world (Gereffi, Garcia-Johnson, and Sasser 2001; Sasser et al. 2006; Conroy 2007).

Many scholars have also taken into account the involvement of different stakeholders and their interactions in the formation of transnational governance. Abbott and Snidal (2009) use the metaphor of a "governance triangle" constituted by states, NGOs, and businesses to depict the roles of different stakeholders. Bartley (2007) finds that transnational forest and labor certification systems are the outcome of political contestation among states, NGOs, and social movements rather than the purely market-based solutions proposed by some firms. A consequence of the conflicting interests of different stakeholders is the creation of rival systems reflecting the divergent interests of their initiators (Cashore, Auld, and Newsom 2004; Fransen 2011). In fact, research focusing on stakeholder interaction does not deny the potential distributional effects of transnational governance, as some groups always have more influence than others on the design of new governance arrangements (Graz and Nölke 2008; Ponte 2014). Thus, studies taking a critical perspective suggest that transnational governance is likely to favor powerful market actors and reinforce inequality in global value chains (Fuchs, Kalfagianni, and Arentsen 2009; Bloomfield 2012).

More recently, the role of the state in the rise and expansion of transnational governance has increasingly gained scholarly attention. In the field of environmental governance, abundant research finds that states have actively engaged in the initiation of many transnational governance systems, and they have done so in various ways, including providing direct funding and technical advice, setting necessary regulatory frameworks, and orchestrating the activities of relevant non-state actors (Andonova 2014; Eberlein et al. 2014; Hale and Roger 2014). Considering the dynamics in the transnational arena, Green (2014) further suggests that the heterogeneity of state preferences is a key factor in determining the form of the governance authority that private actors can have. Regarding the interaction between states and transnational governance, the European Union has been found to be one of the most interesting regions where public authority has strategically and selectively intervened in a number of transnational governance programs in order to protect domestic producers and reduce policy costs (Gulbrandsen 2014; Renckens 2020). Hence, researchers seem to no longer debate whether or not states make influence on transnational governance, but instead look more carefully at how they influence the functioning of relevant systems.

In terms of their empirical focus, early studies primarily investigate a few archetypes of transnational governance, such as the Forest Stewardship Council (FSC) or organic and fair trade certification (e.g., Raynolds 2000;

Cashore 2002; Pattberg 2005; Taylor 2005). Gradually, however, the literature has seen the proliferation of transnational governance across sectors and issue areas and tried to explain such spillover effects and compare relevant governance programs. Highlighting the critical roles played by transnational environmental NGOs, like the World Wide Fund for Nature (WWF), and multinational brands in diffusing the certification model across sectors, Auld (2014) shows that the market and political conditions these actors have faced shaped the early characteristics of the governance rules and certification standards that relevant programs adopt. Other researchers draw on sociological perspectives to describe the cross-sectoral spillover of transnational governance systems as the rise of an organizational field, which embodies shifting norms and discourses on the legitimate procedures to achieve sustainability (Dingwerth and Pattberg 2009). Additionally, a growing population of eco-certification programs has triggered more and more large-*N* comparisons to identify the determinants of credibility, rigor, and transparency in each program (van der Ven 2015; Darnall, Ji, and Potoski 2017; Schleifer, Fiorini, and Auld 2019).

Although the field of transnational governance has increasingly grown to capture a range of questions related to the rise and continuous expansion of relevant programs, for a very long time, the mainstream literature primarily focused on questions of institutional design and legitimacy. As a result, little is known about the functioning of transnational governance "on the ground," including how it has been practiced in different places, the influence it has had on different stakeholders, and whether it has achieved its intended impacts (Bartley 2018; van der Ven and Cashore 2018). Meanwhile, early scholarship has shown a regional bias toward developed countries, where most certification schemes were originated (e.g., Cashore, Auld, and Newsom 2004; Gulbrandsen 2010; Gale and Haward 2011). This bias seems to paint an incomplete picture of the role of transnational governance in today's global value chains in which the Global South (and large emerging economies in particular) has moved to a central position. Therefore, to assess the potential of transnational governance for maintaining sustainability of the Earth system, it is time to turn our focus to the involvement of emerging economies in relevant programs.

Regarding emerging economies, three important questions remain largely unanswered. First, to what extent are actors in emerging economies willing to accept the existing modes of transnational governance, such as eco-certification? To date, the implications of growing production and consumption in emerging economies for the global spread of transnational governance are still under debate. On one hand, several studies have found that South-South trade undermined the rise of transnational sustainability governance in commodity-producing countries in the developing world, meaning that buyers and consumers in emerging markets do not require their suppliers to adopt high standards (Kaplinsky, Terheggen, and Tijaja 2011; Schleifer 2016; Adolph, Quince, and Prakash 2017). On the other hand, there has been evidence of a growing uptake of transnational certification programs in some Southern markets, suggesting that companies and consumers in the Global South may be interested in sustainable products (Pickles, Barrientos, and Knorringa 2016; Schleifer and Sun 2018). Therefore, the existing literature has yet to carefully interrogate how market and political conditions in fast-growing emerging economies may influence the uptake of transnational sustainability governance.

Second, what could incentivize actors in emerging economies to support transnational governance? Given the power imbalance in global value chains and relatively low consumer demand for sustainable products, previous studies often assumed that businesses in the Global South lack the agency to voluntarily join eco-certification programs. In other words, Southern actors may only adopt transnational rules under pressure from their Northern customers. Yet recent firm-level research finds that some Southern businesses have proactively upgraded their sustainability standards to differentiate their products (Malesky and Mosley 2018; Bloomfield 2020). Moreover, as businesses in emerging economies have been well integrated into global value chains and frequently socialized with other stakeholders, they may become familiar with relevant transnational governance systems and find some benefits to adopting sustainable practices. However, the interest of these Southern firms in sustainability governance does not necessarily translate into support for existing transnational rules, as they may develop—often together with other Southern stakeholders—homegrown systems, including standards and certification programs, to complement or supplement Northern-developed programs (Schouten and Bitzer 2015; Wijaya and Glasbergen 2016; Sun and van der Ven 2020). Hence, it is crucial to investigate to what extent Northern-developed transnational governance meets the needs of actors in emerging economies and the responses of the latter to the transnational programs introduced into their respective countries.

Third, past research tends to see emerging economies as a unified category with very few comparative studies, not only across countries but also within countries. However, in addition to the huge discrepancies among emerging economies, each country is highly diverse across different sectors and regions. As research has suggested that the value chain characteristics and the political economy in each sector shape the initiation and development of transnational governance (Auld 2014; Bartley et al. 2015; Fransen and Conzelmann 2015), we must also study such sectoral factors to understand how transnational rules are spread in emerging economies. Such within-country variation is a particularly salient issue for China due to the country's size and the varied institutions and regulations across industries and issue areas.

1.2 China: An Important but Underresearched Case

As the world's largest emerging economy, China should be among the most important destinations for transnational governance. Besides its sheer size, China's authoritarian regime also makes the country unique by posing nontrivial risks for transnational non-state actors. Unfortunately, the mainstream literature on transnational governance has largely focused on places where political economy differs significantly from the Chinese context.[8] As a consequence, we are still not sure how transnational governance functions under China's authoritarian regime and to what extent this new governance mode could contribute to the country's sustainable development. The answers to these questions have large implications for the future of the Earth system governance and, ultimately, our planet's sustainability.

In the past, the authoritarian rule in China has made many researchers on sustainability governance concerned about the transformative capacity of transnational rules and standards in this important country. This pessimistic view is based on the limited space left by the party-state for potential private regulators, such as environmental activists or social enterprises (Drezner and Lu 2009; Kaplinsky, Terheggen, and Tojaja 2011; Economy 2014). In fact, experiences around the world seem to suggest that a strong civil society is conducive to the rise and growth of transnational governance, as NGOs could serve as independent watchdogs and organize boycott campaigns to put pressure on businesses for adopting good practices (Sasser et al. 2006; Conroy 2007; Bloomfield 2014; Toffel, Short, and

Ouellet 2015; Chrun, Dolšak, and Prakash 2016). By contrast, existing studies on non-democracies has suggested that authoritarian states are likely to restrict transnational governance due to their unwillingness to accept the rule-making authority of non-state actors (Buckingham and Jepson 2013; Malets 2015; Bartley 2018).

At the same time, consumer research on China has repeatedly reported growing awareness of corporate social responsibility and sustainability standards, as well as some degree of stated willingness to purchase products made by companies certified as socially responsible (Xu et al. 2012; Cai and Aguilar 2013; Y. Li et al. 2016). This trend seems particularly salient among urban, well-educated Chinese consumers, who are not always sensitive to price when making their purchasing decisions. In other words, certain market conditions in China already may be suitable for the rise of transnational sustainability governance. Indeed, those who have been observing China have seen opportunities for eco-certifications and standards to bridge some regulatory gaps left by the Chinese state across different issue areas, including food safety, the trade of illegal wood, and fisheries management (Hanson et al. 2011; Hoare 2015; Yasuda 2015). Data reported by many certification programs have actually shown a continuous increase in the number of certified producers in China (ISEAL Alliance 2015; Willer et al. 2019). However, without in-depth research on the relevant processes, questions remain about how these programs were introduced into and quickly spread throughout China and whether variation exists across different sectors and programs. More fundamentally, linking such development to the country's authoritarian context, the question of how the Chinese state views transnational governance remains unanswered: Does it see rules and standards made by transnational non-state actors as a threat to its own authority or as an opportunity to bridge governance shortcomings in managing sustainable development? Given the government's strict regulations on the activities of foreign NGOs and businesses, the rise and growth of transnational eco-certification in China seems puzzling.

1.2.1 Key Argument

To explain the promise and limits of eco-certification in China, this book takes into account the institutionalized processes in the country's domestic governance landscape, which differ significantly from the dominant processes in Western democracies (Guttman 2015; Young et al. 2015). To do so, I unpack China's state bureaucracy and its interactions with the market to identify various forces that may drive companies to embrace eco-certification programs created by transnational non-state actors. These forces include pressure from foreign buyers and investors, activities of private governance programs, and the structure of domestic industry. Therefore, in this book, I first build a framework for considering these factors in the political economy of China and how their interactions condition the rise of transnational governance.

Applying this framework to investigate three of China's agri-food supply chains, I find that some actors in the Chinese bureaucracy, especially state-sponsored industry associations, may be willing to accept the authority of transnational governance, and their support can lead to a rapid spread of eco-certification in the country. In contrast, without such domestic support from the state, transnational certification programs would have a difficult time attracting businesses in China. While reaffirming the state's influence on non-state actors, this finding shows a more nuanced picture of the interactions between transnational governance programs and the Chinese state than the pessimistic projections offered by many existing studies on the future of eco-certification in emerging markets. It thus spurs further reflection on the "private" nature of transnational governance when the relevant systems operate in China, a country where the boundary between "state" and "non-state" is often blurry. The Chinese case also contrasts with conventional wisdom that the diffusion of private rules and standards are primarily driven by global markets. Additionally, in order to gain interest and support of Chinese state actors, transnational governance programs and their supporters need to proactively engage with their potential allies in China and make these Chinese stakeholders realize the benefits they can get from transnational governance.

An important caveat of this study is that it focuses only on the adoption of eco-certification programs by businesses without assessing the sustainability impacts ultimately made by these programs. The latter will be determined by several factors beyond the mere adoption of relevant standards, including the nature of the standards, their enforcement, and preexisting natural conditions. Hence, we cannot assume a causal relationship between rule adoption and positive environmental and social impacts. However, although it is not sufficient, adoption is a necessary condition of impact, because without a critical mass of adopters, transnational governance cannot change widespread practices of supply chain actors in ways that lead to improvements in the biophysical environment and socioeconomic outcomes (Espach 2005; Auld, Bernstein and Cashore 2008; Kalfagianni and Fuchs 2015). Additionally, by looking at who adopters are and their importance in the relevant industry, we can make some conjectures about the impact. In fact, as this book will show, eco-certification has only reached a small niche of the Chinese market so far and, therefore, is unlikely to provide substantive reforms on sustainable production and consumption.

Another important question beyond the scope of this book is the rigor and credibility of transnational standards, as some programs may be deemed as "greenwashing" due to their flawed rules and lack of compliance.[9] Supporting these programs makes little, if no, contribution to sustainable development. To reduce noise caused by this factor, my study only focuses on the well-known programs that are likely to set credible standards. Even with this research design strategy, I recognize that some standards may still not be stringent enough to ensure sustainability.

Despite these caveats, through in-depth, systematic analysis of the rise and functioning of eco-certification in China, this book makes three contributions to the field of environmental governance and sustainable development. First, it complements existing theories on the diffusion of transnational governance by investigating the unique case of China, which differs from Western democracies. In this regard, my study joins a burgeoning literature on the interaction between public and private governance by shedding light on ways in which the state engages with transnational institutions in the world's largest emerging economy (Andonova, Hale, and Roger 2017; Bartley 2018; Renckens 2020). Second, my study uncovers the agency of Chinese stakeholders—both state and non-state actors—in sustainability governance. Past research tends to suggest transnational influences as the major driver of sustainable practices in emerging economies, but this view may be too simplistic to capture the various motivations of Southern actors for changing their policies and behavior toward sustainability (Glasbergen 2018; Sun and van der Ven 2020; Starobin 2021). Hence, to examine the potential of transnational governance in China, we need to carefully investigate the incentives for domestic actors from their own perspective and understand their decision-making processes. Third, the book provides new insights into sustainability governance in China's agri-food sector. While China's importance in the global agri-food system is undoubtedly demonstrated by its production and trade volume, the country remains terra incognita for both researchers and practitioners in commodity supply chain governance. My study aims to fill this knowledge gap by showing the opportunities and challenges in China for promoting sustainable production and consumption. It can, therefore, suggest practical recommendations for how to increase the uptake of eco-certification, as well as leverage other useful policies and tools in the emerging economy context.

1.3 Research Approach

This book examines the spread of transnational eco-certification in China at three levels of analysis: namely, across different commodity sectors, different certification programs, and different firms in the same sector. At the broadest level, I look at the growth of eco-certification in the three selected sectors (seafood, palm oil, and tea) to identify the factors leading to the rise (or lack thereof) of the relevant certification programs. In this comparison, I consider not only the current level of market uptake but also the progress over time in each sector. Moreover, when studying each sector, I assess variation among different certification programs and discuss how their features and strategies condition their uptake in China. Lastly, I use firm-level data to probe the determinants of firms' decisions about joining certification programs. This part of my study not only assesses the motivations of leading certified companies in each industry but also draws on statistical analysis—when industry-wide survey data are available—to discover the businesses' motives for supporting relevant standards.

The outcome variable of interest is operationalized as companies' adoption of the sustainability standards set by transnational certification programs (i.e., whether or not companies are certified). For comparison across sectors, I use the percentage of certified production over the industry's total output as a basic measure and the proportion of certified producers in the industry as a proxy.[10] As data are not always available, sometimes I consider the adoption of eco-certification by leading companies (for instance, the 10 largest seafood companies by sales revenue) as an alternative indicator. Moreover, given the importance of China's domestic consumption, I also look at the sourcing policies announced by large retailers in the Chinese market, which could significantly affect the uptake of certified products. At the firm level, I consider companies' certification status, as well as their efforts to promote certified products in the marketplace, such as their self-stated targets. Beyond considering the uptake level at any one point in time, my analysis pays special attention to the trajectory of each certification program since it entered China until 2018, which allows me to compare strategies and paths of growth in the country.

As mentioned above, the three Chinese agri-food supply chains covered by the book are seafood, palm oil, and tea. This small-*N* comparison at the sectoral level was chosen in order to find comparable cases for comparative research (Lijphart 1971; Collier 1993). More specifically, by focusing on the agri-food sector, I limit the variation between my cases in terms of product characteristics, which could otherwise significantly affect firms' reputational risks and, accordingly, their incentives to accept private governance (Mayer and Gereffi 2010; Fransen and Conzelmann 2015). Moreover, I only examine transnational certification programs akin to "hard laws"—namely, those requiring specific rules for production processes, third-party verification, and product labeling—in order to control for variation in the enforcement and monitoring mechanisms of private governance schemes, as these institutional features can affect firms' incentives for participation (Prakash and Potoski 2007b; Auld, Bernstein, and Cashore 2008).

The selection of these commodity chains is based on three criteria. The first and foremost criterion is that the three sectors vary in several market and political factors identified in chapter 2, which can significantly influence the spread of transnational governance in China. For example, they have different degrees of dependence on Northern markets and hence, do not receive the same level of pressure for the adoption of eco-certification from Northern buyers or investors. Specifically, the export to Northern markets remains important for China's seafood sector, its palm oil sector is under the influence of Northern multinationals, and the tea sector has very little connection to Northern markets. Meanwhile, the value chain structure varies in the three cases. This difference can condition the uptake of eco-certification, as large agribusinesses are more likely to support transnational sustainability governance. Comparing the three sectors shows that multinational traders are highly influential in China's palm oil supply chain and large seafood producers achieving vertical integration have arisen, but China's tea industry is still dominated by small-scale producers.

Furthermore, the likelihood of transnational certification programs receiving support from Chinese state actors also differs among the three chains due to the variation in domestic governance systems. In this respect, regulation is highly concentrated in China's seafood chain (largely controlled by the Ministry of Agriculture), less so in the palm oil chain (the Ministry of Commerce regulating the import but not downstream industries), and very fragmented in the supply chain of tea.

These three sectors also vary in the number of transnational certification programs operating in the market and the existence of domestic certifications. With three major transnational programs and the domestic organic certification, the tea sector is a fragmented field for sustainability governance compared to the palm oil sector, which has only one transnational certification program (Lernoud et al. 2017). In the global seafood market, certifications are separate for wild capture and for aquaculture. To date, one transnational program focuses on wild capture, two on aquaculture, and another one on both; in addition, the Chinese government also created domestic certification programs for organic production and good agricultural practices (Potts et al. 2016). Hence, my cross-sectoral analysis can also probe the effects of the fragmentation of governance on business support for transnational sustainability standards (Fiorini, Schleifer, and Taimasova 2017). The existence of domestic programs may also influence the position of Chinese state actors on transnational governance if they are interested in supporting domestic programs.

Table 1.2 summarizes the abovementioned variations across the three commodity chains of China selected for this study. This research design is helpful for investigating the existence of the causal relationships between the hypothesized explanatory factors and the outcome of interest at the sector level (i.e., the entry and growth of certification programs in China; King, Keohane, and Verba 1994).

The second, but also important, criterion of selecting these three commodity sectors is that they have significant economic, ecological, and social impacts. In fact, all three commodities are critical sources of food and beverages for millions of people in the world, but their production and consumption have been associated with serious sustainability challenges (Clay 2004). For this reason, eco-certification has great potential to make critical contributions to the necessary sustainability transformations in the relevant supply chains. The third criterion of my case selection is that China has always been a major player in the global supply chains of these three commodities, as a leading producer, consumer, or both. Accordingly, Chinese

Table 1.2
Variation across three sectors for case selection

Sector	Degree of dependence on Northern markets	Regulatory agencies	Influence of large agribusinesses	Number of certification programs
Seafood	*Moderate to high* for processed products (23% of processed seafood exported, mostly to *developed* countries)	Ministry of Agriculture, supervising a national industry association	*Medium* with increasing industry consolidation	Two transnational programs for wild capture, three for aquaculture (existence of domestic programs for aquaculture)
Palm oil	*Extremely low* (0.1% of the import palm oil re-exported)	Ministry of Commerce regulating the import of the commodity, supervising a national trade association, but other agencies regulating downstream industries (e.g., food and chemicals) could be also relevant	*High* in the trading segment	Only one transnational program (no domestic program)
Tea	*Low* (16% of tea exported, but mostly to *developing* countries)	Regulatory functions shared by three ministry-level agencies, no leading association in the industry	*Low* due to many small-scale producers	Three transnational programs (existence of domestic programs)

Note: The percentages in the "degree of dependence" column are calculated based on the FAO's estimations of average production and export volume in China in the 2010s.

actors' support for eco-certification would have important implications for the overall effectiveness of the relevant programs in reducing sustainability impacts.

The comparison across these three commodity chains is undertaken by a qualitative analysis following a narrative approach to contextualize every step of the complex causal processes (Büthe 2002). This approach is well suited for my study on the emergence and spread of eco-certification in China, as the relevant processes involve dynamic interactions among stakeholders and the forces leading to businesses' adoption of relevant rules may only emerge from such interactions (George and Bennett 2005). In each of these case studies, I trace the process through which transnational certification programs were introduced in China and gradually gained support from relevant stakeholders, allowing me to assess whether the presence of the forces identified in chapter 2 led to the increase in the number of certified firms (Bennett and Checkel 2014). This historical approach enables me to show how different certification programs have evolved since they were introduced into the Chinese market. To identify the "critical junctures" in these processes, I highlight those changes having a profound influence on the subsequent development of eco-certification programs in the Chinese market, such as a change of position by the government or the support of leading companies (Mahoney 2000). This qualitative analysis draws mainly on primary data gathered from intensive fieldwork, including 106 formal interviews with practitioners working for a range of organizations involved in the relevant diffusion processes (see details on this part of the data collection in appendix A). The interview data are complemented by secondary data from academic and grey literature.

In addition to qualitatively examining the entry and spread of certification programs across the three sectors, I use novel datasets composed of firm surveys in the seafood and tea industries to quantitatively investigate factors that could motivate Chinese firms to adopt transnational eco-certification. This approach allows for testing with additional rigor some specific hypotheses on the incentives and structural constraints that businesses have in the Chinese context. The firm-level analysis is only feasible in the seafood and tea sectors, where China produces the relevant commodities domestically. In contrast, companies using palm oil as a raw material are dispersed across different industries, so that similar surveys could not be conducted.

In the case of seafood, the main aim of the quantitative analysis is to test the influence of transnational markets (i.e., export and foreign investment) on firms' decisions to adopt sustainability standards during an early stage of certification diffusion (see details in chapter 3 and appendix B). For the study on the tea sector, I conducted an original survey with researchers at the Tea Research Institute of the Chinese Academy of Agricultural Sciences in 2018. The survey drew a geographically balanced sample of more than 200 tea producers in China. As sustainable tea certification remains largely absent in the Chinese market, this survey included a framing experiment to probe which types of benefits might motivate firms to join relevant transnational certification programs. Specifically, I randomly assigned the respondents to groups that received information emphasizing different types of certification benefits (see details in chapter 5 and appendix C). The advantage of this approach lies in the possibility of disentangling different plausible drivers in an experimental setting and measuring their effects on firm managers' preferences.[11] By revealing which kind of information is more effective in motivating businesses, the results will have important policy implications for the future of transnational sustainability governance in China.

1.4 Outline of the Book

The rest of the book is organized as follows. Chapter 2 develops an analytical framework to identify the forces that are likely to condition the functioning and rise of transnational sustainability governance in China. The framework pays attention to the specificity of governance processes in China to unpack the interests of different stakeholders and the interactions among them in such processes. On each factor that may influence the uptake of transnational governance, I generate specific hypotheses with observable implications at different levels of analysis. While the framework primarily focuses on the politics of private governance in China, it may also shed light on the diffusion of transnational governance in other emerging economy contexts.

Chapters 3–5 provide in-depth empirical studies on the three different commodity sectors. In chapter 3, I examine the initial entry and subsequent development of sustainable seafood certification in China since the mid-2000s. I use both qualitative and quantitative data to investigate the key forces that have driven the rise of eco-certification in the Chinese market. My findings show that since 2013, a government-sponsored national industry association has leveraged its influence in the supply chain to effectively facilitate the growth of seafood certification, and it did so in the hope that certification would contribute to upgrading the Chinese industry and the market expansion of its member companies. Yet the analysis also shows that the rise of sustainable seafood certification in China is likely to boost only the consumption of luxury, higher trophic seafood, which may, ironically, increase the country's ecological footprint.

Chapter 4 investigates the uptake of the Roundtable on Sustainable Palm Oil (RSPO)—the leading transnational certification program for palm oil—in China. It traces the processes through which the RSPO has entered the Chinese market. Unlike the other two commodities studied in the book, palm oil is not produced in China but only imported from other developing countries for consumption. While this trade pattern limits the influence of foreign buyers on Chinese businesses' support for certification, the chapter shows that between 2015 and 2018, the RSPO quickly increased the number of its members and certified facilities in China after it had collaborated with a large, government-sponsored trade association and gained support from some large Chinese agribusinesses. However, when looking more closely at the purchase volume of certified palm oil by Chinese companies, I find that Chinese businesses have yet to reform their sourcing policy toward sustainability, and the government remains reluctant to provide further support for the RSPO, given that palm oil is not a critical commodity for the country.

In chapter 5, I investigate the diffusion of sustainable tea certification in China—a hitherto underexplored commodity in the literature of transnational governance. Although China is the world's largest tea producer and consumer, I find that the potential forces driving the rise of eco-certification remain largely absent in the Chinese tea industry. First, a large, profitable domestic market with unique product types has limited the influence of Northern buyers and investors in China's tea industry. Moreover, transnational certification programs have made little effort so far to engage with domestic state actors and to promote their standards, so that all levels of government officials in China's agricultural sector remain largely unaware of the relevant programs. In the absence of domestic champions, impetus for the rise of sustainable tea certification has not yet occurred in China. Nonetheless, the results of my survey experiment show a potentially large market for sustainable tea certification in China if the relevant programs were to actively inform Chinese producers about the benefits of adopting their standards. An effective approach could be aligning their goals with the Chinese government's policy on sustainable development.

Chapter 6 summarizes the results from my comparative study across the three sectors. It draws useful lessons about successful strategies and common challenges for transnational sustainability governance in China. I then assess the validity of the book's framework in three other major emerging markets (Brazil, Russia, and India) and pose pressing questions to be addressed by future research. Considering the evolving role of the state in China and other emerging economies, the chapter closes by offering thoughts on three scenarios for interaction between public authority and transnational governance and their implications for sustainability impacts. The conclusion reminds researchers and practitioners on Earth system governance to turn their gaze to emerging economies and identify effective tools for steering sustainability transitions in these new centers of the global economy.

2 Between Markets and States: Grounding Transnational Governance in China

There is little doubt that emerging economies present a different environment than do developed markets for transnational governance. The unique on-the-ground functioning of the relevant transnational rules and organizations requires us to investigate specific governance processes in the host country. Even among emerging economies, China seems to be an anomaly due to its size and political system. These characteristics make China a new laboratory for understanding the role of transnational governance in domestic settings and the interaction between public and private authorities. In this chapter, I present an explanatory framework for the rise of transnational governance in China. It accounts for the different causal mechanisms through which relevant stakeholders and their interactions might drive businesses to adopt transnational rules. I argue that while global markets are a key channel for bringing transnational governance into China, domestic state actors, by shaping policy and market environments in the country, play a more critical role in the dissemination of private rules. To substantiate this argument, I unpack the interests of actors in the Chinese state and the ways in which they exert influence.

Understood as private institutions operating across borders, transnational governance creates order and reduces uncertainty via rules and norms. But this definition has a political dimension, as institutions are purposive artifacts that serve the interest of certain groups (North 1990; Bates 2014). For this reason, we must explain the rise of transnational governance or the lack thereof through the perspectives of the relevant stakeholders. When a governance program is introduced to a new territory, it always interacts with actors embedded in the relevant domestic sociopolitical context. In this process, the domestic context may condition actors' abilities and willingness to acquire information and make behavioral or normative changes. At the same time, we cannot overestimate the power of the context, as actors' interests are gradually (re)shaped through dynamic interaction with others. Over time, transnational governance could also build constituencies that may provide the impetus for its further spread. Therefore, to account for the roles of different stakeholders in driving (or preventing) the spread of transnational governance, I consider how the Chinese context may influence their interactions as well as how these actors may exercise agency within this context.

To introduce my framework, I begin with a discussion of two major characteristics of China's sustainability governance system: the lack of NGO campaigns and the limited influence of consumers. These characteristics determine who might influence the rise and spread of transnational governance in the context of China's political economy and how they might exert influence. I then draw on the literatures on transnational governance and Chinese politics to identify the major stakeholders that may be involved in the process of introducing and promoting transnational governance in China, such as foreign exporters and investors, transnational governance programs, and domestic state actors. When considering each type of stakeholder, I hypothesize specific mechanisms through which actors can influence the adoption of transnational rules by Chinese companies. Additionally, the structure of domestic industry could pose constraints on the rise of transnational governance. For this reason, I consider how specific structural features, such as supply chain types, may affect the influence of different stakeholders on businesses' willingness to adopt new rules. This factor helps us better understand the challenges that transnational governance faces in becoming mainstream in the Chinese market.

An important mechanism in this framework is the interaction between transnational governance and the Chinese state. To understand the dynamics of such interactions, I look at the bureaucratic structures in China to identify who in the state bureaucracy might play an important role in influencing the operation of transnational governance. Based on insights drawn from scholarship on Chinese politics, I unpack the incentives that relevant actors potentially have when providing support for transnational governance. Taking into account the interaction between state and non-state actors, I anticipate that the combination of two conditions—engagement of transnational actors and domestic regulatory structure—shapes the Chinese state's intervention in transnational governance.

By putting these elements together, this analytical framework offers a comprehensive understanding about the initial entry and subsequent growth of transnational governance in China. It can also shed light on the dynamic interactions between transnational and domestic actors in the context of other emerging economies. In chapter 6, I discuss how the inferences drawn here can be applied to other countries.

2.1 Political Economy of Sustainability Governance in China

Globalization and the consequent diffusion of rules and norms do not happen automatically. To introduce new institutions, policies, or practices to a place, transnational actors follow specific pathways, and domestic political and economic environments can affect the feasibility of these pathways (Bernstein and Cashore 2012). In other words, transnational governance does not happen in a regulatory void but is always grounded in sites that are "crowded with different actors, agendas, and rules" (Bartley 2018: 44). Therefore, China provides a unique context for the operation of transnational sustainability governance, due to its political system and institutionalized governance processes (Young et al. 2015; Zhao et al. 2020). Two characteristics are especially noteworthy.

The first is the lack of public campaigns—especially boycott campaigns—under Chinese authoritarianism. In China's environmental governance landscape, the state-society relationship has quickly evolved over the past two decades. In this area, research has shown cases where increasing participation by NGOs and citizens in policymaking processes successfully shifted government policies (Johnson 2010; Zhan and Tang 2013; Fedorenko and Sun 2016). Such changes have happened in the context of legislative reforms of public participation and consultation in China's environmental policy, which have brought greater opportunities for civil society groups to engage in policy advocacy. The Chinese government also adopted the Environmental Information Disclosure Measures in 2008, which enabled many non-state actors, including NGOs, media, and the public, to push for information disclosure and transparency in environmental governance (Zhang, Mol, and Li 2016). From this perspective, some scholars have anticipated the rise of new modes of environmental governance in China, including information-based certification led by non-state actors (Mol and Carter 2006).

However, the increasing public participation and the empowerment of NGOs do not mean that the Chinese government has relinquished control over civil society. Despite the involvement of non-state actors in China's environmental governance, these actors are still under close scrutiny by the country's party-state (van Rooij, Stern, and Fürst 2016). As such, civil society groups in China remain "embedded" in the state, so that their predominant strategy is to use their networks with government officials to exert influence on policies (Ho 2007; Teets 2017). In this context, "name and shame" campaigns or boycotts have not yet become a popular form of advocacy. For example, when NGOs in China directly asked companies to disclose pollution information according to government regulations, their requests were met with little to no reaction (Tan 2014). This situation contrasts with Western democracies, where NGO activism has been a key driver behind the rise of transnational governance, especially for many environmental and labor certification schemes (Gereffi, Garcia-Johnson, and Sasser 2001; Sasser et al. 2006; Dauvergne and LeBaron 2014). Therefore, in China's sociopolitical context, the influence of NGOs on the spread of transnational sustainability governance is unlikely to be exerted directly through public campaigns against firms.

The second (and related) characteristic is that in a large, middle-income economy like China, consumers' opinions on sustainable consumption remain indecisive and therefore can hardly become a key driver of any new rules or practices. Over the past two decades, the norm of ethical and responsible consumption quickly emerged and went global, even being reflected in the 2030 Agenda for Sustainable Development.[1] This new norm led to political consumerism in the form of boycotting (i.e., refusing to buy from irresponsible companies) and buycotting (i.e., buying from companies acting responsibly) (Barnett et al. 2011; Stolle and Micheletti 2013). As a result, even if individual consumers do not always show strong willingness to pay for sustainable products, as an imagined collective, consumers have exerted—in a latent way—an important influence on the decision-making processes of businesses concerning the adoption of new rules or higher standards (Bullock and van derVen 2020). But when looking more closely at the movement of political consumerism, one realizes that it flourishes primarily in the Northern hemisphere, especially in postindustrial societies (Boström, Micheletti, and Oosterveer 2019). As a result, similar dynamics may not have appeared yet in emerging economies.

Indeed, despite the presence of a giant middle class and its growing consumption in China, the role of Chinese consumers in the country's sustainability transition remains uncertain. An important reason for such uncertainty is that middle-class consumers still may be price sensitive and unwilling to pay for certified products (Guarín and Knorringa 2014; Y. Li et al. 2016). At the same time, most consumers in China are unaware of the impacts of their consumption behavior (Fesenfeld et al. 2020; Fesenfeld et al. 2021). In addition, the issue of the credibility of standards and eco-labels is salient in China and may reduce consumers' likelihood of buycotting (Cai, Xie, and Aguilar 2017). All these factors make it very difficult to predict whether Chinese consumers will be politically motivated in their everyday choices and opt for more environmentally friendly products (Lei, Liu, and Oosterveer 2019). In this context, the pressure of consumers—even as an imagined collective—is unlikely to enter the equation when businesses consider the adoption of better practices.

Taken together, the two characteristics discussed above provide important background information on the landscape of sustainability governance in China. With respect to sustainable consumption, they can also interact with each other to constitute a vicious circle that may prevent the rise of eco-certification in the market. More specifically, Chinese consumers' unwillingness to pay for certified products is likely to be reinforced by the lack of NGOs' boycott campaigns, because consumers have little chance of receiving information on the negative consequences of their consumption behaviors. Due to these unfavorable conditions, many observers are quite pessimistic about the prospects of transnational sustainability governance, including eco-certification programs, in China (Bartley et al. 2015). Nonetheless, these structural factors do not necessarily indicate the absence of opportunities for transnational sustainability governance in the Chinese market and society. Instead, other mechanisms may exist in China for transnational programs making contributions to sustainable production and consumption. For instance, taking into account the increasing importance of non-state actors in China's environmental governance, we can expect NGOs to use different strategies in China than in developed markets for promoting eco-certification. To understand these opportunities for transnational governance to introduce changes in China, we must turn to the market and political dynamics of the country.

2.2 Introducing an Explanatory Framework

Transnational governance programs are brought to a new country when local businesses accept the relevant rules made by non-state actors operating across national borders. This process is usually triggered by some external stakeholders providing information and putting pressure on businesses (Chrun, Dolšak, and Prakash 2016; Lambin and Thorlakson 2018).[2] Such interactions among actors are especially important in the diffusion of transnational rules from the Global North to emerging economies in which local businesses were not involved in the creation of relevant programs and standards. Therefore, to understand the entry and expansion of transnational governance in China, we need to identify which stakeholders can influence the decisions of businesses and the mechanisms through which they exert influence. I introduce an explanatory framework here and discuss its key elements in detail in the following sections.

As shown in figure 2.1, my framework puts forward three broad types of stakeholders and conceptualizes the ways in which they shape businesses' incentives to support transnational sustainability governance: transnational market agents, transnational governance programs and their NGO supporters, and domestic state or quasi-state actors. These stakeholders differ in the fields in which they operate. Transnational market agents concerned about sustainability issues are buyers based in Northern markets or multinational companies headquartered in developed countries; private governance (certification) programs and the NGOs supporting them are transnational organizations that have local chapters in China; and actors in the Chinese state bureaucracy work at the national or local level.

These stakeholders also vary in their mechanisms of influence due to the different types of authority they have. Through this lens, we can classify the influence of external stakeholders according to the two broad types of motivation they bring to businesses: material and normative concerns.[3] The power of foreign buyers and multinational corporations in global supply chains is based on their ability to control market access (Cutler, Haufler, and Porter 1999; Haufler 2001). For environmental NGOs and certification programs having the status of nonprofit organizations, their influence is mainly derived from their moral high ground on sustainability issues; as a result, businesses adopt relevant rules not only for concerns about potential economic loss but also for normative reasons (Hall and Biersteker 2002;

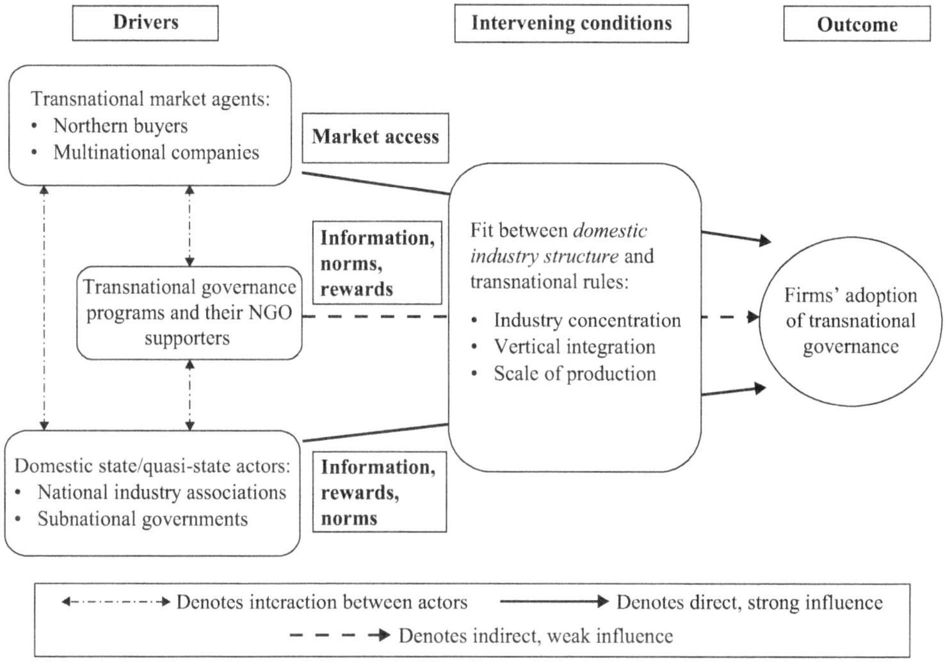

Figure 2.1
A framework explaining the rise of transnational governance in China.

Baur and Palazzo 2011). Both material and normative concerns can exist when state actors exert influence: The pursuit of material benefits leads businesses to change their policies and behavior to avoid further regulations or to gain government support, while the normative obligations play a role when state actors motivate firms through established norms (Harrison 1998; Pattberg 2005b). In the real world, it is always difficult to disentangle these two types of motivation. But material concerns are generally expected to dominate in the initial rise and spread of any new governance systems before they become mainstream in the market (Cashore 2002; Bernstein and Cashore 2007).

A related but more intuitive way to understand different mechanisms through which stakeholders exert their influence is to consider the instruments they use. To distinguish among these mechanisms, we can draw on Vedung's (1998) threefold typology of public policy instruments: regulations (sticks), economic means (carrots), and information (sermons). These instruments are based on different sources of power that organizations use to control or influence others' behavior. Regulations are derived from coercion or physical sanctions; economic means refer to the use of remuneration or deprivation of material interests; and information usually relies—although not always—on moral appeals.[4] While Vedung's typology is used to understand public policy, it also can be applied to instruments that different actors may use to promote private governance systems, given the authority of many non-state actors and their interactions with the state (Hall and Biersteker 2002; Bernstein and Cashore 2007; Green 2014; Renckens 2020).

As transnational governance programs do not derive their authority from state actors, the state generally does not use its coercive power to enforce the relevant rules.[5] Instead, coercion or sanctions for the adoption of transnational governance occur through market mechanisms, such as by granting or blocking market access. This mechanism is especially salient in the context of unequal global commodity trade between Northern buyers and Southern producers, where the former asymmetrically holds market power over the latter (Talbot 2002; Bloomfield 2020). At the same time, through information campaigns, civil society groups can leverage their moral authority to induce firms to adopt new standards or practices. In contrast, without coercion, states still have other means to influence businesses, such as economic rewards, in-kind contributions, and information sharing and knowledge transfer. Because they do not preclude any options, these instruments can be understood as "nudges"—a concept in behavioral economics referring to interventions that can influence people's behavior and decision making without limiting their existing choices—as they can alter businesses' behavior in a more subtle way than hard regulations (Thaler and Sunstein 2009; Sunstein 2014).[6]

All in all, the three groups of stakeholders are likely to follow different routes to introduce and promote transnational governance in China. Yet not all stakeholders were familiar with the relevant transnational programs when they first entered the Chinese market. Therefore, the interactions among different stakeholders could shape their interests and could change, over time, the course of the spread of new standards and practices (see the double-headed arrows with a dash-dotted line in figure 2.1). Such interaction would be especially critical for domestic state actors if transnational actors, including NGOs and market agents, made them aware of the gains and losses that transnational governance might bring. In this process, actors' strategic behaviors have important implications for the rise of transnational governance, or the lack thereof, in a new context.

In addition to the influence of external stakeholders, each industry may face structural constraints when adopting new rules. Many studies have noted the distributional effects of transnational governance, meaning that often it does not provide a level playing field for all actors in the market (Cashore, Auld, and Newsome 2004; Fuchs and Kalfagianni 2010; E. Bennett 2017; Glasbergen 2018). In other words, some types of industries and firms can more easily adopt the standards and practices required by transnational governance programs than others can. Hence, we also need to consider how these structural features of domestic industry condition the spread of transnational governance in China. In sections 2.3–2.7, I form specific hypotheses on the influences of different factors.

2.3 The Power of Transnational Market Agents

To begin with, market transactions are often the most direct mechanism through which the authority of transnational governance programs is grounded. Despite their seemingly "voluntary" nature, governance tools like eco-certification could be imposed on firms and producers by other market actors due to unequal relations among actors along the supply chain (Busch 2014; Lund-Thomsen and Lindgreen 2014). This mechanism is common when market transactions cross national borders and lead firms, based in developed markets, ask their suppliers in the Global South to follow some environmental and social standards. Since the 1980s, the supply chain revolution under globalization has reconfigured the structure of many industries to form "global value chains," linking lead firms in affluent countries with producers in developing countries (Gereffi, Humphrey, and Sturgeon 2005; Gibbon, Bair, and Ponte 2008). These global value chains also connect big brands and retailers to sites of environmental degradation or labor exploitation in countries where domestic regulations are weak. To avoid being associated with these sustainability issues and therefore protect their reputations, lead firms in global value chains, such as IKEA and Walmart, began to use production standards to self-regulate their supply chains (Gereffi, Garcia-Johnson, and Sasser 2001; Conroy 2007; Vandenbergh 2007). In such situations, Southern producers do not voluntarily choose to become certified;

instead, the market power of lead firms make these standards "*de facto* obligatory for access to important markets" (Henson and Humphrey 2010: 1631).

Over the past two decades, an increasing number of lead firms have embraced transnational sustainability governance after they realized the benefits of corporate sustainability for reducing risks and building reputation and competitive advantages (Esty and Winston 2006; Dauvergne and Lister 2013). Almost all of them are based in developed countries, where consumer demand for sustainable products first emerged. In the meantime, China became well integrated into many global commodity chains as a major producer due to its low labor costs and growing production and processing capabilities (Roth et al. 2008; Veeck 2008). Thus, Chinese companies supplying these foreign companies may be compelled to adopt relevant transnational rules; otherwise, they would lose these customers.

Two channels exist for Northern-based market actors to introduce transnational sustainability governance in China. The first is international trade, namely, the export of products to foreign markets where buyers demand certified products. This channel generates the so-called "California effect" identified by Vogel (1995), which suggests that standards used by firms in exporting countries are ratcheted up to match the levels in their trading partners. This "trading up" phenomenon is common when producers in the Global South export to developed countries, and it has actually occurred in the diffusion of many sustainability governance programs, including the International Organization for Standardization (ISO) 14001 and the Forest Stewardship Council (FSC) (Prakash and Potoski 2006b; Perkins and Neumayer 2010; Moeltner and Kooten 2003).

Previous research on China has also shown that transnational standards and certification have often been used by export-oriented Chinese firms as a signal of good sustainability performance to their customers in the Global North (Christmann and Taylor 2001; G. Qi et al. 2011; McGuire 2014). More importantly, in several agri-food supply chains, some transnational standards or certification programs have already become a de facto condition for access to many developed markets (Henson and Humphrey 2010). In other words, they are compulsory in a commercial sense and serve as a trade barrier for producers based in the Global South (Jaffee and Henson 2004). In these cases, to enter certain markets, Chinese companies must comply with transnational governance even if the relevant standards are not required by the governments of importing countries.

It worth noting that the destination of trade flows is critical to the validity of this channel of influence. Compared to North-South trade, South-South trade is unlikely to drive the adoption of higher sustainability standards in Southern producer countries (Schleifer 2016; Adolph, Quince, and Prakash 2017). Therefore, only export to Northern markets, especially Europe and North America, is likely to drive the spread of transnational sustainability governance in China.

Hypothesis 1 Export to Northern markets leads Chinese firms to accept transnational governance.

This export-based channel yields two observable implications. At the sectoral level, the degree of dependence on Northern markets is expected to determine to what extent Chinese businesses are under pressure to adopt eco-certification requirements. At the firm level, both those exporting their products and those planning to enter lucrative Northern markets are likely to get certified.

Observable implication 1a Sectors with a larger proportion of exports to developed countries have higher rates of certified products.

Observable implication 1b Firms that export or are willing to export products to Northern markets are more likely to adopt transnational certification.

The second channel for transnational market agents exerting their influence is foreign direct investment (FDI), namely, when Northern-based lead firms form subsidiaries or joint ventures in China. Like international trade, FDI can introduce better environmental and social practices to firms in emerging economies (Wheeler 2001; Mosley 2010; Stalley 2010). For instance, Prakash and Potoski (2007a) have found that FDI from developed to developing countries drove the global diffusion of ISO 14001 certification—a phenomenon termed "investing up." Garcia-Johnson's (2000) in-depth analysis has also revealed that US investors were eager to push their subsidiaries in Latin America to ratchet up environmental practices beyond local regulations. Similarly, firm-level analysis on China has shown that Chinese firms having multinational ownership were more likely to adopt the ISO 14001 certification (Christmann and Taylor 2001).

Two dynamics may explain the FDI's influence on the spread of transnational governance in China. First, multinational corporations based in the Global North may make commitments to sustainable sourcing in response to activist campaigns, and accordingly, introduce new standards and practices in their global operations (O'Rourke 2006; Pemberton 2011; Bloomfield 2017a). At the same time, these companies may also proactively use transnational sustainability governance as a tool to maximize profits by maintaining a long-term supply of raw materials, achieving efficiency gains, and pursuing first-mover advantage (Vandenbergh 2007; Dauvergne and Lister 2013; Dauvergne 2016). A good example is the global agri-food sector, where many multinational traders, manufacturers, and retailers have made commitments to sourcing only from certified producers (Rueda, Garrett, and Lambin 2017).

Hence, foreign-invested enterprises in China are likely to be more receptive to transnational sustainability governance due to the policies made by their headquarters. For instance, IKEA was among the first actors to introduce the FSC in China and even helped their Chinese suppliers to comply with relevant standards (Ivarsson and Alvstam 2010; Bartley 2018). In such cases, multinational companies require their subsidiaries and suppliers in China to adopt new standards and practices. To clarify, the influence of FDI does not necessarily involve export, as multinational companies may set requirements on their subsidiaries and suppliers regardless of product destinations.[7]

Hypothesis 2 Investment by Northern-based multinational corporations drives the spread of transnational governance in China.

Considering this channel of FDI at the sectoral and firm levels, I draw the following observable implications:

Observable implication 2a The more dominant the position of Northern-based multinational corporations in a supply chain, the higher the rate of certification.

Observable implication 2b Subsidiaries, joint ventures, and suppliers of Northern-based multinational corporations in China are more likely to adopt transnational certification than domestic firms are.

2.4 Activities of Transnational Governance Programs

In addition to being introduced through market transactions, transnational governance programs are agents themselves and can act, often with NGOs sponsoring or supporting them, to directly influence businesses. Through outreach activities, such as awareness raising campaigns, these actors provide new information to firms on issues related to the latter's business and even make moral appeals to pressure firms into changing their behavior

(Cashore 2002; Bartley 2007; Auld 2014; Bloomfield 2017b). For example, certification programs and their NGO supporters can form buyer groups that commit to giving certified producers preferential market access (Cashore, Auld, and Newsome 2004) or organize consumer campaigns directly targeting particular companies (Sasser et al. 2006; Dauvergne 2017). In addition to information campaigns, certification programs and the NGOs supporting them can organize educational events and training sessions and can fund capacity-building projects to help firms adopt relevant standards (Manning et al. 2012; Glasbergen and Schouten 2015). In fact, research has shown that this mechanism of awareness raising and engagement is likely to play an important role in introducing Northern-based governance programs to the Global South, where local stakeholders often lack awareness and knowledge of relevant issues and governance tools (Espach 2009; Peña 2016).

Yet the direct influence of these civil society organizations tends to be weak in the Chinese context. Part of the reason is that civil society groups alone are unable to ensure economic gains or better market access for producers in the Global South (Loconto and Dankers 2014; Carlson and Palmer 2016; DeFries et al. 2017). Unless buyers make contractual commitments, actors in the upstream part of the supply chain often cannot see the tangible benefits of adopting higher standards. More importantly, as discussed at the beginning of this chapter, China does not have a permissive environment for NGOs autonomously launching boycott campaigns. Therefore, the normative pressure that transnational governance programs and their NGO supporters can bring to bear on firms in China is weak at best (as denoted by the dashed arrow in figure 2.1).[8]

That said, in the Chinese context, transnational governance programs and their NGO supporters may trigger policy and behavioral changes of businesses by interacting with some influential stakeholders, including Northern-based multinational companies and domestic state agencies. For instance, certification programs and their partner NGOs could push for changes in the global sourcing policies of multinational brands through campaigns in developed markets or could lobby host governments for public policy support for their programs (Pickles, Barrientos, and Knorringa 2016; Schleifer and Sun 2018; Renckens 2020). The latter strategy could be particularly important in China, as NGOs aligning their issue frames with the interest and discourse of the central state are more likely to influence policy in the country (F. Zeng, Dai, and Javed 2019). For this reason, to understand the influence of transnational governance programs in China, we need to pay significant attention to their interactions with other stakeholders.

The influence of transnational governance programs on the spread of relevant rules and standards often varies according to their strategy and capability at the domestic or local level. I propose two interrelated indicators to capture the strength of such influence. First, the proactivity of the communication strategy in China adopted by a transnational program matters. This indicator reflects on the willingness of each program to increase its presence in China. The more proactive a program's strategy is, the more likely it can reach more businesses and other influential stakeholders in a new market (Gulbrandsen 2010). Second, the human and financial resources that a transnational governance program devotes to a country determine the capability of its local chapter to exert influence or the so-called "local organizational capacity" (Espach 2009). Taking both indicators into account, I expect the following hypothesis.

Hypothesis 3 Proactive communication strategies and a strong local capacity of transnational governance programs contribute to the spread of their rules in China.

This hypothesis can be observed by comparing different programs in the same sector.

Observable implication 3 In the same sector, the proportion of certified products is higher for transnational programs having more proactive communication strategies and more financial and human resources in China.

2.5 Industry Structure That Filters the Diffusion of Transnational Rules

Besides the pressure from businesses and NGOs, the structure of domestic industry can also affect the acceptance of any transnational governance systems in a new market. It is widely recognized that no governance arrangement can provide a "one-size-fits-all" institutional blueprint for diverse contexts (Ostrom 2008). Hence, transnational governance programs do not always have the same effects on different types of supply chains and producers. Drawing on Young (2002), I use the concept of "fit" to denote the compatibility between Northern-developed transnational governance systems and the production methods, norms, and power relations in the relevant Chinese industry.

Abundant research on sustainability governance has shown incompatibility between transnational standards and local production methods due to various barriers that Southern producers face, including the lack of environmental data, the predominance of smallholders, and complex supply chain relationships (e.g., Klooster 2006; Bartley 2010; Pérez-Ramírez et al. 2012; Marschke and Wilkings 2014). Although most certification programs have stated their intention to protect smallholders, empirical evidence on various sectors and standards generally suggests that most existing eco-certification programs favor large, capital-intensive operations and therefore discriminate against small-scale production, which remains popular in the Global South (Raynolds 2004; Gómez Tovar et al. 2005; Cashore et al. 2006; Jacquet et al. 2010). According to Glasbergen (2018), this discriminatory effect is caused by the discrepancy between the sustainability problems prioritized by transnational actors advocating for eco-certification and the needs, interests, and preferences of smallholders in developing contexts. Therefore, domestic industry structure can also influence the spread of transnational governance in China.

Hypothesis 4 Domestic industries favoring industrial, capital-intensive commodity production are conducive to the spread of transnational governance in China.

According to the existing literature, industrial, capital-intensive producers have three key features: market concentration, vertical integration, and economies of scale. Therefore, we can search for evidence supporting hypothesis 4 by examining the existence of these characteristics in Chinese industries. First, market concentration—also called "horizontal integration"—refers to the dominance of a few large players in the market. This feature supports the adoption of transnational governance in a supply chain by alleviating the collective action problem if the relevant programs only need support from a few major players (Cashore, Auld, and Newsome 2004; Gereffi, Humphrey, and Sturgeon 2005; Ponte and Gibbon 2005). For instance, Lee, Gereffi, and Beauvais (2012) have identified four broad types of agri-food supply chains according to the degree of market concentration in the supply and demand segments—buyer-driven chains, producer-driven chains, bilateral oligopolies, and traditional markets—and found that traditional markets that are fragmented in both the supply and demand segments are the least likely to adopt private standards.[9] Hence, we can expect that in a highly concentrated industry, transnational governance will quickly thrive when leading producers or buyers have incentives to use eco-certification to ensure sustainability of production processes as well as product safety and quality (Conroy 2007; Mayer and Gereffi 2010). In this respect, we need to consider the degree of concentration at various nodes along a supply chain, including production, processing, trade, and retailing. Leading firms at any of these nodes of the supply chain can hold significant structural power in the market (Fuchs and Kalfagianni 2010).

Observable implication 4a Market concentration at any stage of the supply chain facilitates the adoption of transnational eco-certification in a given Chinese industry.

The second feature, vertical integration, increases coordination along the supply chain, which facilitates the adoption of eco-certification. In fact, this feature fits the institutional design of most certification programs, as they require the traceability of products along global supply chains and often construct vertically integrated chains tailored for different products (Daviron and Vagneron 2011). Through explicit coordination along the supply chain, hierarchical governance is helpful to the flow of rules required by eco-certification (Gereffi, Humphrey, and Sturgeon 2005; Bush 2018). In contrast, market governance based on ad hoc contracts creates challenges for buyers monitoring the practices of their suppliers (Locke 2013). For commodity producers, being vertically integrated into a chain means long-term, collaborative relationships with downstream buyers, which can increase producers' incentives to adopt and comply with sustainability standards, especially when a price premium exists (Raynolds 2009). Otherwise, suppliers would have greater leeway to switch to buyers who do not ask for certification.

Observable implication 4b Vertically integrated supply chains facilitate the adoption of transnational eco-certification in a given Chinese industry.

Another important feature common to industrial, capital-intensive producers is economies of scale. For most eco-certification programs, the adoption of their standards requires producers to have a relatively strong managerial capacity to establish systems of documentation and record-keeping (Marschke and Wilkings 2014; Bartley 2018). Such requirements are likely to disadvantage small-scale producers and may even exclude them from the value chain (Bush et al. 2013). Even though programs like organic and Fairtrade certification originally aimed to empower marginalized producers in developing countries, the evolution of these programs has significantly increased bureaucratic requirements and certification costs, and therefore the programs become more likely to favor large, agribusiness-style production (Raynolds 2004, 2009; Auld, Renckens, and Cashore 2015). In China, the agri-food sector remains highly diverse, and producers vary significantly in their scales of production (P. Huang 2011). Hence, large agribusinesses are more likely to get certified.

Observable implication 4c Chinese companies engaging in large-scale production are more likely to adopt transnational eco-certification.

2.6 Domestic Champions in the State Bureaucracy

While transnational governance programs are mainly driven by businesses and NGOs operating across borders, domestic actors and institutions can play critical roles in the processes of diffusing relevant rules and standards from the Global North to the Global South (Manning et al. 2012; Berliner and Prakash 2014; Distelhorst et al. 2015; Andonova and Sun 2019). In China, such influence at the domestic level usually stems from the state, which has kept a firm hand on the promotion and regulation of economic development, even though the country has implemented various market reforms in the past 40 years (Y. Huang 2008; Kennedy 2010; Hsueh 2011).[10] Moreover, in China's environmental governance, state planning has become a dominant process through which to exert strong influence on the behavior of businesses and other actors (Young et al. 2015). In fact, research has shown that the rise of some sustainability standards and corporate social responsibility initiatives in China is attributable to support from the Chinese government (Lin 2009; Hofman, Moon, and Wu. 2017). As a result, a transnational governance program has a better chance of thriving in China if it gains support from the Chinese state.

But the state is a conglomerate of agencies and individual actors. China is no exception, even though the country is under authoritarian rule. For this reason, scholars of Chinese politics have proposed the notion of fragmented authoritarianism to describe the divergent and sometimes competing interests of different actors in China's large bureaucracy (Lieberthal and Okesenberg 1988; Lieberthal and Lampton 1992). To understand the influence of the Chinese state on transnational governance, the key questions then turn on which actors in the state might have an interest in intervening in the adoption of relevant rules and how they can do so.

Past research based on other countries' experiences suggests that governments cooperate or co-regulate with non-state actors to relieve regulatory burdens and increase overall governance efficiency (Harrison 1998; Andonova 2014; Green 2014). These motivations might also drive some Chinese state agencies to support transnational sustainability governance. Such state agencies in China could incentivize businesses to adopt transnational rules by providing new information, technical assistance, and even financial rewards like subsidies (Auld, Bernstein, and Cashore 2008; Lister 2011; Gale and Haward 2011; Gulbrandsen 2014). However, that transnational governance originates from the Global North and is led by non-state actors could also make it difficult for Chinese state actors to accept the relevant programs and to view this governance mode as legitimate (Bloomfield 2012; Buckingham and Jepson 2013). Therefore, we need to carefully identify the actors in China's bureaucracy that are most likely to engage with transnational governance. Given the governance landscape in the country, two types of state actors are likely to play an important role.

First, subnational governments at the provincial and city levels may interact with transnational governance programs when firms in their jurisdictions plan to adopt relevant rules. Accordingly, the discretion of local officials in implementing policies in the reform era of China has important implications for the rise of transnational governance in China.[11] In fact, such discretion also exists in the state's regulation of civil society, where the central government often sends "mixed signals" about the limits of what is permissible and allows local officials to judge whether activities are acceptable (Stern and O'Brian 2012).[12] This central-local relationship in China largely explains why, for non-state actors, political opportunity structures are often open at the subnational level for collaboration with government agencies and for influencing policy (Mertha 2009; Hale and Roger 2018). Observing this dynamic, Teets (2014) develops the model of "consultative authoritarianism," which features collaboration between subnational Chinese governments and foreign NGOs, driven by local government officials' willingness to leverage transnational actors for the provision of public goods (also see Weller [2012] and Spires [2011] for similar efforts toward this theory building).

Therefore, when transnational sustainability governance is introduced in China, some subnational governments may be able to provide support for relevant programs without Beijing's consent. For transnational programs and the NGOs that support them, local government officials should be also more approachable and easier to engage with than central-level regulators. The interests of subnational governments in supporting transnational governance could be triggered by both economic and political incentives. In many instances, the prospective economic benefits are an important driver for subnational governments to intervene in policy. Research has shown that local governments in China are willing to make reforms and promote transnational standards to attract foreign investment and boost exports (K. Zeng and Eastin 2007; Wang 2015). Accordingly, local government officials may want to provide support for transnational governance when they expect that the adoption of relevant rules or standards can improve the competitiveness of local industry or attract new investors. In this situation, subnational governments strategically use transnational governance as a tool to further promote local economic development.

Moreover, transnational governance may also help Chinese government officials attain some sustainable development policy goals, and for this reason, subnational governments may encourage businesses to comply with relevant rules. Over the past two decades, central policymakers in China increasingly have paid attention to environmental and social issues associated with economic development and have set a range of targets on sustainability (Zadek 2012). In this political context, the actions taken to promote sustainable development are sometimes a criterion in the central government's evaluation of local officials; accordingly, better policy outputs and outcomes for environmental or sustainability governance is helpful in the promotion of local officials (Y. Qi et al. 2008; Kostka 2016). Due to this career incentive, local government officials could be eager to promote sustainable development. But they may lack the necessary resources to attain policy goals on sustainability and therefore need to collaborate with nonstate actors (Schroeder 2011; Teets 2014). The same dynamic could apply for transnational eco-certification when local officials believe that some programs could help them deliver better sustainability outcomes.

These two incentives are not mutually exclusive but often coexist and reinforce each other. They could drive local government officials in China to take a series of actions to support firms and producers in their adoption of transnational eco-certification, including providing financial rewards, removing policy barriers, and organizing campaigns. While financial rewards, such as subsidizing certification costs, hold promise for effectively changing firms' behavior, such support may be rare or insufficient due to the resource constraints of many subnational governments. These governments may prefer to use nudge-like interventions, including awareness raising, policy recommendations, training, and the removal of policy barriers, to generate interest in transnational governance among firms (J. Chen, Innes, and Kozak 2011). Given the subnational government's influence on the local economy, these interventions could still make important contributions to the spread of transnational governance at the subnational level.

Hypothesis 5 Support from Chinese subnational governments contributes to the spread of transnational governance in their jurisdictions.

To test this hypothesis, I compare different regions in China and examine policy changes by firms in regions where subnational governments provide support for transnational governance.

Observable implication 5a The adoption rate of transnational certification is higher in regions where the local governments provide support for relevant programs.

Observable implication 5b Firms decide to get certified after they have received support from their local government.

The second type of actors in the Chinese state bureaucracy that may have strong incentives to support transnational governance is industry-specific associations at the national level. Past research on other countries has found that industry associations play critical roles in channeling the diffusion of transnational governance (Garcia-Johnson 2000; Andonova 2004; Cashore, Auld, and Newsom 2004; Schleifer 2017). In China, these associations are likely to have an even stronger influence on businesses due to their being part of the state bureaucracy.

In the post-reform era after 1978, China has developed a unique form of state organization that diverges from both the Soviet model of "big" bureaucracy, with all services provided by the state, and the liberal market economy model of "small" bureaucracy, with extensive contracting to non-state actors for the provision of public services (Ang 2009). The Chinese state has a bifurcated structure consisting of bureaus (*jiguan danwei*, literarily translated as "administrative units") and extrabureaucracies (*shiye danwei*, literarily translated as "service units") in every governmental sector and at every level of government. In this system theorized by Ang (2009) as "bureau-contracting," each parent bureau manages a group of extrabureaucracies and has some control over the latter's operations, finances, and personnel appointment, while extrabureaucracies perform a range of tasks delegated to them by their parent bureau, including providing public services, enforcing administrative rules, and even operating commercial activities.

Therefore, unlike their counterparts in liberal market economies, industry associations in China are generally *shiye danwei* and, by nature, part of the state (Guttman et al. 2018).[13] In theory, industry associations do not have regulatory power, but they may have some administrative discretion delegated to them by their parent government agencies, and the leaders of these associations often have the status of civil servants (Ang 2009, 2012). Accordingly, industry associations in China facilitate the implementation of public policies and collect business groups' opinions for policymaking. For most businesses in China, the quasi-state nature of these associations means that their recommendations reflect the direction of government policies. At the same time, being partially dependent on their member companies' financial contributions, industry associations in China are also motivated to protect their members and often serve as effective lobbyists for policy changes (Unger and Chan 1995; Kennedy 2005; Deng and Kennedy 2010).

This unique role played by Chinese industry associations provides them with opportunities to make effective interventions in the adoption of transnational governance. Like subnational governments, their interventions can be driven by both economic and political interests. First, industry associations may support the adoption of transnational governance when relevant standards can bring material benefits to their member firms, such as an expansion into international markets or an increase in productivity (Kennedy 2007). Second, as extrabureaucracies of the state, these associations may encourage the adoption of transnational governance when they find the latter helpful to achieving certain government reforms, such as industrial upgrading and sustainable development. For industry associations' top officials, promoting government reforms through support for transnational governance not only may help their associations get more resources from the relevant parent bureaus but also may create opportunities for their own career promotions.

Given the size of China, we can expect the influence of industry associations on firms' interests in transnational governance to be significant when there is support from national-level associations affiliated with ministry-level agencies. In these situations, the associations' support for transnational governance is seen by their industries as a sign of tacit consent or implicit endorsement of the relevant state regulators. Meanwhile, national associations usually include all major firms in their sectors and therefore can effectively help transnational programs reach many potential adopters and raise awareness of the sustainability issues associated with their industries. Additionally, in China's standardization system, the state often delegates authority to national associations to set industry-specific and group standards. For this reason, their recommendations on new standards are expected to be given significant weight by Chinese firms (Guttman et al. 2018).

To support transnational governance programs, Chinese industry associations generally rely on information sharing and service provision, as they can neither impose regulations nor provide financial rewards like subsidies. Yet they still have some administrative discretion to "nudge" businesses toward the adoption of transnational rules. For instance, they can communicate the benefits of eco-certification to businesses, provide technical advice for the adoption of relevant standards, and even seek to create an industry culture of sustainability through stakeholder forums and training workshops (J. Chen, Innes, and Kozak 2011). They can also bestow excludable benefits on certified producers by endorsing these producers in the marketplace. In this sense, industry associations in China can play a role similar to that of agencies that implement industrial policy in East Asian developmental states (e.g., Taiwan) to change business practices by providing a kind of "industrial extension service" (Wade 2004, 2010). For this reason, I expect the following to hold:

Hypothesis 6 Support from national industry associations in China contributes to the spread of transnational governance in relevant sectors.

Evidence supporting this hypothesis can be observed through comparison across sectors and firms' decision making about the adoption of eco-certification.

Observable implication 6a The adoption rate of transnational certification is higher in sectors where national industry associations provide support for relevant programs.

Observable implication 6b Firms decide to get certified after they have received support from their national industry association.

2.7 Necessary Conditions for Winning Support of Chinese State Actors

While subnational governments and national industry associations are two likely domestic champions of transnational governance, these actors do not necessarily have an interest in intervening in the spread of relevant programs. Even when transnational governance can automatically provide benefits to some actors in China's bureaucracy, the latter may not be aware of the relevant programs originating from abroad or simply may not have the capacity to provide effective support to influence businesses. In the worst case scenario, when Chinese state actors are critical of transnational governance programs—as shown by the case of the FSC—they could hinder the operation of the relevant programs in China and establish competing programs (Buckingham and Jepson 2013; Bartley 2018). Therefore, we must consider the factors that are conducive to the emergence of supporters for transnational governance in the Chinese state.

Any kind of support from Chinese state actors must be based on their own incentives to seek benefits from transnational governance. On this basis, two more conditions seem necessary for state actors to be interested in promoting transnational rules. The two conditions considered in this section can only be *necessary but not sufficient conditions* for the emergence of support of state actors, because other political economy factors must first exist to shape the initial interest of Chinese state actors in transnational governance.

The first condition is the proactive engagement of transnational governance programs and their supporters with Chinese state actors, who may have a shared interest in sustainability governance. In other words, transnational actors advocating for a new governance program need to build a "transnational alliance" with some actors in China's bureaucracy (Farrell and Newman 2015). Frequent outreach and communication appropriate for local contexts are expected to be highly important for the successful diffusion of Northern-developed governance systems in emerging economies, as local stakeholders have little prior knowledge of the relevant governance mode and standards (Garcia-Johnson 2000; Espach 2009; Peña 2016). In the context of China, research has shown that government support for civil society organizations is more likely to occur when personal and professional networks have been established between them (Ru and Ortolano 2009; Teets 2017). Over time, the links between Chinese government officials and transnational non-state actors are likely to create a learning process through which the two sides understand each others' concerns, and such learning can reinforce the collaboration between state actors in China and foreign NGOs (Teets 2014). Thus, the more proactively transnational governance programs engage with state actors in China, the more likely it is that these programs can find supporters.

The second condition is the structure of domestic governance, which can shape the outcome of transnational actors' engagement. In this respect, institutional fragmentation is a critical factor. As suggested by the framework of fragmented authoritarianism, in China, regulatory functions for many issues can be shared by different state agencies, whose interests may diverge (Lieberthal and Oksenberg 1988; Mertha 2009). Such fragmentation increases the costs for transnational programs to find allies in the Chinese bureaucracy, as their managers would need to approach different government agencies or industry associations, which may have different preferences. A fragmented structure also implies that each regulatory agency in the relevant sector has limited capacity and influence, so that the agency cannot provide effective support for the adoption of new standards and practices. By contrast, if a focal state agency—one that is responsible for the regulation of the relevant sector—exists, transnational programs will have a clear target for engagement, and the relevant agency is likely to have enough authority to leverage relevant rules made by non-state actors.[14] In this respect, regulatory fragmentation is expected to bring challenges, rather than provide opportunities, for transnational programs to find supporters in the Chinese state. Therefore, for any transnational governance programs wanting to expand in China, the two conditions discussed above, taken together, are likely to shape the program's likelihood of getting support from domestic state actors.[15]

Table 2.1 shows four idealized types of responses by Chinese state actors to transnational governance according to domestic regulatory structure and the level of engagement efforts made by transnational governance

Table 2.1
Possible outcomes of Chinese state actors' responses to transnational governance

		Domestic regulatory structure in the sector	
		Concentrated	Fragmented
Level of engagement of transnational programs with domestic state actors	High	Strong support	Weak support
	Low	Ambiguous position with the possibility of resistance	Ambiguous position but unlikely to show clear resistance

programs. The basic assumption of these scenarios is that Chinese regulators have no predetermined objection to transnational governance; otherwise, the engagement of other actors alone may be unable to garner support from the relevant state actors. Given this assumption, when a focal state agency exists in a sector, and transnational programs actively engage with this agency or its extrabureaucracies, the relevant government officials are likely to see the benefits of transnational governance programs for China and therefore decide to provide moral or policy support (see the upper-left entry in the table). When all else is equal but the regulatory power is shared by different state agencies, support from actors in the Chinese state would become less likely or weaker due to these actors' divergent interests and the limited authority of each agency (see the upper-right entry in the table). However, when a focal agency exists but relevant transnational programs make little effort to engage with its officials, it is very unlikely to see support from this agency for transnational governance. An even worse possibility in this situation is that the lack of engagement causes misunderstanding and mistrust between transnational and Chinese actors, which can ultimately result in resistance, led by actors in the relevant agency, to the spread of transnational governance in China. Hence, the lower-left entry in table 2.1 suggests that the relevant Chinese state actors are likely to show ambiguity or even resistance to transnational governance. Lastly, when the domestic regulatory structure is fragmented, and transnational programs do not actively engage with actors in different agencies, support from relevant state actors in China remains unlikely. In addition, given the fragmentation of domestic regulatory structure, it is also unlikely for state actors to develop a strong position against transnational governance (see the lower-right entry in the table).

Hypothesis 7 The domestic regulatory structure and the engagement by transnational governance programs together determine the likelihood of winning support from Chinese state actors.

To find evidence supporting this hypothesis, we can look at the conditions in which the most probable allies of transnational governance in China's bureaucracy actually provide support.

Observable implication 7 Subnational governments and national industry associations in China support the adoption of transnational eco-certification when the regulatory power of the sector is concentrated in an agency and certification programs actively engage with state actors.

While hypothesis 7 sheds light on two critical (necessary) conditions for the support of domestic state actors, we must acknowledge the existence of other political economy considerations that can shape the position of Chinese regulators. Among many considerations, potential development benefits of transnational governance for China are likely to constitute an important set of factors, which can include benefits to bridge domestic governance gaps, to make local industry more competitive, and also to increase the authority of the relevant agencies in the state bureaucracy. Given the wide range of these benefits, my framework does not identify specific hypotheses about them, but the analysis in the rest of the book offers insights into the relevant political economy processes and develops propositions to be considered in future research.

2.8 Conclusion

Transnational governance is driven by both market and political forces. Accordingly, the rules and standards set by eco-certification programs do not always automatically flow through market transactions. When transnational programs are introduced, domestic institutions often exert a strong influence over their diffusion and operation. China provides a unique context for the functioning of transnational sustainability governance, characterized by the limited space for NGO campaigns and the lack of political consumerism. This chapter presents an explanatory framework for the rise of transnational governance in this context. The framework maps three types of principal stakeholders involved in the introduction of transnational rules in a given Chinese industry and generates seven hypotheses on the ways in which these stakeholders can generate incentives for firms to adopt relevant rules.

Cross-border market transactions comprise the first and probably the most direct mechanism for introducing and spreading non-state governance arrangements from the Global North to China. Foreign buyers (hypothesis 1) and investors (hypothesis 2) drive this process by requiring their Chinese suppliers or subsidiaries to adopt relevant rules, standards, and practices. In this case, transnational governance is used by Chinese firms as a tool for securing or expanding their access to the global market. Beyond market forces, transnational governance programs themselves can act as civil society organizations to raise awareness among local firms and make moral appeals. These programs can also influence other stakeholders, such as multinational corporations and domestic regulators, who have the means to directly change firms' behaviors. Hence, for any transnational governance programs, proactive outreach strategies and a well-resourced local chapter in China should be conducive to their spread (hypothesis 3). In addition to the influences of different transnational actors, the framework considers the conditioning effects of domestic industry structure on the uptake of transnational governance. This structural factor is crucial due to the challenges of applying Northern-developed transnational rules to the developing context. Hence, I expect that the more a local industry engages in industrial, capital-intensive production, the more easily it can adopt transnational governance (hypothesis 4).

More importantly, domestic actors in host countries can play critical roles in grounding transnational governance, and given China's authoritarian context, the state is expected to have the largest influence in this process. Although transnational governance systems were largely initiated by non-state actors based in Western democracies, due to the fragmented nature of Chinese authoritarianism, some actors in China's bureaucracy may still have economic or political incentives to support the spread of transnational sustainability governance. Two types of state actors are the most likely to become supporters of transnational governance: subnational governments and national industry associations. When they find transnational governance helpful for generating economic benefits or attaining sustainable development policy goals, they can nudge firms toward embracing transnational governance through information sharing, capacity building, and even financial rewards. Through such interventions, subnational governments (hypothesis 5) and national industry associations (hypothesis 6) can make important contributions to the spread of transnational governance in China. But these state actors often have limited prior knowledge about governance systems originating outside China and are therefore unlikely to spontaneously develop interest in supporting the adoption of relevant rules. Therefore, to find supporters in the Chinese state, transnational governance programs need to identify a small number of probable supporters in the domestic regulatory landscape and actively engage with them (hypothesis 7).

The framework developed here offers new insights into the dynamic interactions among transnational and domestic, and private and public stakeholders in the process of introducing transnational sustainability governance in China. While recognizing the North-South divide in transnational governance, my framework suggests that proactive engagement with domestic stakeholders holds the promise of bridging this gap. It also brings back the agency of Southern stakeholders in sustainability governance. Rather than assuming that transnational governance is a tool of Northern stakeholders to maintain their powerful position in global supply chains, one can expect that state actors and businesses in China may strategically use transnational governance to meet their own objectives. While not weighing the importance of different factors, I do recognize the possibility that some can be more important than others in certain sectors and during certain times, as well as the need to assess their relative importance in empirical cases.

3 Seafood: The Rise of Eco-Certification Led by a National Industry Association

This chapter presents the first empirical case study in the book. It investigates the entry and growth of transnational sustainability certification in China's seafood industry, including both wild capture fisheries and aquaculture.[1] While providing critical food sources and livelihoods for millions of people around the world, the global seafood sector faces serious sustainability challenges, including the decline of fish stocks, nutrient pollution, and human rights abuses (FAO 2018c; Smith et al. 2010). In the global seafood supply chain, China plays a prominent role as the leading producer and consumer, representing about 20% of the total production in capture fisheries and over 60% in aquaculture (FAO 2018c). Over the past two decades, the country has also transitioned toward becoming a major seafood importer because of a growing domestic market (World Bank 2013). It was in this market context that sustainable seafood certification first entered China 15 years ago, and over time, gained traction in the Chinese market. Despite the continuous growth in the number of certified firms and products, civil society movements advocating for sustainable seafood in China remain in their infancy, and Chinese consumers are largely unfamiliar with the concept of sustainable seafood. What forces, then, have driven the expansion of the relevant transnational programs?

My analysis in this chapter traces the processes through which different eco-certification programs were introduced to China's seafood industry and gradually increased their uptake in the country. It shows that the rise of sustainable seafood certification in China can be divided into two stages. The first stage began in the mid-2000s, when some eco-certification programs were introduced to Chinese firms by Northern buyers. In this stage, adopters of transnational standards were confined to export-oriented producers.

The second stage started around 2013 after certification programs and their NGO supporters had actively engaged with domestic stakeholders, especially the China Aquatic Products Processing and Marketing Alliance (CAPPMA), a national industry association supervised by the Ministry of Agriculture. By interacting with transnational actors, officials in this quasi-state agency saw the benefits of eco-certification for industrial upgrading and sustainable production, and therefore, they decided to provide moral and policy support to relevant programs. As a result, transnational certification programs partnered with Chinese state actors to promote the concept of sustainable seafood and their standards such that an increasing number of Chinese producers began to use eco-certification to expand their business both internationally and domestically.

The seafood case suggests three key findings. First, it shows the limits of transnational market influences in driving significant changes in China's sustainability governance in an era when the Chinese economy has become increasingly less dependent on exports. Although buyers in developed markets were the initial agents introducing seafood certification to Chinese firms, only a very small proportion of China's seafood industry was influenced by these Northern buyers due to the growing domestic market. Second, when Chinese industry associations partner with transnational governance programs, as part of the state, the former can effectively nudge businesses along the supply chain toward the adoption of relevant standards. The rise of sustainable seafood certification in China is indebted to CAPPMA for its awareness-raising activities, technical advice to firms, and its efforts to link producers with retailers. Third, certification programs' strategies of proactive engagement were successful in gaining the support of state actors in China. In this case, CAPPMA's interests in eco-certification were triggered by its interaction with some transnational certification programs and their NGO supporters.

To present this case study, I begin with a brief summary of major certification programs and their current uptake in China. Next, I examine key structural features of the Chinese industry and how they fit with transnational governance of eco-certification. After this, I conduct a process-tracing exercise to show the two stages of the rise of sustainable seafood certification in China, exploring the incentives of major stakeholders in these processes. I conclude by discussing the successes and limits of sustainable seafood certification in China.

3.1 Certification Addressing the Global Fisheries Crisis

For centuries, humans exploited seafood as an unlimited gift of nature. However, rising demand and technology development since the mid-twentieth century posed alarming threats to this sector's sustainability. On wild catch, the percentage of biologically unsustainable marine fish stocks increased from 10% in 1974 to 31.4% in 2013, such that the volume of global wild catches has leveled off at around 80 million tons (FAO 2016). More seriously, prolonged intense exploitation caused the collapse of many fish stocks, which might not be reversed even by extreme restrictions on harvest (Neubauer et al. 2013). Besides the ecological consequences, overfishing also incurs huge economic costs, as much as $83 billion per year according to the World Bank's (2017) conservative estimate. In China, overfishing is a salient issue, as shown by the decline and depletion of many fish stocks in its domestic seas over the past 30 years and the further pressure that has been added to Chinese fisheries' ecosystems by coastal pollution from industrial development and waste (Pan and Wang 2012; Cao et al. 2017).

To sustain the rising demand for seafood, the aquaculture industry has rapidly expanded around the globe since the 1970s, and the volume of farmed fish for human consumption surpassed that of captured fish in 2014 (FAO 2016). But the growth of this subsector has profound implications for the environment due to habitat destruction in coastal lowlands, large inputs of wild fish for feed, introduction of invasive species, and eutrophication and pollution in coastal waters (Naylor et al. 2000; Páez-Osuna 2001; Tilman et al. 2002). Many of these problems are indeed serious in China's fast-growing aquaculture industry, especially water pollution due to the (over)use of antibiotics, which are detrimental to fish, terrestrial animals, and human health (Cabello 2006; S. Zou et al. 2011).

It was in this context of increasing global concern about sustainability of fisheries resources that eco-certification emerged in the 1990s in the seafood sector. For decades, global fisheries governance remained state centered, dominated by public rules that were imposed domestically by individual coastal states and globally by regional fisheries management organizations (Barkin and DeSombre 2013). But the development of a code of conduct for responsible fisheries in 1995 by the Food and Agriculture Organization (FAO) of the United Nations gave a momentum to NGO activism and transnational governance in the seafood sector. Subsequently, some NGOs decided to promote this conservation approach through certification, and the code has also served as a main reference for most schemes (Auld 2014). Below, I present the major certification programs in the global seafood market and their current status in China.

The Marine Stewardship Council (MSC) is the world's first seafood certification program, focusing only on wild capture fisheries. It was created in 1997 by an NGO-business partnership between the World Wide Fund for Nature (WWF), which wanted to model the success of forest certification in the fisheries sector, and Unilever, which had a growing concern about the long-term supplies of its seafood products (Gulbrandsen 2009; Auld 2014). In addition to certifying fisheries that adopted sustainable fisheries management, the program also created a chain-of-custody certification for supply chain actors using or selling certified products, such as possessors and retailers, to ensure product traceability. The program won the support of major retailers in Northern markets in the early 2000s, including Sainsbury's and Tesco in the UK, Migros in continental Europe, and Whole Foods in the US. It thus quickly became the most established certification program for capture fisheries and has continuously increased in market uptake around the world (Jacquet et al. 2010; Pérez-Ramírez et al. 2012; The Press Association 2017). As of March 2017, 315 fisheries in 34 countries have been MSC-certified, representing 12% of the world's marine wild catch (9.5 million tons), and nearly 25,000 labeled products are on sale in over 100 countries (MSC 2017b).[2] Since the mid-2000s, the MSC has made noteworthy progress in China by having certified two fisheries operated by Chinese companies and more than 300 supply chain actors, mostly processors, and by introducing over 150 labeled products into the Chinese market (The Press Association 2017). Notably, the MSC has gained support from many Chinese processors, as shown by the number of chain-of-custody certificates in China, ranked third in the world (MSC 2017b).

Launched in 2006 in Italy by an environmental activist, Friend of the Sea (FOS) is another seafood certification program covering both capture fisheries and aquaculture. Since 2008, the program has experienced significant growth in its certified wild catch production, which reached 9.3 million tons by the end of 2015 (Friend of the Sea 2018). Part of the reason for this surge is the program's more lenient standards compared to the MSC (Auld 2014). The program's impact on the aquaculture industry remains very limited, as its certified producers represent less than 1% of the global production volume. However, in both subsectors, Chinese producers and processors have not yet adopted the program's standards; nor have certified products been sold to China.[3]

For aquaculture, certification programs also emerged in the 1990s as the industry, especially shrimp farming, had become subject to controversies. The Global Aquaculture Alliance (GAA) was established in Seattle in 1997 by businesses and scientists studying shrimp farming to develop a code of practices for the industry. In 2002, the GAA launched its shrimp certification program, named "Best Aquaculture Practices" (GAA-BAP). Covering four aspects of sustainability issues—environmental protection, social responsibility, food safety, and animal welfare—the GAA-BAP specifies standards for farms, feed mills, hatcheries, and processing plants. Since 2005, with the support of large branded retailers, such as Walmart, the program has rapidly increased its market uptake. In 2007, the GAA-BAP started to expand its standards to many other species, starting with tilapia. Today, it is one of the leading certification programs in the global aquaculture market, with 1,850 certified facilities in 31 countries producing more than 2 million tons of products.[4] By the end of 2017, there were 170 GAA-BAP certified facilities in China, mostly in the tilapia and shrimp industries.[5]

The Aquaculture Stewardship Council (ASC), jointly created in 2010 by the WWF and IDH, the Sustainable Trade Initiative, is another major certification program. It resulted from eight multi-stakeholder dialogues organized by the WWF, on developing sustainability standards for farmed seafood. In 2012, the ASC awarded its first certificate to a tilapia farm in Indonesia. Like the MSC, the ASC sets standards for both farms and supply chain businesses (e.g., processors and retailers). Despite being a newer program, the ASC has experienced rapid growth around the world. By the end of 2017, the program had 548 certified farms producing a total of 1.27 million tons of farmed seafood sold in 66 countries; in China, there are seven certified farms (six for tilapia, one for scallops), 49 chain-of-custody certificate holders, and 101 certified products on sale.[6] For both the GAA-BAP and the ASC, their certified companies in China were concentrated in the tilapia industry. In fact, among different seafood industries in China, tilapia has the highest uptake of transnational eco-certification, with an estimate of over 13% of the production by volume in 2015 coming from businesses adopting at least one transnational certification (iFISH 2016).

Additionally, in the early 2000s, transnational certification programs on organic agriculture (e.g., International Federation of Organic Agriculture Movements) and good agricultural practices (e.g., GlobalGAP) developed aquaculture standards (Auld 2014). Although these programs have grown in the global seafood market, their impact in China remains insignificant, partly because they have not focused on species produced in China (Potts et al. 2016; Chen, Han, and Wang 2017). Moreover, the Chinese government developed its own organic (China National Organic Product Certification) and good agricultural practices (ChinaGAP) certification programs in the mid-2000s, making Chinese producers more exposed to these domestic standards. Both the Chinese organic and good agricultural practices certification programs are regulated by a state agency—the Certification and Accreditation Administration (CNCA)—and their standards are only recognized by a few foreign markets, meaning that their certified products are almost all sold domestically. To date, the number of producers certified by ChinaGAP remains very low, whereas organic certified production has surpassed 300,000 tons (CNCA and China Agricultural University 2016; Chen, Han, and Wang 2017).[7] Yet both programs have gained little support from downstream businesses and play a marginal role in the Chinese market.[8]

In summary, the field of sustainable seafood certification is fragmented into several programs differing in their subsectors (i.e., wild capture fisheries or aquaculture), sponsors, and geographical coverage. Table 3.1 lists the programs relevant to the Chinese seafood sector. Of the two leading transnational programs for capture fisheries, the MSC has entered China and made remarkable progress, whereas FOS remains absent in the Chinese industry and market. The aquaculture subsector is a more crowded field for eco-certification due to the existence of government-developed organic and GAP programs. But these domestic programs do not directly compete with transnational programs, as they focus on different species and market segments. Accordingly, both the GAA-BAP and the ASC have been able to quickly increase their uptake in China in the past decade.

As many programs do not disclose their certified production volume in each country, I use the certification status of the 10 largest Chinese companies as an indicator of the influence of eco-certification in China's seafood sector. Table 3.2 shows that half of these companies have been certified by at least one transnational program applicable to them. This pattern suggests that eco-certification has become popular at least among large producers in China's seafood industry.

Table 3.1
Summary of seafood certification programs (as of 2017)

Program	Subsector(s)	Global reach	Uptake in China
Marine Stewardship Council (MSC)	Wild capture	315 fisheries in 34 countries, 12.0% of global marine catch	2 fisheries, 389 supply chain businesses, and 150 labeled products on sale
Friend of the Sea (FOS)	Wild capture, aquaculture	88 fisheries in 45 countries, 12.4% of global marine catch, 1% of global aquaculture production	No certified business
Best Aquaculture Practices (GAA-BAP)	Aquaculture	1,850 facilities in 31 countries, 2.5% of global aquaculture production	84 farms, 12 feed mills, 15 hatcheries, and 59 processing plants
Aquaculture Stewardship Council (ASC)	Aquaculture	548 farms, 1.6% of global aquaculture production	7 farms, 49 supply chain businesses, and 101 labeled products on sale
China Good Agricultural Practices (ChinaGAP)	Aquaculture	Not applicable	23 producers; very low production volume
China National Organic Product Certification	Aquaculture	Not applicable	Over 700 producers; around 0.6% of China's total production

Data sources: Annual reports and websites of the transnational certification programs; L. Chen, Han, and Wang (2017); and CNCA and China Agricultural University (2016). The percentages were calculated according to the total production volume provided by the FAO and China's Bureau of Fisheries.

3.2 China's Seafood Industry in a Changing Market

Before assessing the role of different stakeholders in driving the rise of seafood certification in China, let us first consider how the domestic industry's structure conditions the applicability of eco-certification standards. The analysis in this section shows that the industry remains diverse, with different types of supply chains. On one hand, the industry has been upgraded in the past two decades to become increasingly integrated both horizontally and vertically. This trend indicates the rise of industrial, capital-intensive production, which

Table 3.2
Support of top 10 Chinese seafood companies for eco-certification

Order	Company name	Main business	Certification programs adopted
1	Zhangzidao (Zoneco) Fishery Group	Marine fisheries (scallops)	MSC (sustainable fisheries and chain-of-custody)
2	Zhanjiang Guolian Aquatic Products	Shrimp and fish farming	GAA-BAP, ASC
3	Baiyan Investment Group	Tilapia farming, fishmeal production	GAA-BAP, ASC
4	Dalian Tianbao Green Foods	Seafood, agricultural product processing	MSC (chain-of-custody)
5	Shandong Homey Aquatic	Mariculture and seafood processing	
6	Dahu Aquaculture	Freshwater fisheries, fish processing	China Organic certification
7	Shanghai Kaichuang Marine International	Distant water fishing	
8	Shandong Oriental Ocean Sci-tech	Seafood seed breeding, farming, and processing	MSC (chain-of-custody)
9	China National Fisheries Corporation Overseas Fisheries	Distant water fishing	
10	China Ocean Fishing Holding Limited	Distant water fishing	

Note: The companies are ordered by sales revenues in 2016 as estimated by Harkell 2017b.

can ease the adoption of eco-certification. On the other hand, due to the size of the country, small businesses still represent a large segment of the Chinese industry, especially in the domestic market. These producers face many difficulties in adopting sustainability standards originated in the Global North.

China's seafood production has had a more than 20-fold expansion since the 1950s (see figure 3.1). It is now the world's largest seafood industry, producing around 80 million tons of aquatic products (FAO 2018c). Aquaculture has driven this dramatic growth, especially since the mid-1980s. Marine capture and the freshwater fish farming dominate, respectively, China's wild capture and aquaculture industries (Bureau of Fisheries 2016).[9] This

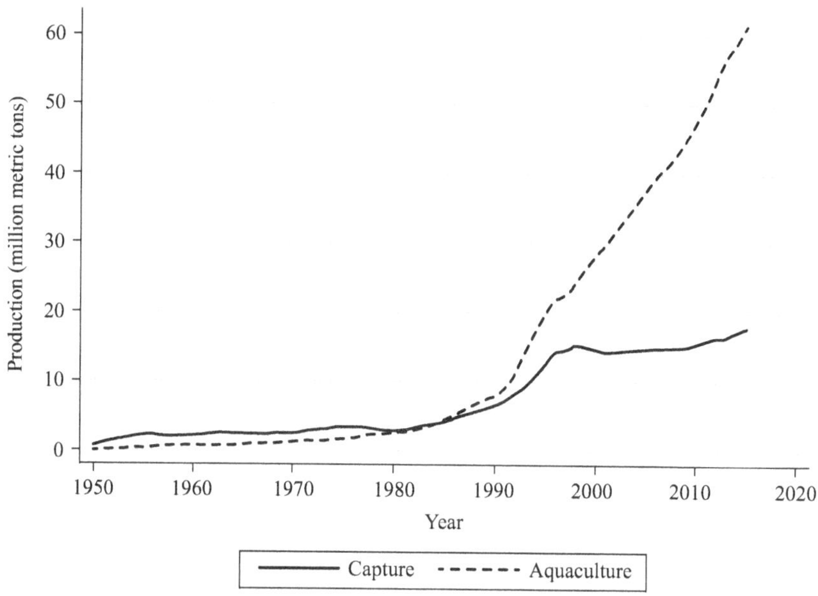

Figure 3.1
Changes in China's production of aquatic products since 1950.
Data source: FAO fishery commodities production and trade database at http://www.fao.org/fishery/statistics/global-commodities-production/query/en.

expansion largely benefited from the country's economic reform in 1978, which improved fishers and fish farmers' production incentives by decollectivizing property rights and introducing market prices. In 1985, market reforms in the seafood sector were deepened by a central government's directive to liberalize the prices of all products, further product circulation and market competition, and relax export controls.[10] The state also set the goal of tripling per capita fish consumption in China by the end of the twentieth century.

Since then, China has begun to develop a modern seafood industry and has gradually become a leading exporter in the market. Figure 3.2 shows the surge in China's fish product exports over the past three decades (these exports have multiplied by 17 in volume and 27 in value). The rise of a large and competitive processing industry is a major driver of this development. Since the mid-1980s, the Chinese government has used a series of supportive policies, including tax reductions and financial credits, to develop the aquatic product processing industry as part of its plan

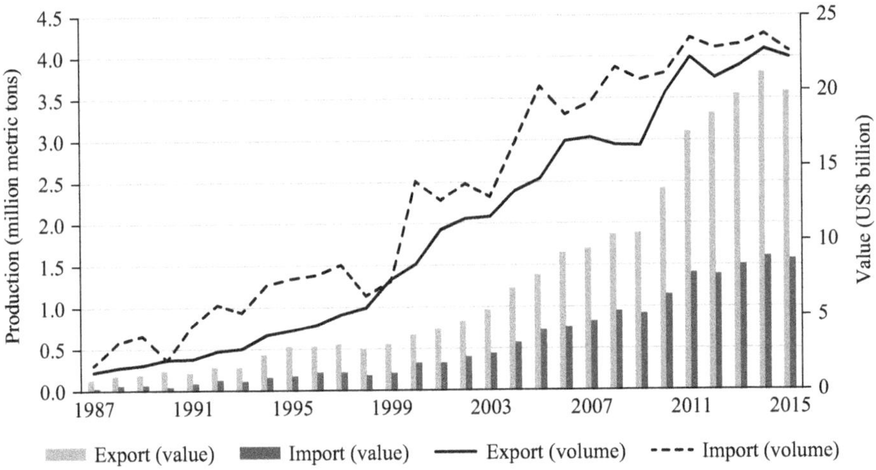

Figure 3.2
Imports and exports of China's fish products.
Note: The data in the figure refer to the trade of the four categories of fisheries products, including fish, crustaceans, mollusks, and other aquatic invertebrates.
Data source: FAO fishery commodities production and trade database at http://www.fao.org/fishery/statistics/global-commodities-production/query/en.

for agricultural industrialization (Yang et al. 2016). These policies have created a thriving industry of frozen processing to export products having higher added value to developed countries. Drawing on cheap labor, Chinese processors rely more on manual filleting, which generates higher yields compared to mechanized filleting (Lindkvist, Trondsen, and Xie 2008). Hence, many Northern producers decided to outsource processing activities to China, making the country the world's largest exporter of fish products since 2002 (FAO 2016). For instance, frozen cod is sent to China from Europe and North America for filleting and packaging, and then is reexported (Hanson et al. 2011).[11] In these supply chains, export-oriented processors are likely to receive certification requirements from their foreign buyers. However, the export volume represents only 6% of China's total production—this figure suggests that a large majority of producers cannot receive information on eco-certification from their customers (Bureau of Fisheries 2016).

Moreover, the global seafood market began to change in the mid-2000s due to decreasing consumption in developed countries and increasing labor costs in China (Cui 2015). Consequently, more and more Chinese producers began to shift their focus to the growing domestic market and introduce premium processed seafood to Chinese consumers. This leads to a trend of industrial upgrading in the industry. Instead of only being suppliers of Northern brands, many Chinese producers and processors started to build their own brands, targeting both the domestic and international markets.[12] For these Chinese firms, seafood certification can provide opportunities for building reputation and creating added value for their products.

In parallel with this trend is the rising consumption of seafood in China. In 2015, the country accounted for 36.9% of global fish consumption, making it by far the world's largest consuming country.[13] Driven by this growth, the consumption of imported premium seafood in China also significantly increased in the past two decades (FAO 2018c; also see the import value and volume in figure 3.2). Foreign species, such as lobster, salmon, and scallops, have become fashionable in China. For instance, Atlantic salmon is considered to be the "Prada of seafood" and has gained popularity among young urban consumers (Undercurrent News 2012). Shrimp is another example: The demand in the Chinese market grew 123% on average between 2005 and 2015 such that China has transformed from a major shrimp exporter into the leading importer in the global market (Anderson, Valderrama, and Jory 2016; Harkell 2018).

In addition to changing consumption habits, Chinese consumers' distrust of food safety standards used by domestic producers has also contributed to the increase in imported seafood products (Villasante et al. 2013). In fact, food safety has become as "a major concern" of most Chinese seafood consumers, and many even believe that "imported products are always better."[14] Seeing this trend, fresh food e-commerce platforms in China have introduced more and more imported seafood products to consumers and have experienced exponential growth in their sales of relevant products (Harkell 2017a). The rise of some e-commerce giants also led to increasing market concentration in the retail segment, which is a supply chain feature conducive to the spread of eco-certification, as discussed in chapter 2.

To better understand the industry's fit with eco-certification, we can identify three typical types of supply chains for both capture fisheries and aquaculture products according to their target markets: *traditional domestic market, domestic premium market,* and *export market*. The first and third chains emerged with different production networks in the mid-1990s, whereas the second one arose in the mid-2000s. They vary in product forms; species; and accordingly, stakeholders involved. This trifurcated structure suggests that transnational certification programs can only be introduced and accepted in some types of supply chains but not in others.

In the traditional domestic market, live products maintain a dominant position due to the consumption habits that see "live" is a symbol of freshness and good quality.[15] Despite the rise of frozen seafood sales in supermarkets, live, fresh fish remains highly popular among Chinese consumers, as freshness is "a culturally-valued institution" (Fabinyi and Liu 2016). Therefore, the chains supplying the traditional domestic market are often short and even informal, with little or no involvement of branded manufacturers. Moreover, species traditionally consumed in China are very different from those in Northern markets. Popular products are mainly caught in China's coastal seas, including largehead hairtail, yellow croaker, cuttlefish, and squid. For Chinese fishers, the costs of entering the domestic market are relatively low, and therefore most of them operate on a small scale, often as family businesses.[16] Due to the collapse of many fish stocks in China's coastal seas, it has become even more difficult for these fishers to increase their scale of production or achieve vertical integration (Cao et al. 2017). On farmed seafood, carp, a low-trophic-level species, has always been the most popular farmed fish in China (Cao et al. 2015; Bureau of Fisheries 2016). Because of low costs and a long production history, most carp are farmed in small polyculture facilities owned by households and sold live without being processed (Smith et al. 2010; Chiu et al. 2013; Yang et al. 2016). Hence, in the traditional domestic market, most products are from unbranded, small-scale producers and are sold in wet markets. All these features can be barriers to the adoption of eco-certification.

The chains supplying the export market focus on the species popular for Northern consumers. Typical wild-caught products are whitefish (e.g., cod or pollack), salmon, and tuna. In these supply chains, fish is first harvested in fisheries outside China and then sent to China for secondary processing to produce fish fillets to be sold in the EU, the US, and Japan. Due to the size of this market, some producers have been able to increase their scale of production and achieve horizontal integration: It has been estimated that in the early 2010s 50 companies produce 60% of China's exported fish fillets

(Hanson et al. 2011). In aquaculture, China has also developed an export-oriented industry, supplying Northern markets with maricultured scallops and high-tropic-level freshwater fish, such as tilapia and catfish. Notably, since the 2010s, China has produced over 40% of the farmed tilapia in the world, and most of these products were exported (CAPPMA 2017). A key feature of these supply chains is that producers, processors, and retailers are often vertically integrated to ensure coordination along the chain. Through capital accumulation, some export-oriented companies in China have also transformed into large agribusinesses, specializing in industrial fishing or faming and high-standard food processing (Godfrey 2014). These producers are likely to have the financial and technical capacity to adopt transnational sustainability standards.

More recently, a new type of chain supplying premium seafood in China's domestic market emerged due to the growing consumption of high-end products. Popular products in these chains include domestically produced species that are deemed healthy and luxurious, such as shrimp, hairy crab, and sea cucumber, and also imported species from developed countries, like lobster and salmon. Instead of going through wholesale markets, this type of supply chain is vertically integrated and involves large, branded producers and retailers. Thus, in these chains, large producers supply high-quality, branded products to Chinese urban middle-class consumers through supermarkets and e-commerce platforms (Undercurrent News 2012). Compared to the traditional domestic market, this rising market favors large businesses, involves fewer intermediaries, and targets consumers who are less price sensitive. Therefore, it provides a favorable environment for the growth of certified sustainable products.

Figure 3.3 illustrates China's trifurcated seafood sector. Of the three market types, the traditional domestic market has the largest share of China's seafood consumption, but it also has the most complex supply chains that fit least well with the governance mode of eco-certification.[17] By contrast, the chains supplying the export market and the domestic premium market are more likely to be vertically integrated and dominated by large producers, processors, and buyers. The prior practices of businesses targeting these markets should also be closer to standards required by transnational eco-certification programs (Broughton and Walker 2010). Therefore, eco-certification is more likely to thrive in these two types of supply chains.

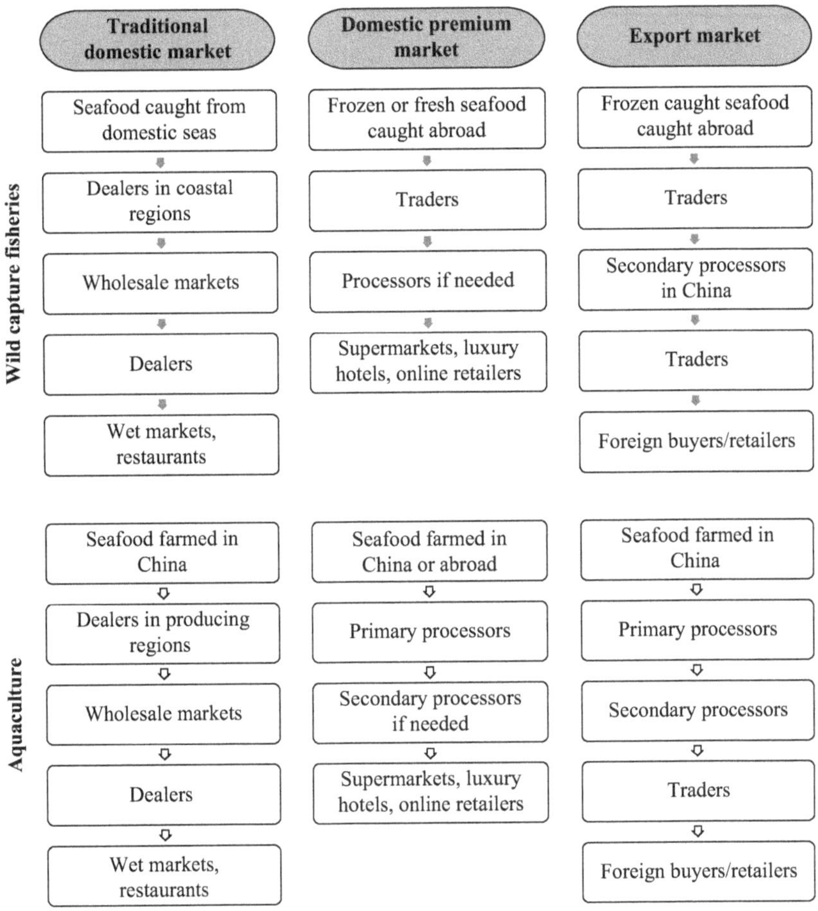

Figure 3.3
Typology of China's seafood supply chains.

3.3 From Limited Spread to Rapid Growth of Transnational Certification

I now turn to the roles played by different stakeholders in the rise of sustainable seafood certification in China. This process has two phases, demarcated by the appearance of supporters of transnational programs in China's state organization around 2013—especially CAPPMA, an influential industry association. Since then, there has been rapid growth in the uptake of eco-certification in the domestic seafood supply chain. In this section, I examine the dynamics in each phase and identify the changing forces driving the adoption of seafood certification programs.

3.3.1 Stage I: Transnational Governance Driven by Northern Markets

Despite the controversy over the impact of seafood production and the creation of several certification programs in the 1990s, eco-certification, as a new governance mode, was not introduced to China's seafood industry until 2005. The first encounter between the Chinese industry and transnational certification programs occurred when Northern buyers asked their Chinese suppliers to comply with relevant standards. But before the early 2010s, transnational programs made little effort to engage with Chinese stakeholders and promote their standards in China's marketplace. Hence, transnational market influences were the predominant driver of seafood certification in China in this phase, and most certified firms were in the chains supplying the export market.

In the subsector of capture fisheries, the MSC was introduced to China's processing industry as a result of the endorsement of the program by major retailers and seafood brands in Northern markets. In Europe, Sainsbury's committed in 2003 to stocking only sustainable wild catch by 2010, and seafood brands like Iglo Group and Findus started to supply certified products in 2004; in North America, Whole Foods Market began to sell MSC-certified products in 2000, and Walmart made a firm commitment in 2006 to purchase all wild-caught fresh and frozen fish for the US market from MSC-certified fisheries (Walmart 2006; The Press Association 2017). The sourcing policies of these retailers and brands sent clear signals in the marketplace of developed countries and led producers supplying these markets to adopt MSC standards (Gulbrandsen 2009).

This new trend in Northern markets had clear implications for Chinese processors located in the middle of this global seafood supply chain. Due to China's position as the leading supplier of processed whitefish to the EU, the MSC chain-of-custody certification was introduced to the country as early as 2006, targeting processors exporting products to Europe, especially Germany.[18] According to the MSC commercial director, the support of Lidl in Germany was "a particularly important milestone because it sent an incredible signal to the supply chain" (quoted in The Press Association 2017). In 2006, five Chinese processors adopted the MSC chain-of-custody standard to prove traceability of seafood from certified fisheries. Since then,

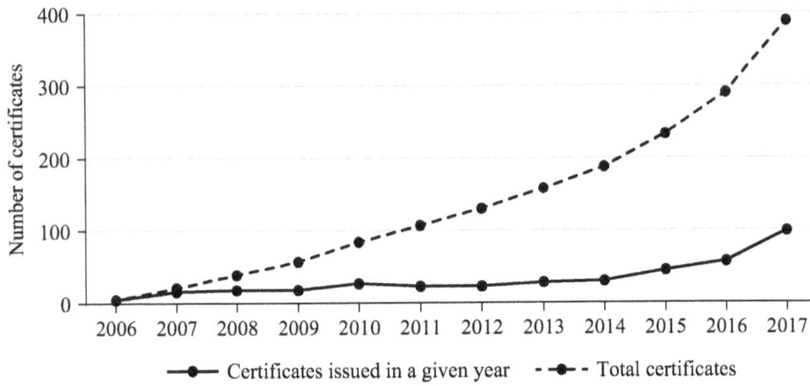

Figure 3.4
Growth of the MSC chain-of-custody certification in China.
Data source: MSC website at http://cert.msc.org/supplierdirectory/VController.aspx?Path=be2ac378-2a36-484c-8016-383699e2e466&_ga=2.39249824.2088586696.1625995511-1562584574.1624224302.

to meet the demand of their foreign customers, an increasing number of Chinese processing plants have been MSC-certified (see figure 3.4). But the figure also shows a relatively constant growth rate until 2014, suggesting that in this early phase, the program could not gain a momentum to attract a wide range of supporters in China's wild-caught seafood sector.

Early MSC-certified firms in China were concentrated in the supply chain of seafood reexports, especially large processing companies. The chain-of-custody certification only requires Chinese processors and traders to ensure that their supplies are from certified fisheries elsewhere and to establish certain traceability and management systems.[19] Thus, the uptake of MSC chain-of-custody certification in China's reexport supply chain did not mean the rise of sustainable seafood in the Chinese market. When the MSC set up an office in China in 2013, there were only three to five types of MSC-labeled products for sale in the country—and all were imported and made by foreign brands.[20] Until that time, the program did not attempt to actively promote its standards in China, as the program's leadership found that domestic conditions were not yet ready for its standards.[21]

Regarding fisheries certification, no Chinese fisheries had adopted the MSC standards before 2011. The first Chinese fishery to be awarded MSC certification was Zhangzidao scallop fishery, managed by Zhangzidao Fishery

Group (also called "Zoneco") in China's Yellow Sea (in the Northwest Pacific). The fishery started the initial assessment in late 2011, and after a long process of assessment and audit, was finally awarded certification in 2015. After Zhangzidao, another Chinese company (Liancheng Oversea Fishery) was certified for its longline tuna fishery in the Cook Islands' Exclusive Economic Zone. By the end of 2017, only these two Chinese companies were operating MSC-certified fisheries, and Zhangzidao was the only certified fishery in China's territorial waters.

The fact that only one capture fishery in the China seas has been MSC-certified reveals the challenges that Chinese fisheries face in following transnational governance on sustainable fisheries management. As a general pattern for fisheries in the Global South, this low uptake level reflects the misfit between the existing fisheries management in China and the MSC standards (Pérez-Ramírez et al. 2012). To date, China's marine fisheries management relies on blunt input control measures (specifically, a seasonal fishing moratorium) instead of output controls, such as total catch limits by fisheries and species, the latter of which are more complex and difficult to implement (G. Shen and Heino 2014; Cao et al. 2017). Yet this governance mode is not in line with the sustainable fishing approach championed by fisheries certification, and therefore, makes it very difficult for Chinese fisheries, especially small-scale ones, to get certified.[22] Notably, data deficiency is a critical barrier for Chinese fisheries to pass the MSC's assessment—even a large fishery like Zhangzidao lacked a record of many ecosystems' data when it decided to apply for MSC certification.[23] Such evidence demonstrates the importance of fit between domestic industry structure and transnational rules, as suggested by the framework developed in chapter 2.

Additionally, both Zhangzidao and Liangchen adopted MSC fisheries certification due to the requirements of Northern buyers. In the case of Zhangzidao, the company's application for MSC certification was originally driven by its strategic move to expand business into developed markets. As one of the largest Chinese seafood conglomerates (the so-called "dragonhead" enterprise specializing in scallop production), the company has established a vertically integrated production chain from harvesting to end-product manufacturing and marketing, and it was listed on the stock market in 2006. Since then, it has identified a strategy of internationalization to become "a respectable and remarkable marine food enterprise in the world."[24] Getting MSC certification was, therefore, part of this strategy, especially to help the company enter the EU market, one of the world's largest scallop buyers with the highest sale price. However, the EU banned the import of all Chinese scallops in 1997 because of *Vibrio parahaemolyticus*, a bacterium found in frozen scallops produced in China (Parker 2016). Therefore, as a leading Chinese brand, Zhangzidao has been eager to rebuild the reputation of Chinese scallops in the global and EU markets, and it considered the MSC certification as a potential seal of approval for entering European markets.[25] But contrary to the company's expectations, its MSC certificate could not effectively help Zhangzidao open the EU market, so that, to date, scallops from this certified fishery are mainly sold in China (Harkell 2017c).[26] Despite this unexpected result, this case again shows that transnational market dynamics were the main driving force of the initial rise of eco-certification in China's seafood industry.

In aquaculture, the GAA-BAP was the first program introduced to the Chinese industry. As for the MSC case, the sourcing policies of large retailers in developed countries were the driving force of the program's entry in China. In late 2005, Walmart announced a commitment to require all of its foreign suppliers of farmed shrimp to be BAP-certified (Walmart 2005). Accordingly, the demand for certified products in the US brought GAA-BAP standards to Chinese aquaculture producers as early as 2006, first to a leading shrimp producer—Zhangjian Guolian.[27] In the early years of aquaculture certification, adopters were mostly large companies having achieved vertical coordination in their supply chains. For instance, Zhanjiang Guolian, as the first BAP-certified producer in China, had acquired industrial farming technologies and an integrated production system (GAA 2014). As the GAA-BAP developed standards for other species, Walmart and other Northern buyers also expanded the scope of their sustainable sourcing policies. These requirements inevitably led more Chinese aquaculture producers to adopt GAA-BAP standards. As China has been an important exporter of tilapia and shrimp to Northern markets, especially the US market, most early adopters of GAA-BAP standards in China were in these two industries (US Department of Agriculture 2018).[28]

As a newer program, the ASC only entered China in the early 2010s, initially through a project under the EU-China Environmental Governance Programme. Funded by the European Commission, the project was carried out by CAPPMA, WWF-China, and the ASC from 2012 to 2014, and it supported Chinese tilapia producers in achieving ASC certification.[29] As a result of the project, three tilapia farms in the Hainan province were certified in 2015, but all of them belonged to large companies focusing on the export market, and these companies had been also certified by the GAA-BAP. Since then, a few other large tilapia producers sought ASC certification in order to expand their international markets, and a large scallop producer was certified in 2017 to meet the demand from its Australian customers.[30] Compared to the GAA-BAP, the program's lower uptake in China can be partly explained by the lack of demand from European buyers—the ASC's major market—for Chinese farmed seafood, such as tilapia (Harkell 2017a). In other words, the demand for Chinese farmed fish in the US market facilitated the initial spread of the GAA-BAP, whereas limited trade interdependence between China and Europe has hindered the ASC's growth. Therefore, the evidence in the aquaculture industry also shows the strong influence of Northern buyers on the certification decision of Chinese producers during the initial spread of the relevant programs in China.

A statistical analysis using firm-level panel data can provide more insights into the forces driving the early growth of transnational seafood certification programs in China. It draws on the data on seafood processors in the Chinese Industrial Enterprise Database (CIED) from 2005 to 2009. Developed by China's Bureau of Statistics, the CIED is composed of time series data of all firms in China whose annual revenue exceeds 500 million RMB (see more details on how I constructed a subsample of seafood firms from the CIED in appendix B). Therefore, the study presented below only focuses on relatively large companies. I employed logistic regression to assess the impact of export, foreign capital, and size and economic capacity on individual firms' certification status as of 2011. This quantitative study is helpful for testing three of the hypotheses developed in chapter 2 on factors influencing the spread of transnational governance in China: hypothesis 1 (influence of export to developed markets), hypothesis 2 (influence of investment by Northern-based multinationals), and hypothesis 4 (influence of domestic industry structure).[31]

The outcome variable was constructed as a binary variable identifying the firms adopting eco-certification and the year they were certified for the first time.[32] Compared to the total number of firms in the dataset, certified firms represent a very small proportion, only about 2.5% ($N=61$). However, this actually reflects the slow growth of sustainable seafood certification in

China until the early 2010s, a period in which transnational programs did not directly engage domestic stakeholders. To address the potential issue of reverse causality, I use a lagged dependent variable in the analysis, as firms decided to get certified after they had received demand from their buyers, and the certification process itself also takes time—at least several months—for audit and assessment.[33] The variables used in the analysis and their summary statistics are shown in table 3.3. We can see that export remains important for Chinese seafood processors in the relevant period as overall the export volume accounted for more than third of their production (measured by the variable *Export ratio*). Meanwhile, the industry was not under strong influence of foreign capital as only 21.6% of the firms had received foreign investment (measured by *Foreign invested*) and only 7% of the whole sample is foreign-owned companies (measured by *Foreign owned*).

Table 3.4 reports the results of the baseline model using the random-effects logistic regression and 1-year lagged outcome variable. This model was chosen as the outcome variable of most cases in the sample is time invariant (i.e., firms remained uncertified in the whole period). Two alternative models were used to check for robustness: the mixed-effects model considering the fixed-effects at the firm level and the complementary log-log model taking into account the highly skewed distribution of the outcome variable. They yield results similar to the baseline model (see appendix B).

The regression results demonstrate statistically significant and substantively strong effects of the export market on firms' adoption of seafood

Table 3.3
Summary statistics

	Mean	Standard deviation	Minimum	Maximum	*N*	*n*
Cert1 (1-year lag)	0.00986	0.0988	0	1	5,677	2,237
Cert2 (2-year lag)	0.00899	0.0944	0	1	6,786	2,397
Export ratio	0.342	0.413	0	1	6,873	2,394
Export value (natural log)	5.270	5.317	0	14.97	6,883	2,397
Foreign invested	0.216	0.411	0	1	6,883	2,397
Foreign owned	0.0696	0.254	0	1	6,883	2,397
Assets (natural log)	8.841	1.515	0	14.54	6,836	2,391
Employees	249.0	538.9	0	12,000	6,883	2,397
Sales (natural log)	10.72	1.335	4.369	15.05	6,873	2,394

Table 3.4

Logistic regression results (random-effects, 1-year lagged dependent variable)

	(1)	(2)	(3)	(4)	(5)	(6)	(7)	(8)	(9)
	Cert1	Cert1	Cert1	Cert1	Cert1	Cert1	Cert1	Cert1	Cert1
Export ratio	1.615***	1.675***	1.606***				1.680***	1.776***	1.664***
	(4.41)	(4.45)	(4.36)				(4.83)	(4.81)	(4.77)
Export value				0.126***	0.150***	0.101**			
				(3.62)	(4.23)	(2.94)			
Foreign invested	0.826**	0.901**	0.888**	0.890**	0.892**	0.981**			
	(2.68)	(2.85)	(2.90)	(2.87)	(2.94)	(3.06)			
Foreign owned							0.830*	0.841*	0.980**
							(2.30)	(2.08)	(2.69)
Assets	0.484***			0.385***			0.512***		
	(4.43)			(3.36)			(5.38)		
Employees		0.000416**			0.000256			0.000448**	
		(2.80)			(1.74)			(2.90)	
Sales			0.636***			0.518***			0.666***
			(5.02)			(3.71)			(6.23)
2007.year	–0.0504	0.0246	–0.0405	–0.0585	–0.0267	–0.0609	–0.0530	0.0243	–0.0431
	(–0.13)	(0.06)	(–0.10)	(–0.15)	(–0.07)	(–0.15)	(–0.14)	(0.06)	(–0.11)
2008.year	–0.484	-0.388	–0.507	–0.474	–0.417	–0.484	–0.498	–0.402	–0.514
	(–1.11)	(-0.88)	(–1.16)	(–1.09)	(–0.97)	(–1.11)	(–1.18)	(–0.91)	(–1.22)
2009.year	0.124	0.293	0.0616	0.143	0.212	0.0826	0.0840	0.271	0.0246
	(0.31)	(0.71)	(0.16)	(0.36)	(0.54)	(0.21)	(0.23)	(0.66)	(0.07)
lnsig2u_ cons	–1.254	0.0756	–1.302	–0.308	–0.416	–0.231	–7.782	–0.129	–8.785
	(–0.20)	(0.05)	(–0.22)	(–0.15)	(–0.16)	(–0.11)	(–0.31)	(–0.06)	(–0.23)
N	5,630	5,670	5,670	5,637	5,677	5,670	5,630	5,670	5,670

Note: *t* statistics in parentheses; $^{*}p<0.05$, $^{**}p<0.01$, $^{***}p<0.001$.

certification. The coefficients for both *Export ratio* and *Export volume* remain positive and statistically significant across different model specifications. The effects of *Export ratio* show that Chinese seafood processors dependent on foreign markets have a strong tendency to support eco-certification. Using an odds ratio to interpret this result, the likelihood of being certified is more than five times higher for firms focusing on export (*Export ratio* = 1) than for those selling their products only in China. Likewise, the size of firms' export business also matters, as reflected by the positive and statistically significant effects of *Export value*. This result provides strong evidence to support hypothesis 1. Moreover, foreign-invested firms are also more likely to get certified, and the likelihood is more than doubled compared to domestic firms. Similar effects also exist when foreign investors own firms in China, as shown by the coefficient of *Foreign owned* in columns 7–9. This finding supports hypothesis 2.

On firms' capacity and scale of production, *Assets, Employees*, and *Sales* remain positive and statistically significant in almost all model specifications. In line with hypothesis 4, these findings show that eco-certification is more likely to be accepted by large and economically powerful processing firms, which can more easily achieve vertical coordination and economies of scale. The effects of these variables confirm the negative impacts of certification on small-scale seafood producers in the Global South, as highlighted by existing literature (Jacquet et al. 2010; Bush et al. 2013).

In short, the changing sourcing policies of Northern buyers drove the initial entry of transnational certification programs into China from the mid-2000s to the early 2010s. In this stage, sustainable seafood certification only arose in the chains supplying the export market. This uptake pattern supports the hypotheses on the influence of transnational market agents (hypothesis 1 and hypothesis 2). But it also suggests that eco-certification was far from popular in China's seafood sector as export-oriented businesses, often engaging in large-scale industrial production, represent a very small niche of the whole industry. However, this situation quickly changed after transnational certification programs had become active in China.

3.3.2 Stage II: Growth in the Chinese Market

In the early 2010s, the spread of sustainable seafood certification in China began to accelerate after relevant transnational programs had attempted to engage with domestic stakeholders. In this new phase, certified seafood has gradually entered China's domestic marketplace, especially the chains supplying the premium market. A key trigger of this development is partnerships between certification programs and a national association in the seafood processing and marketing industry—CAPPMA. Collaborating with this quasi-state organization, certification programs established their local teams and introduced their standards to a wider range of Chinese producers and consumers. As certification programs have paid increasing attention to opportunities in China's domestic market, the demand of Northern buyers became less important—although it still exists—than information and services provided by CAPPMA to incentivize businesses to adopt sustainability standards. Below I trace the process of this transition, showing how CAPPMA has helped the relevant programs increase their uptake in China.

The emergence of support of the national industry association In China's seafood sector, a centralized governance system provides opportunities for transition to sustainable fisheries if the state commands transformational changes (Cao et al. 2017). Being aware of this unique institutional context, several certification programs and their NGO supporters have first sought collaboration with actors in the relevant Chinese bureaucracy when they started to promote their standards in China. Talking about the MSC's China strategy, a top-level official of the organization highlighted that "from [the] beginning (of our activities in China), we explained to the Chinese authorities that we want to work with them and to help them."[34] This example shows that some certification programs understand that their growth in China cannot be solely determined by market dynamics, and they have proactively sought support from domestic state actors. In fact, such efforts have come to fruition in China after CAPPMA, a leading industry association directed by the Ministry of Agriculture, became a champion of sustainable seafood.

CAPPMA is the representative of China's seafood industry at the national level and serves as an intermediary between the government and businesses. Its members consist of major companies engaging in activities along the seafood value chain, including fish harvesting and farming, processing, marketing, and service providing. As a state-sponsored association, CAPPMA is operated as a government agency that has authority delegated by the state to regulate the industry in several domains. Its main functions include collecting production and market data, leading business coordination for market stability, formulating standards on product quality, and supervising seafood export according to international regulations.[35] The last two functions mean that the association plays a central role in setting production standards and introducing international regulations to Chinese businesses. For this reason, CAPPMA has always been a key information source for actors in China's seafood industry to learn rules and standards from abroad.

Indeed, designated by the Ministry of Agriculture to represent China in international events on commercial cooperation and negotiations, CAPPMA officials were among the first actors in China's state organization to get in touch with sustainable seafood certification in the late 2000s.[36] Since then, increasingly more frequent interactions between CAPPMA and transnational certification programs gradually helped relevant Chinese officials understand the governance mode of eco-certification and its potential benefits. As described by hypothesis 7 in chapter 2, the fact that CAPPMA is the only state-sponsored association representing China's seafood industry and the proactive engagement of transnational programs with the association's officials together provide enabling conditions for the rise of CAPPMA's support for seafood certification. As a result, the leadership of this quasi-state association has generated a strong interest in promoting some transnational certification programs in the Chinese industry, which was shaped by the changing contexts in both the marketplace and domestic policy in the mid-2000s.

On the market side, new challenges emerged in the late 2000s for China's seafood industry due to decreasing profits of reexport business caused by shrinking seafood demand in Northern markets and rising labor costs in China. This change led many Chinese processors to build their own global brands in the retail market in order to add more value to products (Cui 2015). In this new context, CAPPMA's top-level officials saw the opportunities provided by transnational eco-certification for Chinese producers to increase their competitiveness in global markets as certification can secure or expand their access to developed countries.[37] More importantly, the decline of Northern markets has led many Chinese producers to shift their focus to their domestic market. To help the industry better explore the potential of a large domestic marketplace, CAPPMA saw the necessity of reforming the industry to upgrade production standards to address food safety issues and increase trust in product quality of Chinese consumers (Cui 2015). As a well-functioning national system to monitor product quality and safety has yet to be established in China, CAPPMA was willing to first draw on eco-certification as private institutions to facilitate the industry's self-regulation and rebuild the reputation of the seafood industry among consumers (J. Shen 2017). In other words, when being introduced into China, the focus of transnational certification programs on sustainable fisheries management has often been less emphasized than their requirements for traceability to ensure product quality.[38]

On the policy side, the concept of sustainable fisheries promoted by transnational certification programs is in line with the directions of fisheries governance set by the Chinese government since the mid-2000s. In 2006, the Ministry of Agriculture identified "sustainable fisheries" as a "strategic goal" in China's five-year plan for fisheries development, which highlights the sustainable use of natural resources and reduction of environmental impacts (Ministry of Agriculture 2006). Since then, sustainable production in both capture fisheries and aquaculture has remained an important component of China's fisheries policy. Hence, promoting eco-certification also allows CAPPMA to help the Chinese government reach policy goals on sustainable fisheries, and the association's move has actually been welcomed by many government officials.[39] In fact, the actions taken by CAPPMA to introduce transnational eco-certification in China and support the adoption of sustainability standards have been helpful for the relevant officials to raise the profile of this quasi-state agency as well as of themselves in the state bureaucracy.[40] From this perspective, political incentives of officials in CAPPMA are also an important driver of the association's support for transnational eco-certification.

Effects of CAPPMA's support CAPPMA's support for eco-certification has been threefold. First, it has led the organization of the annual "Sustainable Seafood Forum" during the China Fisheries and Seafood Expo, the largest seafood fair in Asia. The initiative started in 2009 after the WWF, the MSC, and a US-based NGO (Sustainable Seafood Partnership) had succeeded in collaborating with CAPPMA, and through CAPPMA reached out to the Bureau of Fisheries in the Ministry of Agriculture. The forum brought together environmental NGOs, seafood producers and buyers, certifiers, and government officials to discuss transnational initiatives promoting sustainable seafood and to introduce relevant certification programs to Chinese stakeholders.[41] Since 2011, the forum has been institutionalized and expanded as a partnership between CAPPMA and WWF-China, the MSC, and the ASC. As a co-organizer, CAPPMA has invited to the forum a range of important domestic stakeholders, including businesses and governmental officials.

For Northern-based certification programs, this forum has provided a critical opportunity to raise awareness about sustainable seafood in the Chinese industry and establish conversations with key Chinese stakeholders to explain their objectives, methods of working, and potential benefits. As reflected in an observation by a seasoned participant of the forum: "Over the years, we've seen an increase in the range of people [who] actually participated in that discussion (within the forum) . . . and the number of companies with an interest in these environmental and social issues," and through these forums, "we [were] . . . able to offer a value proposition to those businesses, to the retail channels, that there is enough value in what we do and in the sort of risk mitigation that we provide."[42] Therefore, the forum has presented new global trends on sustainable seafood governance to Chinese stakeholders and has been helpful in generating the interest of some businesses in eco-certification.

Second, CAPPMA has supported the work of several certification programs in China through bilateral partnerships. For the MSC, CAPPMA has been an important ally for nearly a decade in organizing fishery improvement projects and promotional activities in China.[43] For the ASC, as mentioned earlier, the program's initial introduction was achieved through an EU-funded project carried out by CAPPMA and WWF-China. In this project, CAPPMA introduced the ASC standards to major Chinese tilapia producers and coordinated with the regulatory agency on certification (CNCA) to facilitate the undertaking of audits.[44] Even after this project ended, CAPPMA continued to support the ASC in introducing its standards to a wider range of Chinese producers. A remarkable example is the development of the ASC standard for flatfish, a mariculture species mainly produced and consumed in East Asia. The proposal for developing this new standard was raised in 2016 by some Chinese producers wanting to use sustainability standards to ensure long-term development of their industry after CAPPMA had introduced the ASC to them. CAPPMA also helped the ASC convene Chinese experts and stakeholders in the subsequent processes of drafting standards and initiating public consultations.[45]

GAA has also built a close partnership with CAPPMA. In June 2014, the two organizations signed a memorandum of understanding (MoU), according to which CAPPMA helps the program certify more producers and identify marketplace endorsers in China, while GAA promotes certified Chinese products to retailers and foodservice operators worldwide (GAA 2015). The endorsement of CAPPMA has largely facilitated GAA's work in China and also has helped the program establish collaborations with other agencies in the Chinese state. In 2016, GAA organized its annual conference in China and signed MoUs with CNCA and China Entry Exit Inspection and Quarantine Association to increase the GAA-BAP's impact in China (Undercurrent News 2017). In 2017, with CAPPMA's support, GAA strengthened its presence in China by opening a local office in Shanghai, and since then has begun to more proactively approach Chinese businesses. These efforts in China have led to a rapid growth of certification uptake: Within a year, the program won the support of major Chinese e-commerce platforms and introduced its standards to producers of species other than tilapia and shrimp (BAP 2017).

For transnational certification programs, establishing direct collaboration with a quasi-state industry association like CAPPMA has important implications in the Chinese political context. Beyond engagement activities assisted by CAPPMA, the association's implicit or explicit endorsement has increased the legitimacy of these programs in eyes of the Ministry of Agriculture and has reduced their political risks of being opposed by other state agencies.[46] Additionally, for many Chinese firms, CAPPMA, as part of the state organization, is to communicate the government's recommendations and to send signals about future policies. Hence, as described by a certification program's manager, some Chinese producers interpreted CAPPMA's endorsement for her program as "a government requirement" on production standards.[47] CAPPMA has also helped transnational programs to communicate their standards to firms and producers in a way that is "better received" in Chinese culture.[48] The effects of CAPPMA's support on the growth of eco-certification can be seen by comparing FOS with the programs that have partnered with CAPPMA. To diffuse its standards in China, FOS's strategy has been to directly approach businesses without engaging CAPPMA or any other state actors.[49] However, such endeavors have received very little reaction from the Chinese industry, as the program has not yet persuaded any company to get certified.

Third, as part of its work on sustainable consumption, CAPPMA has played a central role in introducing seafood certification to Chinese retailers and consumers. In 2013, CAPPMA joined the China Sustainable Retail Roundtable initiated by the China Chain Store and Franchise Association (CCFA) and WWF. Through this initiative, CAPPMA has engaged in two projects helpful in generating retailers' interests in seafood certification. The first project is consumer campaigns in the annual "Sustainable Consumption Week." Since 2014, sustainable seafood has become a main theme at this event, during which certification programs like the MSC organize promotional and educational activities in both retail stores and online platforms across the country (MSC 2016). According to the CCFA's estimate, Sustainable Consumption Week has quickly grown from activities in only four big cities in 2013 to national campaigns reaching more than 35 million consumers in 93 cities in 2015 (Pei 2016). Hence, consumers in China's premium seafood market have gained familiarity with eco-certification. For instance, consumer surveys conducted over the years by CCFA show that MSC-certified products have become increasingly recognizable and acceptable to Chinese consumers, especially in wealthy regions (Y. Li, Zhang, and Jin 2017).

The second project is the development of a "Guideline on Responsible Seafood Sourcing" to raise awareness about sustainable seafood among Chinese retailers and help them implement responsible sourcing policies. The first version of the guideline was published in 2015 jointly by CAPPMA, CCFA, and WWF-China. The guideline follows a goal-based governance approach and lays the basis for diffusing the norm of sustainable sourcing. By introducing different certification programs and listing the number of certified producers of key species consumed in China, it recommends that Chinese retailers prioritize certified products in their sourcing and establish direct connections with certified producers (China Sustainable Retail Roundtable 2015). In 2017, CAPPMA and CCFA gathered more stakeholders to update the guideline.

Beyond awareness raising, this guideline sent a clear signal to the Chinese retail sector and helped transnational certification programs approach large retailers to promote sustainable seafood. After the guideline's release in 2015, several certification programs intensified their efforts to engage with Chinese retailers. As in Northern markets, they first tried to convince multinational retail and catering brands to source more certified products in China; but large retailers like Walmart were hesitant to make sourcing commitments to the Chinese market.[50] Despite limited support from multinational supermarkets, with the assistance of CAPPMA, transnational certification programs have successfully reached out to Chinese e-commerce giants, who have been major drivers of the growth of China's retail market since 2010. In contrast to the continuous decline in the growth of most physical retailers, China's online retail market has rapidly expanded to become the world's largest and to reach a transaction scale of $581.8 billion in 2015 (Deloitte China 2017). Hence, the online market of fresh food, including seafood, in China is deemed a promising way to target wealthy consumers who value food safety and quality, and it has been booming since the mid-2010s on major Chinese e-commerce platforms, such as Alibaba's Tmall and JD.com.

Important progress was achieved in 2017, as reflected by the signing of MoUs between GAA and JD.com and between the MSC and Tmall to promote sustainable seafood. Expecting eco-certification to increase their sales of high-quality seafood, these e-commerce giants set ambitious sourcing targets: By 2020, Tmall aims to sell 20% of its seafood with the MSC label, and JD.com is committed to ensuring 50% of its farmed seafood supply and over 80% of its private label farmed offerings are at least two-star BAP-certified (MSC 2017a; BAP 2018).[51] To convince Chinese e-retailers to change their sourcing policies, CAPPMA has served as a broker to connect them with certification programs.[52] E-retailers' commitments have quickly influenced producers targeting the domestic premium market. For instance, in October 2017, a Chinese hairy crab producer, eager to expand its online market, became the first BAP-certified hairy crab farm in the world (BAP 2017). Hence, with support from large e-retailers, sustainable seafood certification has gathered momentum in China's domestic market.

Table 3.5 lists the activities promoting sustainable seafood in China carried out by transnational certification programs with the support of CAPPMA since the early 2010s. At this stage, certified firms in China expanded from export-oriented producers to those supplying the domestic premium market, and large Chinese e-retailers made strong sourcing commitments for certified seafood. Given the country's size, certified products are likely to represent a small niche in the whole Chinese industry. Nonetheless, transnational certification programs, including the MSC, GAA-BAP, and the ASC, have grown much faster since 2013. CAPPMA is a key contributor to such growth by introducing and recommending the relevant programs to Chinese producers and retailers.

Table 3.5
Major progress on sustainable seafood movement in China supported by CAPPMA

Date	Activities
Since 2011	"Sustainable Seafood Forum" taking place annually during the China Fisheries and Seafood Expo
Since 2013	"Sustainable Consumption Week" organizing annual consumer campaigns on sustainable seafood through large retailers
2012–2014	An EU-funded project for Chinese tilapia producers to adopt the ASC certification
2014	The MoU between GAA and CAPPMA to help certify more aquaculture producers and identify marketplace endorsers in China
2016	The MoUs between GAA and the Chinese regulatory agency on certification and a leading trade association to increase the impact of GAA-BAP
2015, 2017	Publications of the *Guideline on Responsible Seafood Sourcing* for the Chinese retail sector
2016	The development of the ASC flatfish standard led by Chinese producers
2017	The MoU between the MSC and Alibaba's Tmall, with the latter's commitment of having 20% of seafood sold with the MSC label by 2020; The MoU between GAA and JD.com, with the latter's commitment of having sourcing for 50% of its farmed seafood to be at least two-star BAP-certified by 2020

3.4 Conclusion

As the world's largest seafood producing and consuming country, China's support has profound implications for the overall effectiveness of eco-certification programs aiming to promote sustainability transition in the global seafood supply chain. The modernization of China's seafood industry since the 1990s has consisted of enabling conditions for the adoption of eco-certification, especially by producers supplying the export and domestic premium markets. In this market context, different sustainable seafood certification programs were introduced to the Chinese industry in the mid-2000s. By examining the entry processes of the relevant programs and survey data from Chinese processing firms, I find that, prior to 2012, demand in Northern markets was the main driver of the uptake of eco-certification in China's seafood industry. In addition to the requirements of foreign buyers, rising Chinese seafood brands proactively adopted eco-certification standards in the hope of gaining access to foreign markets, as shown by the case of Zhangzidao. Overall, the evidence in this initial stage supports my first two hypotheses (hypothesis 1 and hypothesis 2) in chapter 2 on the influence of transnational market agents.

But this uptake pattern changed in 2013, as transnational certification programs began to actively engage with Chinese stakeholders to promote their standards and build partnerships with CAPPMA, a national seafood industry association supervised by the Ministry of Agriculture. Through interactions with certification programs and the NGO supporting them, CAPPMA's top-level officials realized that eco-certification could provide economic benefits to the association's members through upgrading and branding, as well as political benefits for the association itself through the promotion of sustainable fisheries—an important element of China's fisheries policy. Thus, CAPPMA has collaborated with transnational programs, and its endorsement and direct support for eco-certification led to the quick expansion of seafood certification in China's industry and marketplace. Although the association cannot provide financial rewards to its members, by leveraging its connections with the central government, it has successfully nudged some producers toward using eco-certification and has encouraged large e-retailers to include certification in their sourcing policy. Therefore, at this stage, domestic state actors, rather than transnational market agents, played a critical role in driving the growth of seafood certification in China. This finding strongly champions hypothesis 6 on the influence of quasi-state industry associations. As suggested by hypothesis 3, the efforts by transnational certification programs to proactively engage with CAPPMA and to build their local chapters have also been helpful for increasing their uptake in China. Additionally, CAPPMA's increased support is also in line with the expectation of hypothesis 7, as the regulatory structure in China's seafood sector is concentrated.

To summarize, unlike experiences in the Global North, the recent rise of sustainable seafood certification in China was not led by a bottom-up civil society movement; instead, it was achieved in a top-down manner, driven by a quasi-state national industry association. Given growing consumption in China, this rising momentum for certified seafood in the Chinese market holds the promise of limiting or even reducing environmental burdens on global fisheries resources. That said, we must be cautious and not be too optimistic about the ultimate outcomes of seafood certification in China for several reasons. First, most Chinese producers, especially those in the capture fisheries subsector, remain unable to adopt sustainability standards, as their unsophisticated management measures are not compatible with the approach advocated by eco-certification. Moreover, in line with hypothesis 4 on the fit of eco-certification with large, capital-intensive production, certified producers in China are mainly confined to the chains supplying the high-end market segment, whereas the majority of seafood in the domestic market is still sold in wet markets without labeling. Additionally, the quality of standard implementation can also be questionable, as well-functioning traceability systems have yet to be established in China's seafood industry, and certification does not necessarily lead to better performance and the continual improvement of compliant producers (Tlusty and Tausig 2015; Sun and van der Ven 2020). Finally, the increasing popularity of eco-certification may increase consumption of high-trophic-level species in China, such as salmon and catfish, which could, paradoxically, put further pressure on global fisheries resources and introduce negative ecological impacts. These are important questions to be considered if we want to better harness eco-certification to achieve a sustainable seafood sector in China and globally.

4 Palm Oil: The Entry of the RSPO with Lukewarm State Support

Used in a variety of products, including food, cosmetics, and cleaning products, palm oil is a critical commodity for many industries. From 1970 to 2010, its global production experienced a 23-fold surge, but this boom has caused large-scale deforestation and biodiversity loss, especially in Southeast Asia (Byerlee, Falcon, and Naylor 2017). In light of this surge, some environmental NGOs and business stakeholders initiated a transnational certification program—the Roundtable on Sustainable Palm Oil (RSPO)—to reduce the industry's environmental and social impacts. As the only certification program focusing solely on palm oil, the RSPO quickly expanded its influence in the global supply chain and has been eager to win support from Chinese companies. But the market structure that China has—no oil palm plantations and only imports of the commodity from other developing countries—presents challenges for the RSPO in engaging with Chinese stakeholders, who generally lack awareness of relevant sustainability issues. Additionally, palm oil is only used as an ingredient in different products, which further increases the difficulty of targeting a specific industry and gaining support from consumers. In this challenging situation, what can drive the rise of palm oil certification in China?

This chapter investigates the evolving process through which the RSPO was taken up in China's palm oil supply chain and identifies the key forces shaping this process. It shows that the program's fast growth in China since 2015 was mainly attributable to efforts made by the RSPO and its NGO supporters to proactively engage with Chinese stakeholders, especially actors in the state organization. As the outcome of such efforts, the RSPO has partnered with a quasi-state industry association—the China Chamber of Commerce for Import and Export of Foodstuffs, Native Produce and Animal By-Products (CFNA)—to build awareness of sustainable palm oil in China and reach out to domestic enterprises holding dominant positions in the market. This finding underscores the positive effects of proactive communication strategies and strong local capacity on the promotion of transnational eco-certification in China. It also confirms the important role of state actors, especially national industry associations, in influencing the spread of transnational governance in China. Nonetheless, the study also reveals that Chinese state actors have been hesitant to provide stronger policy support to incentivize firms to change their sourcing behaviors, as the direct benefits of palm oil certification for the country are deemed limited. Such hesitation has prevented a significant increase in the volume of certified palm oil imported to China.

The chapter begins with a summary of the RSPO's history and its growth in China. Next, I consider the structure of China's palm oil supply chain, assessing its fit with the governance model of eco-certification. I then examine the RSPO's efforts for increasing its uptake in China and its progress over time. My analysis shows the importance of partnerships between the RSPO and Chinese state actors and illustrates such dynamics through the case of the largest state-owned agribusiness—China National Cereals, Oils and Foodstuffs Corporation (COFCO). In the conclusion, I draw lessons from the RSPO's China strategy and discuss the limitations of palm oil certification in transforming the Chinese market.

4.1 Palm Oil Controversies and the Emergence of the RSPO

As a cheap edible oil, palm oil is highly saturated and solid at room temperature, and it has a neutral taste and smell. Therefore, it became an appealing ingredient for food, cleaning, and toiletry products (Saxon and Roquemore 2011). It is also used as the primary cooking oil in many developing countries. Due to growing demand, the commodity has become the most used vegetable oil in the world in the past two decades.[1] Southeast Asia has been always the leading supplier in the global palm oil market, and Indonesia and Malaysia together represent around 85% of global production (see figure 4.1).

The rapid growth of palm oil industries in the two leading producer countries resulted in a phenomenal expansion of plantations at the expense of natural forests (Koh and Wilcove 2008; Pirker et al. 2016). For economic reasons, both governments have strongly supported the expansion of palm oil

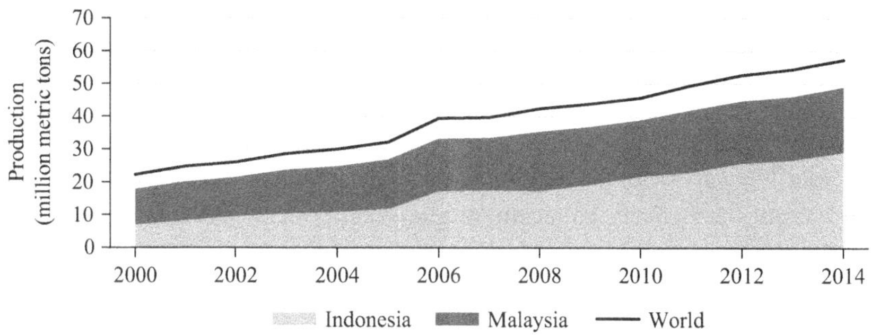

Figure 4.1
Changes in global palm oil production since 2000.
Data source: FAO 2018a.

export and have paid less attention to the consequences of land-use change (IFC 2011). But the tropical land converted to oil palm plantations contains species-rich and carbon-rich tropical forests, including peatlands, which are important biodiversity and carbon stocks (Koh et al. 2011; Vijay et al. 2016). As a result, large amounts of greenhouse gases have been released into the atmosphere, and the survival of many endangered species, such as the orangutan and Sumatran tiger, has been threatened (Greenpeace 2008; Rainforest Action Network 2013; Henders, Persson, and Kastner 2015). Human rights violations have also been associated with the expansion of oil palm plantations, including the failure to protect local communities' land rights and the use of forced and child labor (Colchester 2011; Rainforest Action Network 2013; Amnesty International 2016).

Seeing huge environmental and social impacts caused by the palm oil industry, in the late 1990s, WWF decided to partner with industry representatives and investors to promote sustainability governance in the global palm oil supply chain. The outcome was the creation in 2004 of a certification program—the RSPO—that aims to "transform markets to make sustainable palm oil the norm."[2] The RSPO is a membership-based organization, where businesses and civil society groups can join as members to participate in its decision-making processes and obtain access to its information. Business members can take a further step to get certified for producing or using sustainable palm oil. At the heart of this certification program are the RSPO Principles and Criteria, a set of guidelines for producing palm oil sustainably, against which assessments of producers are made by third parties. Businesses in the downstream part of the supply chain using certified palm oil also need to have their management system verified to obtain a supply chain certificate (like the chain-of-custody certification for seafood). On paper, the RSPO's Principles and Criteria cover every aspect of sustainable development to promote economically viable, environmentally appropriate, and socially beneficial management and operations (RSPO 2013; Pye 2016). But the program's standard-setting processes have been dominated by industry groups with little involvement of smallholders, and many loopholes exist in the implementation (Pichler 2013; Richardson 2015). Field investigations by environmental NGOs found cases where certified producers destroyed natural forests or violated the rights of local communities and workers.[3]

In terms of supply chain certification, the RSPO has four systems: book and claim, mass balance, segregated, and identity preserved.[4] In the "book and claim" system, downstream manufacturers and retailers who want to support sustainable palm oil can buy credits from RSPO-certified producers without physically purchasing and using certified palm oil. "Mass balance" allows downstream users to mix certified and uncertified palm oil but provides no guarantee about the percentage of certified palm oil in the resulting products and, therefore, may help in "greenwashing" (Rainforest Action Network 2013). Only the "segregated" and "identity preserved" systems monitor the whole supply chain by separating certified products, and the "identity preserved" system even traces sustainable palm oil back to the individual supply bases. While these systems imply different levels of commitment and use of certified products, the RSPO does not require downstream businesses to communicate the systems they choose to end consumers, and this has further sharpened observers' criticism (Ruysschaert and Salles 2014).

In response to external critics, the RSPO reformed its governance and strengthened its standards, and these efforts have made the program's requirements substantially more stringent than regulations in most producer countries (Schouten and Glasbergen 2011; Garrett et al. 2016). Accordingly, holding the promise of reducing the sustainability impacts of the global palm oil market, the RSPO has experienced rapid growth since 2008. As of June 2018, the RSPO had attracted 3,920 members and had more than 3.1 million hectares of certified oil palm area, which collectively produced 13.6 million tons of palm oil—approximately 19% of the global production volume (RSPO 2018a). Hence, the RSPO has been considered by some analysts to be one of the most successful eco-certification programs in the past decade

(Lernoud et al. 2017). To transform the global market, the RSPO needs to engage with emerging economies, which have become major end markets for palm oil (Schleifer 2016; Dauvergne 2017). In addition to the EU, China, India, and Indonesia were three major consumers in the past decade, together accounting for nearly 40% of global consumption.[5] But advocates of sustainable palm oil have been worried about these new end markets and have even warned that the demand by emerging markets for cheap palm oil is now the key driver behind agricultural expansion and deforestation in Indonesia and Malaysia (Greenpeace India 2012). In response to this market change, in the early 2010s, the RSPO decided to make efforts to promote certified products in emerging economies.[6]

The RSPO has set time-bound plans for uptake in these markets—for China, the goal is to have 10% of palm oil certified by 2020 (RSPO 2016). The target in China is relatively pessimistic compared to other Southern markets (e.g., 30% for India and 50% for Indonesia). While the rationale behind these targets remains unclear, the modest goal for China reflects the many obstacles that have been expected in transforming the country's palm oil sector.[7] In 2011, the RSPO was first introduced to Chinese companies, and in 2015, the program began to accelerate its spread in the country (see figure 4.2). Such progress is rather surprising for the RSPO, as the number of its members and supply chain certificates has always been higher in China than in India—an outcome contrary to the program's initial expectations for the two markets (Schleifer and Sun 2018).

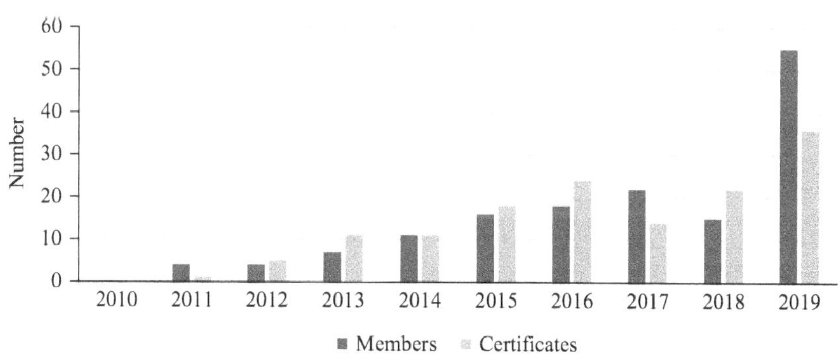

Figure 4.2
The RSPO's annual growth in China.
Data source: RSPO website at https://rspo.org/certification/search-for-supply-chain-certificate-holders.

Table 4.1
Support for the RSPO from major trading companies in the Chinese market

Company	RSPO membership	RSPO-certified facilities in China
Wilmar	✓	✓
Cargill	✓	✓
COFCO	✓	✓
Sinograin	✓	✗
Julong[a]	✓	✗
Sinar Mas	✓	✗

Note: This list was suggested by a commodity trader specializing in the Chinese palm oil market (Interview BBJ11). The imports of these companies represent more than half of the total palm oil consumed in China.
[a]Julong was a private Chinese company specializing in palm oil trade, but since mid-2016, the company has suffered from financial problems and withdrew its membership.

Growing support for the RSPO in the Chinese market is also reflected by the position of the commodity traders dominating China's palm oil supply chain. Table 4.1 shows that, as of mid-2017, nearly all major traders of palm oil in the Chinese market were RSPO members, and three of them had supplied certified palm oil to buyers through their facilities in China. Despite these encouraging trends, we must recognize that the uptake of certified palm oil in the Chinese market remains very low—only up to 1.5 % of the total volume imported to China, according to data for 2017–2018 (RSPO 2018a).[8] This figure shows a substantial gap between the physical uptake of certified products and the RSPO's target of 10%. To explain the RSPO's progress and limitations in China, we need to consider the industry's structure and the influence of key stakeholders.

4.2 China's Palm Oil Supply Chain

Over the past 25 years, China has become a major player in the global palm oil market by quintupling its consumption volume. Accounting for 17% of the country's vegetable oil consumption, palm oil is now the third-most popular vegetable oil in the country after soybean and rapeseed oils.[9] As the climate in China is not suitable for the growth of oil palm, all palm oil consumed in the country is imported, mostly from Indonesia and Malaysia.[10] Figure 4.3 illustrates China's import volumes and its position in the

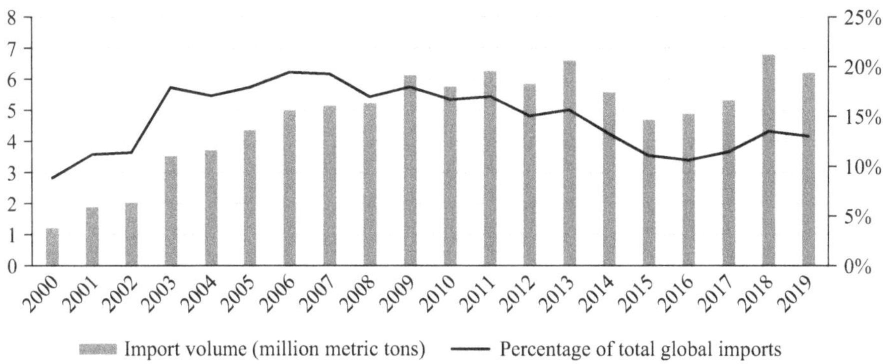

Figure 4.3
China's imports of palm oil.
Data source: US Department of Agriculture's reports *Oilseeds: World Markets and Trade* at https://usda.library.cornell.edu/concern/publications/tx31qh68h?locale=en.

global palm oil trade since 2000. Despite some fluctuations, China always has been one of the top palm oil importers in the world.[11]

The surge in the demand for palm oil has been driven by the development of China's food and chemical industries since the late 1990s. Trade liberalization policies in the agricultural sector, as a result of the country's accession to the World Trade Organization, further facilitated the import of palm oil for Chinese industries (Orden et al. 2007). In 2006, China finally opened its import market by abolishing all quotas and only setting a tariff rate of 9% for palm oil.[12] Due to this liberalization reform, an increasing number of private traders, including foreign-owned ones, were able to enter China's vegetable oil market (Martin 2005).

Nearly all palm oil imported to China is used to produce products consumed domestically, and only an insignificant amount is used in exported products (CFNA 2010). Being a large end market of palm oil poses challenges for the rise of palm oil certification in China, as the strategy of targeting Northern multinationals may be problematic due to the limited influence of these companies on the Chinese market. Unlike the case of the seafood processing industry, very few users of palm oil in China seek market access to developed countries. Hence, we are unlikely to observe the situations assumed by hypothesis 1 in chapter 2. This market structure has indeed made many practitioners pessimistic about the prospects of sustainable palm oil in China.[13]

In terms of industry structure, China's palm oil supply chain consists of three main stages: commodity trading, manufacturing of consumer goods, and retail. Involving very different companies at each stage, this chain often lacks lead firms seeking vertical coordination along the chain. In other words, downstream companies wanting to source certified products could face technical barriers to tracing their materials and identifying certified producers. Nonetheless, horizontally, the commodity trading industry in this chain has been concentrated in a small number of large companies—a feature that can be conducive to the spread of eco-certification. In the absence of official data, market analysts have estimated that fewer than ten trading companies control more than half of the supply of palm oil to China (also see table 4.1).[14]

Some top importers in this list are large multinational agribusinesses, which play a dominant role in the global agricultural commodity trade.[15] Originally established as grain traders, these companies have been transformed into "agricultural value chain managers" on a global scale by undertaking a range of activities from production and processing to distribution and finance (Clapp 2015). For their business in palm oil, companies like Cargill and Wilmar have their own integrated supply chains with plantations and crushing mills in producer countries.[16] Because of their influence on global trade, multinational agribusinesses have been the main targets of various eco-certification programs (Ponte 2014). This is also the case for the RSPO, which has proactively engaged these agribusinesses since its creation. Moreover, under pressure from NGO campaigns, consumer goods manufacturers have also asked these companies to provide a "license to operate" through certification or other governance initiatives (Rueda, Garrett, and Lambin 2017). As a result, major agribusinesses in the global palm oil market, such as Wilmar and Cargill, have decided to support the RSPO and have been committed to making 100% of their supply compliant with RSPO standards.[17] If these foreign traders follow through on such commitments in their business in China, they will constitute a key driving force of the rise of sustainable palm oil.

Besides multinational companies, the Chinese government has also aggressively supported the so-called "dragonhead" agribusinesses, and some state-owned companies, such as COFCO and Sinograin, have become top palm oil importers and strongly influence the Chinese market. More recently, Chinese agribusinesses have followed the state's "agricultural going out" policy to merge multinational commodity traders and purchase farmland and processing plants abroad (Schneider 2017). For instance, in 2014, COFCO acquired the majority stake of two major international grain traders, Nidera and Noble Agri, a move that would enable China to get closer to the source of oilseeds (Clapp 2015). Hence, if large, capital-intensive Chinese agribusinesses find the RSPO helpful in building their global reputation and improving their supply chain management, they may help the program to promote eco-certification in the Chinese market.

Additionally, a few private companies also became major palm oil importers in the 2000s (Potts et al. 2014). However, most of them are not traditional commodity traders but have used palm oil as collateral to get cash loans from banks and then put cash into higher-yielding investments (Ng 2013). To get loans from banks, private traders cash out their imported palm oil at a discounted price in China's local market, which discourages traditional commodity traders (i.e., agribusinesses) and palm oil users from importing directly from producer countries. However, to repay their loans, these companies must continue to increase their import volume, even though actual demand remains unchanged, and this has led to a vicious circle that further decreases the price in the Chinese market.[18] As a result, for several years, the price of palm oil in China was consistently lower than the imported price (Reuters 2014). This trading model, with a distorted price status, constituted a major challenge for the import of certified palm oil, as relevant trading companies are highly price sensitive and have little incentive to build relationships with producers. Fortunately, since 2014, most companies engaging in commodity financing have been gradually eliminated from the market, as the price discounts have become too high to maintain and the government also has tightened regulations on bank loans after a fraud case, in which traders pledged the same collateral for multiple loans (Reuters 2014). This market change has important implications for palm oil certification in China, as, compared to financial market speculators, large agribusinesses are more likely to support eco-certification to maintain long-term supply and corporate reputation.

Moving to the stage of consumer goods manufacturing, some large users of palm oil in China are branded companies that produce food or chemical products. In the 2000s, more than 70% of the palm oil imported to China was used in the food industry and around 15–20% was for the oleochemical industry (CFNA 2010; Ng 2013). In China's food industry, palm oil is not used as a major cooking oil, nor is it sold in bulk. Hence, most palm oil in China is used by convenience food manufacturers, and this market has become increasingly concentrated in large brands: For instance, a few companies control China's instant noodle industry (X. Zou 2013). In the oleochemical industry, palm oil is used to produce various personal care products and candles. The scale of production is relatively large and major manufacturers include both multinational and domestic chemical companies.[19] In this market, we see multinational brands like Unilever, which have adopted strong sustainability policies and may serve as important agents to introduce sustainable palm oil certification in China. However, given the scale of the country, it has been estimated that over 5,000 small companies in China use palm oil, many of which target the country's less developed regions.[20]

In the last stage of this chain, China has a fast-growing and increasingly concentrated retail sector, with the rapid expansion of Northern big-box supermarkets in the past two decades (Allen 2012; Dauvergne and Lister 2013; Pickles, Barrientos, and Knorringa 2016). Meanwhile, large Chinese supermarket chains have also become popular in urban areas (Hu et al. 2004). Accordingly, many products containing palm oil are likely to be sold by these large, branded retailers, who could play a key role in raising awareness and increasing the uptake of palm oil certification in China. For instance, the RSPO's growth in China would be accelerated if multinational retailers such as Walmart extended their sustainable sourcing commitments to the Chinese market (Dauvergne 2017).

Figure 4.4 illustrates the key parts of China's palm oil supply chain from production sites to retail stores. While vertical integration remains limited, the RSPO could leverage a few dominant traders, especially multinational ones, to promote certified palm oil in the Chinese market. Additionally, large, branded manufacturers using palm oil are prospective supporters of eco-certification. These structural features suggest opportunities for the RSPO to gain traction in China, although sustainability impacts of palm oil production remain largely unknown to most local stakeholders. Below I examine how the RSPO gradually entered and expanded its operations in China.

4.3 The Progress and Limitations of Sustainable Palm Oil Certification

The RSPO was initially introduced to Chinese stakeholders in the late 2000s.[21] However, until 2011, no companies based in China had joined the RSPO, nor had any certified palm oil been sold to the country. Since 2011,

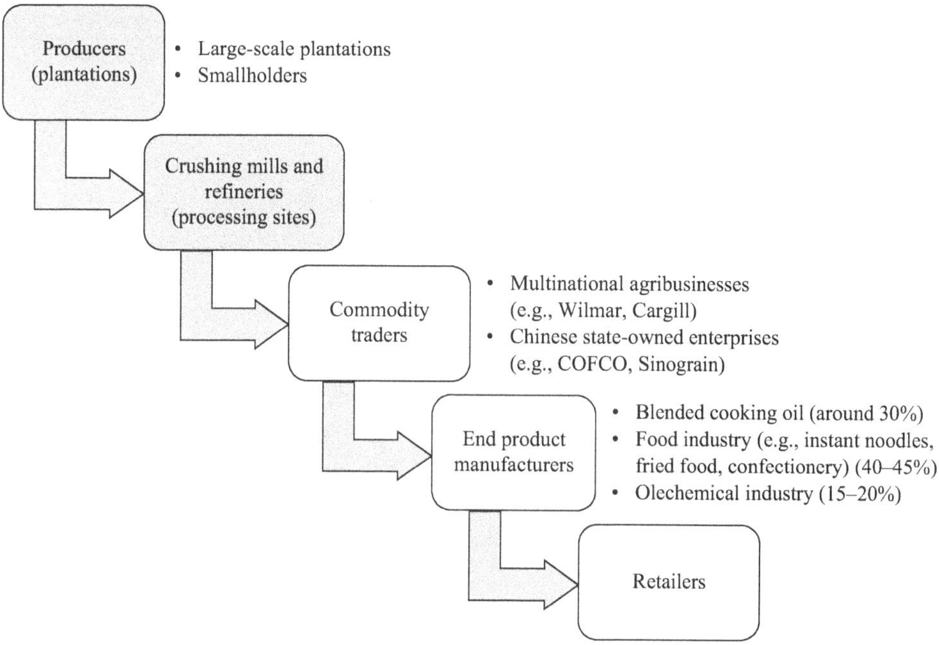

Figure 4.4
Structure of China' palm oil supply chain.
Note: Shaded boxes refer to stakeholders located outside China. Large multinational agribusinesses usually have integrated supply chains up to the stage of production, by owning plantations and crushing facilities in producer countries. But this is not the case for Chinese state-owned agribusinesses.

some companies began to show interest in the RSPO by becoming members and even obtaining supply chain certificates to physically handle certified palm oil. The RSPO gathered further momentum after 2014, as reflected by a surge in the number of new members and certificates every year (see figure 4.2). This progress is remarkable, although the sales volume of certified palm oil to China remains low. It can be attributed to the RSPO's efforts to engage with domestic stakeholders and the subsequent support from some actors in China's state organization. This section first examines the roles of different stakeholders in the relevant processes and then zooms in on the case of COFCO, a major state-owned commodity trader in China.

4.3.1 Transnational Market Influences on the Initial Entry of the RSPO

RSPO-certified facilities began to appear in China in 2011. As only an insignificant part of palm oil is used in China to make products for export, the influence of Northern buyers on the adoption of palm oil certification by Chinese firms should be limited. Nonetheless, in line with the mechanism specified by hypothesis 1 in chapter 2, a few export-oriented manufacturing companies were among the earliest RSPO certificate holders in China due to the demand by their customers in developed countries. The first-ever RSPO supply chain certificate holder in China was Beltek (Huizhou) Foods Co., a producer of instant noodles that not only supplies China's domestic market but also many developed countries, such as the US, the UK, Canada, and Germany since the early 2000s.[22] In its Communication of Progress to the RSPO, the company stated that to follow requirements on sustainable palm oil in foreign markets, 22% of the palm oil it had purchased in 2013 was from certified plantations.[23] This is a typical case, in which sustainability governance has flowed from Northern buyers upstream in the global palm oil supply chain. Hence, a few companies in developed markets sourcing products from China that contain palm oil were the drivers of the initial entry of the RSPO into China before 2015.[24]

In the same period, foreign-invested multinational corporations in China seemed to play a more significant role in introducing the RSPO to the Chinese industry and market by adopting relevant standards in their facilities and setting requirements for their suppliers. Most of them sought certification for their global operations due to the social pressure concerning palm oil that they had experienced from other countries. Accordingly, their certified facilities in China have served as a prerequisite for them to meet their global sourcing commitments, even if they did not immediately switch to certified palm oil in their Chinese business. In line with hypothesis 4, these foreign-invested companies tend to be large and have the capacity to implement traceability in their supply chains. These early supporters included companies at different stages of the supply chain, from commodity traders to consumer goods manufacturers and retailers.

Among commodity traders, large multinational agribusinesses like Wilmar and Cargill became major contributors to the initial rise of the RSPO in China after they had decided to support sustainable palm oil certification in their global networks. A notable example is Wilmar, a Singapore-based agribusiness that is one of the largest oil palm plantation owners in Indonesia and Malaysia and is also the largest edible oils refiner and specialty fats manufacturer in China.[25] As of mid-2017, the company had the most RSPO-certified facilities in China, holding 13 out of the 87 supply chain certificates listed on the RSPO's website. The company is among only a few agribusinesses in the world that have built an integrated system of palm oil production, encompassing cultivation, processing, and trading, and therefore has been able to adopt RSPO standards in its vertically integrated supply chain.

Wilmar's support for RSPO certification has been largely driven by criticisms from civil society groups about its environmental and social impacts in producer countries (Colchester et al. 2011). For instance, NGOs launched campaigns against the company and submitted complaints to the RSPO and also to the World Bank's International Finance Corporation, which financed the company's plantations (Balaton-Chrimes and Macdonald 2016). Under such pressure from civil society and investors, Wilmar announced a far-reaching policy commitment of "No Deforestation, No Peat, and No Exploitation" in 2013 (Poynton 2013; Wilmar 2013). With this commitment, the company began to adopt the RSPO standards in its global operations, including China, where it has always been a leading supplier. In late 2013, Wilmar adopted the RSPO supply chain standard in its processing plants in China, and a year later, it began to supply palm oil from certified plantations to China.[26] While the company has expressed its willingness to support the uptake of sustainable palm oil in the Chinese market, it has not announced any target for the volume or percentage of certified commodity in its Chinese business, nor has it set out explicit requirements for their Chinese buyers.[27] In other words, if downstream companies do not demand the certified commodity, Wilmar's support for the RSPO seems unlikely to increase the actual sales volume of sustainable palm oil in China.

In China's industry of consumer goods manufacturing, a few Northern-headquartered, branded companies were among the earliest promoters of sustainable palm oil in China. A widely cited example is Mars, Incorporated, an American manufacturer of chocolate and chewing gum. Partly as a response to activist campaigns in Northern markets, in 2010, the company joined the RSPO and set a target of sourcing only RSPO-certified palm oil by 2015. Since then, the company has implemented this policy in its global operations, including in China. To achieve its target, Mars has made great efforts to explain the importance of sustainable palm oil and potential benefits of eco-certification to its suppliers in China.[28] By the end of 2013, all palm oil purchased by the company around the globe was RSPO-certified according to the mass balance model. Hence, this case shows that the sourcing requirements of some foreign branded manufacturers in China provided another important pathway for the initial rise of certified palm oil in China in the early 2010s.

In the retail sector, multinational supermarkets' policies on responsible sourcing also facilitated the initial entry of the RSPO into the Chinese market. For example, Walmart and Carrefour committed to ensuring the use of 100% sustainable palm oil in their private brand products by the end of 2015. While both companies have prioritized Northern markets—North America for Walmart and Europe for Carrefour—in implementing their policies, they have also introduced the RSPO to their suppliers in China, driving a few Chinese manufacturers to support sustainable palm oil.[29] However, in their 2016 Communications of Progress to the RSPO, both retailers reported that their Chinese business represented only 1% of the total certified palm oil that they purchased globally.[30] Given the size of the whole Chinese market, these figures suggest that the existing policies of multinational supermarkets had only a marginal influence on the rise of sustainable palm oil.[31]

In summary, in the early 2010s, multinational companies in China were key actors in introducing the RSPO to Chinese businesses in the palm oil supply chain. As illustrated by figure 4.5, before 2014, 12 out of 13 RSPO supply chain certificates in China were held by foreign-invested companies. These

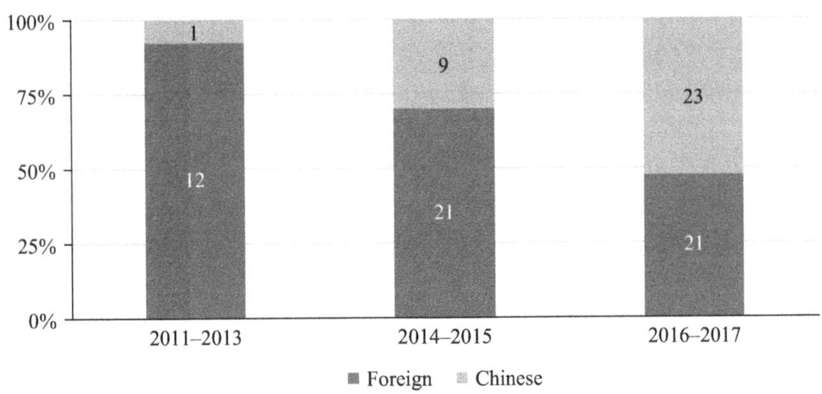

Figure 4.5
Evolution of RSPO supply chain certificate holders in China.
Note: The figures appearing in the bars indicate the number of certificates.
Data source: RSPO website at https://rspo.org/certification/search-for-supply-chain-certificate-holders.

companies drove the initial uptake of sustainable palm oil in China due to the pressure they received in other markets—a phenomenon that is in line with hypothesis 2 in chapter 2. Yet, as reflected by the RSPO's slow growth before 2015, the influences of transnational market agents remained weak in China's palm oil supply chain. This made the RSPO and its NGO supporters further realize the importance of gaining the support of Chinese stakeholders.

4.3.2 Engagement of the RSPO with Actors in the Chinese State

Soon after its creation, the RSPO acknowledged the importance of the Chinese market and began to devote efforts to engage with stakeholders in China's palm oil supply chain. The program has adopted a strategy to proactively leverage the influence of actors in the Chinese state to incentivize businesses for sourcing sustainable palm oil. According to a former top official of the RSPO, "to increase the uptake of sustainable palm oil in China, you should move the government first and get the right people on board."[32] Under this strategy, since 2008, the RSPO has invited representatives of the Chinese government and industry to the RSPO annual roundtable meetings and also organized, with support from some partner NGOs, several visits by Chinese stakeholders to producer countries for awareness raising.[33]

While the RSPO has gradually built connections with some government officials through these exchanges, the program was not present in China until 2015. Prior to that, it had mainly relied on transnational NGOs advocating sustainable palm oil to engage with Chinese stakeholders. In this respect, WWF, as a founding member of the RSPO, played an important role. WWF-China was the first organization to raise the issue of palm oil in China in 2007 and helped the RSPO establish contacts with some government agencies and businesses.[34] Another important partner is Solidaridad, a Dutch development NGO, which has worked on palm oil issues since 2009 and has actively advocated sustainable palm oil in the global market. Since 2013, Solidaridad, with the support of the Dutch government, has organized several roundtable dialogues with Chinese stakeholders as well as study tours in Europe and Indonesia in order to raise Chinese stakeholders' awareness of sustainability problems related to palm oil.[35]

For both WWF and Solidaridad, their main approach is to engage the attention of major companies in the supply chain through communication and collaboration instead of campaigns or boycotts. To incentivize companies in the palm oil supply chain to support eco-certification, both NGOs first attempted to partner with the relevant government agencies or industry associations supervised by these agencies. This strategy has been deemed particularly important in China, because the government cannot be bypassed in the rise of transnational governance. According to the team leader of the market transformation program in WWF-China, "The nature of voluntary standards changed when they entered China[,] as the country remains an incomplete market economy . . . the Chinese government has a strange position as it would like to represent everyone including companies, civil society, and consumers."[36] As I show below, over time, proactive engagement by the RSPO and its NGO partners with Chinese state actors has come to fruition, as reflected by the establishment of a partnership in 2013 with the CFNA, a national trade association supervised by the Ministry of Commerce (MOFCOM).

In China, the MOFCOM is the national agency regulating commodity import, and it naturally became the first target of engagement by the RSPO and its NGO supporters. As mentioned earlier, in 2008, the RSPO invited officials of the MOFCOM to attend its annual meeting and visit plantations in Indonesia. Despite sending their officials to these activities, the MOFCOM viewed the RSPO as a foreign NGO and remained unwilling to start formal collaborations with it.[37] For transnational NGOs, the MOFCOM has been one of the most difficult Chinese ministries to approach, as it lacks experience working with civil society groups and has demonstrated little interest in sustainability issues outside China.[38]

Nonetheless, the RSPO and WWF-China found opportunities in a trade association on oils and oil seeds under supervision of the MOFCOM (i.e., CFNA). Representing China's agri-food industry involved in import and export, CFNA comprises more than 6,900 members, including all major firms in different stages of China's palm oil supply chain. Like most other national industry associations in China, it is a quasi-state organization responsible for passing on the opinions of the industry and providing policy advice to national regulators, in this case the MOFCOM. Accordingly, the association has played a bridging role in communication between the state and the companies importing oils and oilseeds, and it has influence on China's palm oil market by providing important policy and market information.[39] Due to the role of CFNA in China's palm oil supply chain, its top officials also joined the Chinese delegation at the RSPO annual meeting in 2008. This trip made CFNA's officials realize that eco-certification has become such an important governance mode in the global palm oil market that Chinese businesses could no longer ignore this new trend.[40] Therefore, CFNA showed interest in starting a dialogue with the RSPO. Seeing this as an opportunity to find supporters in China's state organization, the RSPO and its NGO supporters proactively approached CFNA about a collaboration to promote sustainable palm oil in China.

As a result, CFNA began to work with the RSPO on several awareness-raising activities to introduce the concept of sustainable palm oil and RSPO certification to Chinese businesses. In 2009, CFNA assisted the RSPO in organizing a dialogue on sustainable palm oil held in conjunction with the China International Cereals and Oils Industry Summit, and CFNA invited major importers and users of palm oil in China to participate in the dialogue. These participants agreed on a statement of support for the promotion of sustainable palm oil, based on which the "China Sustainable Palm Oil Network" was created later in the year as a platform for sharing information among major companies in the palm oil supply chain, the RSPO, and its NGO partners. From 2009 to 2011, this network organized several stakeholder meetings and identified a strategic plan to help companies increase the procurement and use of sustainable palm oil.[41]

These meetings have allowed CFNA officials and representatives of its member companies to regularly interact with transnational actors supporting sustainable palm oil and to better understand the sustainability impacts of palm oil production.[42] As a result of such interactions, CFNA and some of its members have gradually increased their interest in supporting sustainable palm oil. Collaboration between CFNA and the RSPO has been further strengthened since 2010 through a study sponsored by the UK's then-Department for International Development (DFID) on developing policy recommendations for sustainable palm oil in China.[43] As the Chinese party executing this project, CFNA organized three multi-stakeholder forums from 2011 to 2012 and published a report on the "Prospects and Challenges of Sustainable Palm Oil for China" (CFNA 2010). The project has enabled CFNA's leadership to further realize the influence of the RSPO on the global palm oil supply chain and the changing positions of key market actors on eco-certification.[44] Seeing the need to inform Chinese companies sourcing palm oil of such changes, in May 2013, CFNA decided to formalize its partnership and strengthen collaboration with the RSPO in a Memorandum of Understanding (MoU). By signing this MoU, CFNA has started to "fully endorse RSPO certification and [be] committed to working with [the] RSPO to promote the procurement and use of sustainable palm oil in China."[45]

Winning the moral support of this trade association has been a key achievement for the RSPO, allowing it to further diffuse knowledge about sustainable palm oil and its certification in the Chinese market. For the RSPO, CFNA became a "comrade" in promoting sustainable palm oil and further helped the program engage with major Chinese companies in the supply chain.[46] For CFNA, collaboration with the RSPO has allowed the group to expand its areas of work to sustainability issues and gain more traction both within the state and internationally. In 2014, following the first study project, CFNA led another project funded by DFID on developing a code of best practices for Chinese companies investing in palm oil production. The result is the "Guide for Overseas Investment and Production of Sustainable Palm Oil by Chinese Enterprises" (CFNA 2015). The development and publication of this guide and related outreach activities have further raised awareness among Chinese businesses about the sustainability challenges associated with palm oil, providing an impetus for the growth of RSPO certification beyond transnational market influences. Hence, although the RSPO could not collaborate with the MOFCOM, its partnership with CFNA, a quasi-state organization connected to the MOFCOM, has been helpful in promoting sustainable palm oil in the Chinese market.

In retrospect, the partnership with CFNA constitutes a critical juncture for the RSPO to attract members and certified companies in China. In this process, the endorsement of CFNA has helped the program establish contacts with large state-owned commodity traders, such as COFCO, and also, through stakeholder forums and meetings, has raised awareness of the sustainability issues associated with palm oil among a wide range of downstream companies in the supply chain. For many Chinese companies, the information and advice provided by CFNA has been deemed credible and even interpreted as a signal of future government policy.[47] As a result, the MoU between the RSPO and CFNA and the resulting efforts to promote certified palm oil in China have given incentives to an increasing number of Chinese companies, especially large ones, to support sustainable palm oil. As shown by figure 4.5, before 2014, all but one of the RSPO supply chain certificates in China were held by multinational companies, and no certified palm oil had been physically imported to China; but since 2016, the share of domestic companies over the total number of RSPO-certified plants in China has significantly increased, and a few of them have physically purchased certified palm oil.[48] Although the sourcing policies of multinational companies also contributed to this growth, CFNA's nudge-like interventions, including information sharing and awareness raising, have been a critical force driving this progress.

With CFNA's support, the RSPO also began to strengthen its organizational capacity in China in late 2015 by opening a local office in Beijing with a full-time national representative. Since then, the program has further intensified its marketing efforts in China. In 2016, it launched a Chinese website and organized a stakeholder forum. As in the case of the seafood sector, the RSPO and WWF-China began to collaborate in 2016 with the national industry association in the retail sector—China Chain Store and Franchise Association (CCFA)—to organize a yearly "Say Yes to Sustainable Palm Oil" consumer campaign.[49] In 2017, 156 supermarkets, department stores, and appliance stores participated in this event (RSPO 2018a). These activities were associated with an accelerated growth of the RPSO in China, where the number of RSPO-certified facilities increased by 40% from mid-2016 to mid-2017 (RSPO 2017b). The growing presence of the RSPO in China has also gained the attention of researchers working for an advisory body of the State Council, who suggested using the RSPO to green China's palm oil supply chain in a 2016 report (CCICED 2016).[50]

More recently, with sustainable development increasingly gaining importance on the Chinese government's agenda and palm oil becoming a salient issue in global arena, CFNA has continued its support for sustainable palm oil by creating with the RSPO and WWF the "China Sustainable Palm Oil Alliance," a platform aiming to facilitate communication among stakeholders in China's palm oil supply chain for increasing the uptake of certified palm oil (RSPO 2018b). In short, since the late 2000s, the RSPO has proactively approached Chinese state actors and formed a partnership with CFNA, the national trade association affiliated with the MOFCOM. CFNA's endorsement has further facilitated the RSPO's engagement with major Chinese companies in the supply chain. Table 4.2 summarizes the milestones in this process and the role of CFNA.

Despite the momentum gained by the rise of RSPO certification in China, a caveat must be added about the program's actual impact due to the very low volume of certified commodity imported into the country. CFNA's support has been effective in raising awareness about sustainability impacts of

Table 4.2
Milestones in the rise of sustainable palm oil in China

Date	Activities
2013	The MoU signed between the RSPO and CFNA forming a strategic partnership to promote the procurement and use of sustainable palm oil in China
2014–2015	A DFID-funded project, implemented by CFNA, producing the "Guide for Overseas Investment and Production of Sustainable Palm Oil by Chinese Enterprises"
2015	The opening of a local RSPO office in Beijing
2016	The launch of a Chinese website of the RSPO; The organization of the first RSPO-China forum bringing together stakeholders in China's palm oil supply chain
Since 2016	The "Say Yes to Sustainable Palm Oil" campaign in supermarkets and stores, organized by the RSPO, WWF, and CCFA
2018	The "China Sustainable Palm Oil Alliance" created by CFNA, the RSPO, and WWF

palm oil and introducing the RSPO to Chinese businesses. However, simply relying on the provision of information and technical advice without financial rewards cannot offer businesses strong incentives to change their sourcing practices. Furthermore, unlike seafood, the product characteristics of palm oil as an ingredient, instead of end product, and its bad reputation among Chinese consumers for being unhealthy have made many food manufacturers unwilling to openly promote certified palm oil in the market.[51] Consequently, Chinese companies may become RSPO members and even get supply chain certificates as a preemptive strategy to prepare for potential market changes, but without proactively changing sourcing behavior.

Seeing the limitations of the current partnership between the RSPO and CFNA, many advocates of sustainable palm oil have stressed the need for "building a business case through more concreate policies," such as public procurement or reduced tariffs for certified palm oil.[52] Unfortunately, according to several observers, CFNA had no intention of advocating for further policy support from the MOFCOM to increase the physical uptake of sustainable palm oil, partly because the Chinese government is unlikely to pay for sustainability benefits in producer countries.[53] For CFNA, the fact that palm oil is much less important than soybean oil in China's vegetable oil market also limits the association's incentives to make additional efforts lobbying the government to subsidize importers of certified palm oil. Indeed, despite some efforts by transnational NGOs and foreign governments in persuading the Chinese government to set a sourcing target like some European countries do, no state agency in China has ever expressed interest in taking further actions to promote sustainable palm oil.[54] Therefore, the support of Chinese state actors for palm oil certification has remained lukewarm and has made little contribution to the physical uptake of the certified commodity.

4.3.3 Case Study: COFCO's Support for Sustainable Palm Oil

The analysis in this section shows how the RSPO's engagement with domestic stakeholders and the subsequent support from CFNA has led to growing interest in sustainable palm oil in China. Considering the progress that the RSPO has made in the country, one of the greatest achievements is winning support of state-owned agribusinesses, which are major palm oil suppliers in the Chinese market. In this respect, the commitments on sustainable palm oil made by COFCO are remarkable. I now delve into this case to show how COFCO has been approached by the RSPO and has gradually generated incentives for supporting sustainable sourcing.

Being state owned, COFCO is the largest Chinese agribusiness operating on a global scale in a range of commodity sectors. In China, it is a top importer of oilseeds, including soybean and palm oil. In recent years, the company has risen in the global commodity market by acquiring some international grain traders and increasing its investment in commodity production in other developing countries (Clapp 2015; Schneider 2017). Due to the company's scale and its importance in China's palm oil supply chain, RSPO founding organizations attempted to involve COFCO in the program's initial creation; as a result, COFCO joined the RSPO in 2005 due to corporate social responsibility considerations.[55] However, because of the uncertainty in China's palm oil market and changes in the company's internal governance, COFCO did not further engage in the RSPO's activities and soon withdrew its membership.[56]

In the early 2010s, when the RSPO and its NGO supporters approached the company again, at a time when the Chinese government was paying increasing attention to sustainable development, COFCO returned to the RSPO to support sustainable palm oil. The change in COFCO's palm oil policy occurred after advocates of sustainable palm oil, especially WWF, had partnered with CFNA to establish dialogues with the then-top managers of COFCO. Through these dialogues, COFCO's leadership learned about the benefits of the RSPO and concrete ways to make progress on sustainable sourcing.[57] As a result, COFCO resumed its RSPO membership in late 2012, and a few months later, it received its first supply chain certificate following the RSPO's mass balance model.

Since its return to the RSPO, COFCO has made a strong commitment to sourcing sustainable palm oil. The company has seen its support for the RSPO as part of China's action to combat climate change and pursue sustainable development. As the Chinese government has strengthened its climate and sustainability policies, COFCO has also announced its ambitious commitment to sustainable commodities at several international events. In December 2015, during a side event at the Paris Climate Summit, the then-chairman of the company, Ning Gaoning, introduced a plan to promote sustainable consumption in China:

> We will not buy products grown from areas of deforestation or conversion of natural habitats, or the crops produced by using a lot of pesticides, water and other chemicals due to poor management of farming practices. . . . We will strive to establish green and sustainable global supply chains, because we are in a great position to decide what product[s] we buy or do not buy to meet the increasing demand of Chinese consumers for environmentally friendly agriculture products.[58]

At the 2017 World Economic Forum in Davos, the company's president again underscored the commitment to purchase sustainably produced commodities and called on global commodity traders to "turn our pledge into concrete measures" (Elliott 2017). For some observers, these statements by a Chinese company marked a historical shift by China's leadership on global climate action (Tabuchi 2017). Therefore, in addition to concerns about corporate social responsibility, COFCO, as a state-owned enterprise (SOE), has also drawn on transnational sustainability governance to support broad policy goals set by the top Chinese leaders.

Beyond these statements, COFCO has also taken concrete steps to support the RSPO and sustainable palm oil. The company is among the four Chinese members that have maintained the best reporting records by disclosing their purchased volume of certified palm oil every year.[59] Thus, in terms of reporting and transparency, COFCO has been one of the most compliant companies in China with respect to the RSPO's requirements. Moreover, beginning in 2013, COFCO has begun to purchase certified palm oil, and since then, its sourcing volume of sustainable palm oil has gradually increased (see figure 4.6). However, the purchasing volume has remained very low, showing that COFCO has a long way to go before completely switching to sustainable sourcing. A main obstacle to this fundamental change seems to be the price premium, which makes certified palm oil unlikely to become mainstream in the Chinese market, even though COFCO has made efforts to promote certified commodity to its downstream buyers.[60]

Therefore, the case of COFCO shows that Chinese SOEs can become strong supporters of transnational eco-certification without pressure from Northern markets. According to NGO officials interacting with COFCO, the company's progress should be attributed to its top managers, who are also government officials and, therefore, sought to use eco-certification to support the Chinese state's policy on sustainable development.[61] Hence, at a deeper level, COFCO's support for sustainable palm oil has been motivated by the increasingly strong position of the Chinese state on supporting sustainable development. In this case, the shadow of the state has contributed to the adoption of corporate sustainability policy by Chinese SOEs. Nonetheless, we also see only slow progress by COFCO in delivering on its

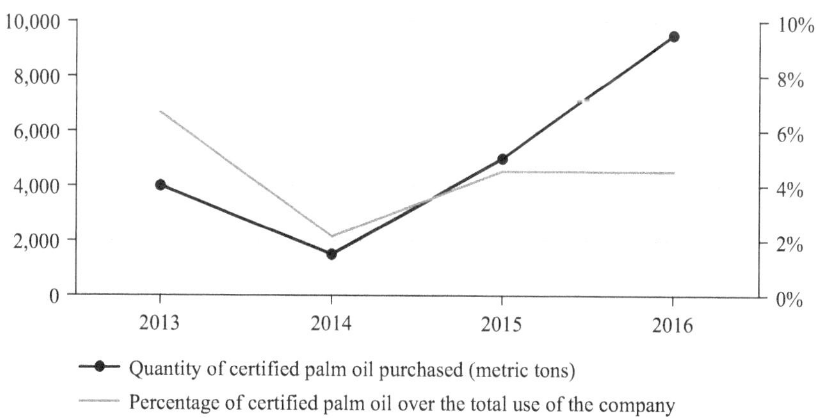

Figure 4.6
COFCO's purchase of certified sustainable palm oil.
Data source: Annual Communications of Progress submitted by COFCO to the RSPO in 2013–2016, at https://www.rspo.org/members/1928/COFCO-Corporation/group-member, last accessed on August 13, 2018.

commitment, which provides evidence casting doubt on the potential of sustainable palm oil in the Chinese market.

4.4 Conclusion

The case of palm oil demonstrates the challenges for the rise of transnational eco-certification in China when the influence of Northern market agents remains weak. In the early 2010s, the RSPO was little known in China's palm oil supply chain, although several multinational corporations had introduced the program and set sourcing requirements for their subsidiaries and suppliers. In other words, despite evidence supporting the hypothesis on the contribution of foreign investment (hypothesis 2 in chapter 2), this mechanism could not lead to a rapid expansion of sustainable palm oil in China.

Yet, with the RSPO's proactive strategy to engage with local stakeholders, sustainable palm oil certification has still taken off in this difficult market environment since the mid-2010s. In this process, the strategic partnership with CFNA—a quasi-state trade association—has helped the program approach a larger number of companies and raise their awareness of sustainable palm oil. For instance, the case of COFCO shows that some Chinese SOEs have become willing to use eco-certification to show their support for China's policy on global sustainable development and climate action. As a result, an increasing number of companies in China, especially domestic ones, have become RSPO members and have even become certified. Hence, the recent momentum of palm oil certification in the Chinese market lends support for both hypothesis 3 on the importance of proactive communication and the local capacity of transnational certification programs and hypothesis 6 on the support of national industry associations.

The partnership between CFNA and the RSPO also corroborates hypothesis 7 on the conditions enabling the emergence of Chinese state actors' support for transnational governance. The existence of the MOFCOM, as the only agency regulating palm oil import, and CFNA, as the relevant association supervised by the MOFCOM, has facilitated the RSPO in identifying its target of engagement and concentrating its efforts. On this basis, the efforts of the RSPO and its NGO supporters, especially WWF, to initiate dialogues and organize study tours have been helpful in building the trust of Chinese officials and have ultimately paved the way for establishing the

RSPO-CFNA partnership. Compared to the seafood case (see chapter 3), state actors' support for palm oil certification has been weaker and less determined. Such variations may be explained by the fact that China can gain fewer economic benefits from palm oil certification, given that the country does not produce the commodity.

Additionally, this chapter shows that, to date, Chinese companies supporting the RSPO mainly consist of large agribusinesses and manufacturers of food and chemical products. In these cases, market concentration and economies of scale reduce the marginal costs of certification. This uptake pattern, in combination with the challenges that many downstream companies face in tracking materials along their supply chains, supports hypothesis 4 on the fit between domestic industry structure and the governance model of eco-certification.

The palm oil sector also shows the limits of eco-certification in transforming the Chinese market. Despite the progress made by the RSPO since the mid-2010s, the sales volume of certified palm oil has been less than 2% of total consumption in China. In fact, several barriers are likely to persist in the foreseeable future to prevent significant growth of the import of certified palm oil by China. First, unlike seafood, which is consumed as an end product, palm oil remains largely unknown by consumers. More work is needed from the RSPO and its supporters to educate Chinese consumers and subsequently develop their demand for the certified commodity. But this task seems extremely difficult, as the negative consequences of the palm oil industry are not perceived as a major issue in Chinese society. Relatedly, without strong consumer demand, retailers and consumer goods manufacturers are reluctant to change their sourcing practices. This is even less likely for this commodity, as certified palm oil is more expensive than its conventional counterpart. With a lack of demand from their downstream businesses, commodity traders can hardly translate their responsible sourcing commitments into an actual increase in the sales volume of certified palm oil. As shown by the cases of COFCO and Wilmar, traders have been unwilling to impose certified commodity requirements on their buyers, given the competition in the market. This situation may result in gridlock in the supply chain, where businesses at different stages wait for others to move first, despite everyone claiming to support sustainability. Finally, although CFNA has played a central role in promoting the RSPO in China, its nudge-like interventions have limitations in generating market demand for certified palm oil. State agencies like the MOFCOM could use regulations or rewards to break the abovementioned gridlock. However, the Chinese government has shown no intention of taking stronger actions to promote sustainable palm oil. Looking ahead, hopes may lie in China's eagerness to take a leadership role in global environmental governance through some sourcing commitments, but it remains to be seen whether the Chinese state wants to draw on transnational governance to achieve this goal.

5 Tea: Fertile Ground without Seeds for Transnational Eco-Certification

As an important cash crop across five continents, tea constitutes the most consumed manufactured drink in the world (Chang and Brattlof 2015). While the commodity has played a critical role in rural development and poverty reduction in the Global South, its production is anything but sustainable for the environment, farmers, and workers due to issues like chemical pollution, biodiversity loss, and labor abuses. Realizing these challenges, several Northern-based transnational initiatives have stepped into the sector to certify sustainable tea over the past two decades. While the uptake of certified products quickly increased in the global tea market in the 2010s, the relevant programs have made little progress in China—the world's leading tea producer and consumer country, accounting for, by volume, more than 40% of the global production and 33% of the global consumption (Chang 2015; FAO 2018a; Willer et al. 2019).[1] What has prevented the rise of sustainable tea certification in China?

Drawing on a range of data, including field interviews and surveys, this chapter examines the challenges facing transnational certification programs in China's tea industry and the possible pathways for soliciting support from Chinese producers for sustainable tea certification. The analysis highlights three takeaways. First, the structure of China's tea industry limits the influence of transnational market agents on the spread of eco-certification to the country. More specifically, a large, self-sufficient domestic value chain, where the type of dominant products differs from that in developed markets, has made China a difficult territory for multinational brands—the main advocates of sustainable tea certification. Second, transnational certification programs have shown little intention to engage with Chinese stakeholders, and a fragmented regulatory structure in China's tea sector has further reduced the likelihood of collaboration between transnational programs and Chinese state actors. As a result, the relevant programs have yet to harness support from influential actors in China's state bureaucracy to increase their market uptake. In this sense, the tea case contrasts with those of seafood and palm oil by relying primarily on market forces to spread transnational governance to China, and this dynamic further explains the low adoption rate of sustainable tea certification among Chinese producers. Third, through a survey experiment with a sample of Chinese tea producing companies, I find that seeking linkages with China's goals on sustainable development and policy support from local governments can be an effective strategy for transnational programs to increase their uptake in China; by contrast, Chinese producers have little interest in using certification to gain access to foreign markets. This quantitative study provides further evidence of the state's influence on the rise of transnational governance in China.

In this chapter, I first introduce different eco-certification programs in the global tea market and their uptake in China. Next, I analyze the structure of China's tea industry and examine its fit with transnational standards. I then investigate the slow progress of each transnational program in China and show that the forces that can potentially drive the spread of sustainable tea certification have been largely missing in the past two decades. In section 5.4, I present the results of a survey experiment conducted as part of the Organic Tea Producer Survey (see details on this survey in appendix C), which suggest the strong influence of state policy on businesses' interest in sustainable tea certification. I conclude with some recommendations for promoting sustainability governance in China's tea industry.

5.1 The Rise of Eco-Certification in the Global Tea Market

Located in tropical and subtropical areas, most tea production regions are ecologically sensitive and underdeveloped. The commodity has therefore been associated with several sustainability issues. Biodiversity loss and land-use change are deemed the key environmental challenges, due to the expansion of monoculture plantations at the expense of tropical forests (H. Li et al. 2012; Owuor et al. 2018). Another major concern is the overuse of agrochemicals as pesticides and fertilizers, which have negative effects on both consumers' health and the local environment. For instance, residues of hazardous pesticides have been found to be higher than the recommended limits in many tea products sold in China and India (Greenpeace

2012, 2016; Greenpeace India 2014). Moreover, labor rights violations—including exploitation, unsafe working conditions, and child labor—are prevalent in tea plantations across developing countries (van der Wal 2008; Wu 2009). Additionally, in the global tea supply chain, the value distribution has been highly uneven between upstream producers and a handful of multinational brands focusing on blending, packing, and marketing, and as a result, Southern producers hardly benefit from market growth and have few resources to improve their practices (Talbot 2002; van der Wal 2008; LeBaron 2018).

Despite the salience of these issues, tea was relatively late in becoming a dynamic field of eco-certification compared to other tropical commodities, such as coffee and cocoa. By the late 2000s, only a small group of stakeholders in the global tea supply chain were aware of corporate social responsibility and sustainability standards (van der Wal 2008). But rapid progress has been made since then with the development of tea standards by large transnational certification programs like Rainforest Alliance (RA). In the past decade, sustainable tea certification has experienced remarkable growth: as of 2017, around 19% of the area on which tea is harvested globally was certified to sustainability standards to supply at least 20.9% of the global production volume (Willer et al. 2019).[2] At the time of writing, Fairtrade International, RA, and UTZ are the three major transnational eco-certification programs for tea, whereas organic certification is subject to national regulation in most countries.[3] I now discuss these programs and their market uptake in China.

Fairtrade was the first transnational certification program to enter the tea sector back in the 1990s. The "fair trade" movement originally emerged in Europe to promote more equitable North-South trade by empowering producers to combat poverty, strengthen their position in value chains, and take more control over their lives through a premium set above world market prices (Raynolds 2000). Fairtrade International was created in 1997 as a global membership organization to coordinate different fair trade schemes that supported the sustainable development of small-scale producers and agricultural workers through a range of social, economic, and environmental requirements.[4] In 2016, the program certified 3.1% of the global tea area (representing 4.3% of the global production volume), and most Fairtrade-certified areas were in Kenya, Uganda, and India (Lernoud et al. 2018). Fairtrade certification was introduced to Chinese producers relatively early, with the first certificate awarded in 2001 to a cooperative in Jiangxi.[5]

However, the program has had little growth since then in China: as of 2016, there were only nine certified cooperatives with a total annual production of less than 3,400 metric tons (BRECC 2017; Lernoud et al. 2018).

RA has been the program with the highest uptake in the global tea market since 2011. As an NGO dedicated to environmental conservation and sustainable livelihoods, RA developed its certification program on sustainable agriculture in the 1990s.[6] The program began to certify tea through a partnership with Unilever, the owner of Lipton and PG Tips, with the aim of promoting sustainable tea certification in the mainstream market (Henderson and Nellemann 2012). In May 2007, Unilever announced its goal of certifying all tea in Lipton and PG Tips teabags sold in Western Europe by 2010 and in the world by 2015. Soon thereafter, other tea brands, including Twinings and Tetley, made similar sourcing commitments (Braga et al. 2010). With support from these brands, RA soon became popular in the global tea industry: In 2016, the program certified 11.4% of the global tea area (469,000 hectares), producing more than 1.08 million metric tons of tea (Lernoud et al. 2018). The program was initially introduced to producers in China in 2012 by Unilever due to Lipton's sourcing requirement.[7] However, compared to other major producer countries, RA has made little progress in spreading its standards to Chinese producers: As of March 2017, only 26 tea farms with a total area of 6,515 hectares were certified in the country, which produced only 1.4% of the total volume of RA-certified tea (Newsom and Milder 2018).[8] Hence, despite its influence on the global supply chain, the program remains marginal in the world's largest producer country.

The third transnational program is UTZ, a Dutch initiative originating in 2002 to promote sustainable farming in the coffee sector. The program aims to ensure social and environmental sustainability and improve farm management. UTZ entered the tea sector in 2007; had its first certified tea producer in Malawi in 2009; and has since received support from several European tea brands, such as Pickwick and Messmer.[9] As a younger program, UTZ has rapidly increased the uptake of its tea certification since 2010, although its certified area has been much smaller than that of the two aforementioned programs. In China, UTZ remains largely unknown: As of 2016, it had only certified 1,040 hectares of tea farms in the country, with an estimated annual production volume of less than 3,000 metric tons (Lernoud et al. 2018).

Table 5.1 shows that, compared to their global reach, the three transnational programs have gained little traction in China's tea sector. The

Table 5.1
Uptake of sustainable tea certification (including organic certification)

Certification program	Global reach	Uptake in China
Fairtrade International	3.1% of the global harvested area; 4.3% of the global production volume	0.1% of China's harvested area; 0.15% of China's production volume
Rainforest Alliance	11.4% of the global harvested area; 18.4% of the global production volume	0.28% of China's harvested area; 0.48% of China's production volume
UTZ	1.7% of the global harvested area; 2% of the global production volume	0.05% of China's harvested area; 0.13% of China's production volume
China National Organic Product Certification	2% of the global harvested area; 1.5% of the global production volume	2.1% of China's harvested area; 2.2% of China's production volume

Note: Data are as of 2016, drawn from Lernoud et al. (2018), and the percentages of the certified volume over the total production volume are calculated using the relevant data from FAO 2018a.

proportions of their certified areas and production volumes in China are all below 0.5%. By contrast, we find that organic certification, which has more stringent environmental standards than these programs promoting sustainable agriculture, is much more popular among Chinese tea producers. In fact, since the late 2000s, China has emerged as the world's leading producer country of organic tea (CNCA and China Agricultural University 2016; Lernoud et al. 2018). Nearly all organic tea producers in China have been certified by the national certification program run by the government, which has not been recognized by most foreign countries. This means that organic tea produced in China has been sold mainly domestically.[10] While the rise of organic tea certification in China has benefited from some supportive government policies, it also suggests important developments in China's tea industry that are relevant to sustainability governance (CNCA 2014). To understand the limits of transnational sustainability certification and the relative success of national organic certification in China's tea sector, we first consider the structural features of the Chinese industry.

5.2 Characteristics of China's Tea Industry

For centuries, tea was produced exclusively in China, due to specific agro-climatic requirements and manufacturing processes that were unknown to the rest of the world. In the early seventeenth century, tea began to be exported to Europe by the East India Company and soon became a fashionable drink, especially in Britain. Growing tea consumption also caused large trade deficits for the British Empire with Qing China, which became a major cause of the First Opium War in 1839 and later led the East India Company to commission botanists to take tea seedlings from China for replantation in India (Rose 2010).[11] Hence, in the second half of the nineteenth century, many large-scale plantations emerged in British India and Ceylon, which challenged China's position as the leading exporter in the global tea market (Gupta 2008). In the first half of the twentieth century, China's production and export fell dramatically because of foreign invasion, civil war, and economic dislocation; it was only after the Communist Party took power that the tea industry slowly began to recover (Etherington and Forster 1993). Figure 5.1 illustrates the growth of the global and Chinese tea industries in the past half century. It shows that, since the mid-1980s, the tea harvest area and production volume in China increased by 2.5 times and 3.8 times, respectively, and this rapid expansion has been a key driver of the global tea market. While the rejuvenation of China's tea sector has benefited from modern technologies and economies of scale, the

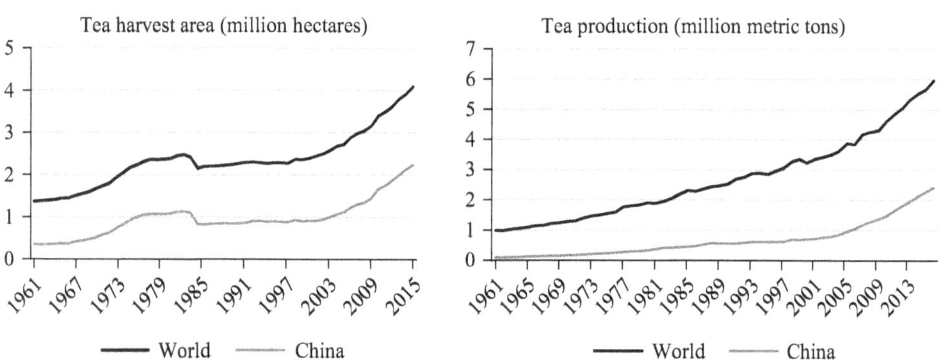

Figure 5.1
Expansion of tea production in China and the world (1961–2016).
Data source: FAO 2018a.

industry itself has several unique characteristics compared to those of other major producer countries. Three of these characteristics are likely to condition the rise of sustainable tea certification: trade patterns, degree of market concentration, and scale of production.

5.2.1 Trade Patterns: A Large Domestic Market and Rising South-South Trade

First, China's position in the global tea market has limited the influence of Northern buyers on Chinese producers' adoption of eco-certification. Although China had regained its position as the world's largest exporter country of tea in the mid-2010s in both volume and value, the relevant trade patterns have limited the exposure of its tea industry to the certification requirements of transnational market agents. In fact, as shown in figure 5.2, the importance of the export market for China's tea industry has continuously decreased from 35.8% in 2001 to only 13.9% in 2016. In other words, tea is no longer an export commodity for most Chinese producers. Meanwhile, the domestic tea market in China is huge and has grown very rapidly since the early 2000s. Between 2006 and 2013, the amount of tea consumed in China almost doubled, surpassing 1.6 million tons and accounting for one-third of the world's total consumption (Chang 2015).[12] Hence, for Chinese producers, more opportunities seem to exist in the domestic market.

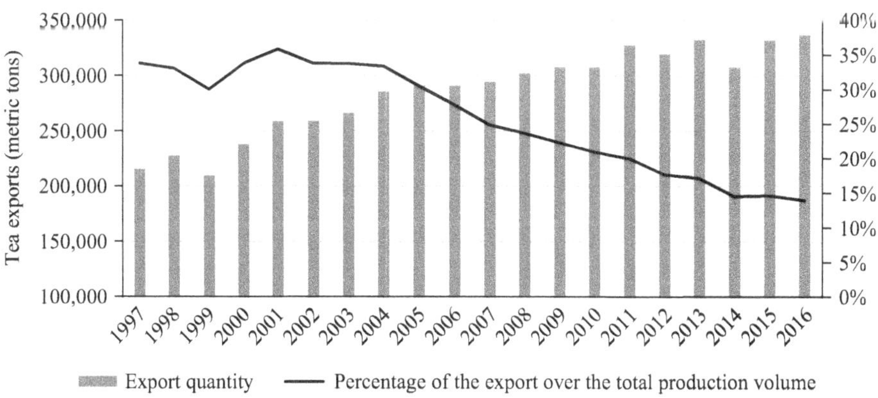

Figure 5.2
Evolution of China's tea exports (1997–2016).
Data source: FAO 2018b.

More importantly, the Chinese market has been increasingly more profitable than foreign markets, even those in developed countries, due to the special cultural meanings of tea. For the Chinese, tea is not just a hot beverage but a symbol of hospitability and entertainment, and it is therefore always considered to be a luxury consumer item (Etherington and Forster 1993). This unique understanding of the commodity is well reflected by the large gap between the price in China and that in the export market. According to estimates by the China Tea Marketing Association (CTMA 2017), in 2016, the average sales price in China's domestic market was RMB 110 per kilogram (around $16.6), which was more than three times higher than the average export price ($4.5). In fact, prices in the domestic market have been driven by a variety of high-end teas, for which 1 kilogram can cost more than $1,000; by contrast, in the export market, Northern buyers offer lower prices in order to minimize the costs and compete against coffee and soft drinks.[13]

In addition, given the country's long history of production, the Chinese consume a much richer variety of teas than do consumers in the rest of the world. Beyond green and black teas, tea in China has been broadly classified into six categories according to different processing methods, and these classifications have been further refined by other product features, including the variety of bush, shape of the leaf, time of plucking, and region of production (Z. Chen and Yang 2011). Accordingly, for many Chinese producers, the value of their products can hardly be understood by foreign buyers and consumers, and as a result, these producers have focused on the domestic market. In that market, producers can also build their own brands by marketing their geographic origins and specific manufacture methods, whereas in Northern markets, they can only serve as suppliers to foreign buyers without any chance to promote their own brands.[14]

Relatedly, the tea culture in China has led to different consumption habits from those in developed markets. In Europe and North America, tea is mainly brewed using teabags made from broken tea leaves, which is usually blended and flavored. However, broken tea signals low quality in China, where most teas are in the form of dried whole leaves that are not blended with products from different regions and rarely have other flavors added. Hence, teas that are highly ranked in China have yet to become attractive to European consumers.[15] In other words, the products that Northern markets need the most require different types of leaves and manufacturing methods from those that are considered popular and of high quality in China. This mismatch between China's supply and Northern markets' demand in terms of product categories has further limited the industry's export, because for many Chinese producers, expanding export business is not cost effective.[16]

Additionally, in China's export market, developing countries, not developed ones, have become major destinations for Chinese tea. Figure 5.3 shows the top 15 importers of Chinese tea by volume from 2007 to 2016. Africa has become the most important market for China's tea industry, representing more than half of the country's tea export by volume, and Morocco alone accounted for 20% of China's export in 2016. This market trend began in the early 2000s and has been driven by growing tea consumption in the developing world, especially in countries having large Muslim communities with whom tea is a highly popular beverage.[17] This expansion of Southern markets has been also coupled with strict food safety standards, such as the maximum residual limit of pesticides imposed by developed countries, which have further prevented Chinese producers from exporting tea products to Northern markets, especially the European Union (Wei, Huang, and Yang 2012; Yue et al. 2010). Considering both market changes and food safety regulations, many Chinese producers in the export market have decided to move their business to developing countries. More recently, China's Belt and Road Initiative has given another impetus for the expansion of China's tea export to Southern markets (Y. He 2015; Ministry of Agriculture 2016).

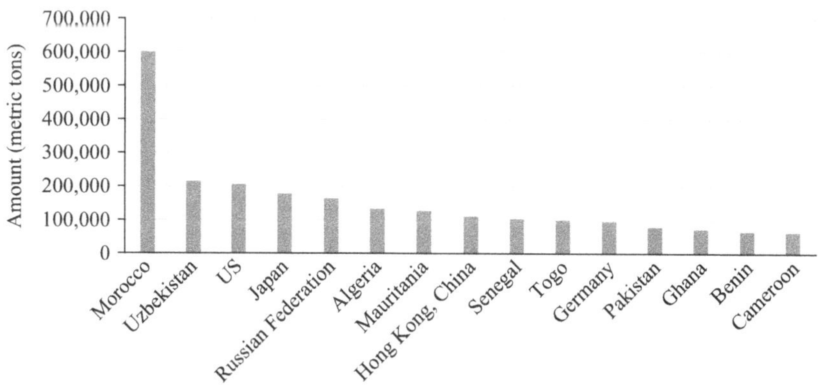

Figure 5.3
Major destinations of China's tea exports (2007–2016).
Data source: United Nations Comtrade database at https://comtrade.un.org/data.

5.2.2 Degree of Concentration: Lack of Dominant Brands

The second key feature of China's tea industry is horizontal fragmentation due to the rise of many local brands since the 1990s. This makes the Chinese market different from Northern markets, which are dominated by a small number of major brands in the downstream part of the supply chain. As mentioned above, this fragmentation is partly caused by the diversity in the categories of teas produced and marketed in China. As distinctive teas are grown and produced in 20 provinces and thousands of counties, horizontal integration is very costly and technically impossible, such that each producer or brand can only be specialized in a limited number of product categories.[18] China's rich tea culture has also made Chinese producers unwilling to follow the strategy of Northern brands of marketing tea products in a less differentiated way (Wu 2009).

Moreover, market reforms in China have further exacerbated this trend of fragmentation, as the state no longer has a monopoly on tea marketing. In the pre-reform era, China's tea industry had a centrally planned system, in which farmers sold their leaves to a dedicated government agency. The latter allocated raw materials to state-owned manufacturers, who then sent final products to trading companies that were also controlled by the government for distribution in the both domestic and export markets. But this system was completely dismantled by the market-oriented reforms in the late 1980s, which also led to the privatization of many tea manufacturing and trading companies. Subsequently, producers in different places began to market their products themselves, often by emphasizing their production regions, and this marketization process has generated thousands of small brands created by entrepreneurial farmers or manufacturers.[19] Hence, the industry has been highly fragmented since the 1990s in both the production and marketing stages of the supply chain. According to data reported by the Ministry of Agriculture in 2016, 90% of the 66,000 tea manufacturing companies in China remain small enterprises with an annual revenue of less than RMB 5 million (approximately $750,000), and the sales value of the top hundred Chinese tea brands represents only 12% of the industry's total sales (Xinhua 2017a).

Seeing this fragmented structure, Western observers generally believe that "Lipton is more powerful than 70,000 Chinese tea companies" (Miller 2010). Some have even suggested that "the tea brand with the greatest market share in China is Lipton" (Sigley 2015: 336). However, these claims are not grounded in accurate data. Instead, in contrast with their dominance in other markets, big Northern brands like Lipton have a very small market share in China, as they only offer teabags, which represented a mere 4% of the teas consumed by the Chinese and only 2% of the total sales in China's domestic market in 2014 (China Economic Net 2014; Yicai 2017). In other words, Northern-based multinational brands remain marginal in the Chinese tea market.

Moving to the retail stage, teas in China are sold through many different channels, including supermarkets, specialty stores, tourist shops, and e-commerce platforms, due to a wide variety of product grades (CTMA 2016). Moreover, as different varieties of teas have their own niche markets in specific regions, many producers have been able to establish long-term relationships with their major customers and directly supply them without going through other intermediaries. Indeed, in my survey conducted in 2017, direct sales were reported as the most popular sales channel by a nationally representative sample of Chinese organic tea producers (see table 5.2). In contrast, the same survey also suggests that the supermarket is not a key channel to sell tea in China. More recently, an increasing number of Chinese producers has joined the movement of e-commerce by opening their own online shops to sell tea products. Nonetheless, unlike the development in the seafood sector, large Chinese e-retailers have yet to invest in the tea market. In summary, the industry structures have remained highly fragmented across all stages of China's tea supply chain. According to hypothesis 4 in chapter 2, this characteristic is likely to remain a challenge for the rise of sustainable tea certification in China.

Table 5.2
Retail channels used by Chinese tea producers

Type of channels	Number of companies	Proportion of the total sample (%) (*N*=215)
Direct sales to regular customers	195	90.7
Supermarket	31	14.4
Specialty store	63	29.3
Membership subscription	26	12.1
E-commerce	101	47.0

Note: Companies were asked to indicate all channels they used in the survey, so the sum of the numbers in the second column of the table is more than 215.
Data source: Organic Tea Producer Survey.

5.2.3 Small Scale of Production but Increasing Vertical Integration

The third important characteristic of China's tea industry is the predominance of smallholders. The lack of economies of scale is reflected by the average yields of tea farms in China over the past two decades, which were much lower than those of other major producer countries (see figure 5.4). In fact, early research has shown that around 80% of tea land in China was operated by individuals or individual households on small farms after the introduction of land ownership reforms in the 1980s (Etherington and Forster 1993). In this respect, the land tenure system in the post-reform era has prevented Chinese tea farmers from consolidating their lands to form large plantations, which could help them increase productivity and improve quality (Miller 2010). As a result, many smallholders have struggled to secure the resources to adopt sustainability standards and market their products (Blackmore et al. 2012). Assessing this structural feature against the observable implication of hypothesis 4 on economies of scale, we can conclude that this relatively small scale of production is likely to hinder the adoption of eco-certification programs by Chinese tea producers.

However, two important caveats should be added to this pessimistic view on the potential of sustainable tea certification in China. First, in addition to the country's fragmented land tenure regime and the limited capability of farmers, low yields in China's tea industry have historical

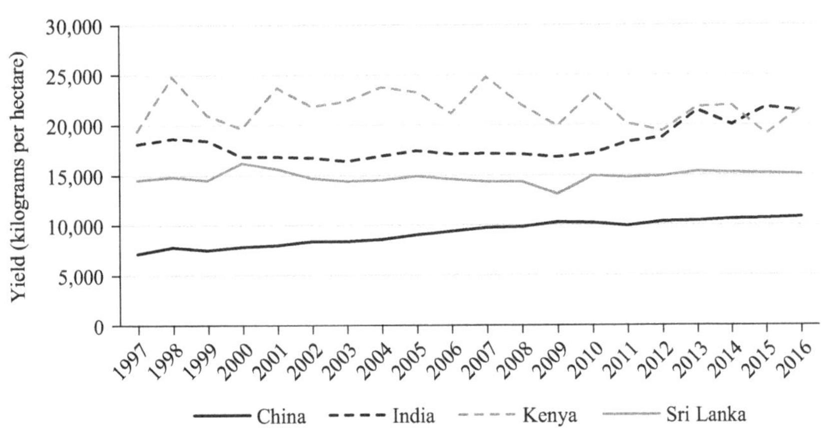

Figure 5.4
Tea production yields in major producer countries (1997–2016).
Data source: FAO 2018a.

roots that could be conducive to the rise of eco-certification. For thousands of years, tea production was a family affair, and except for experiments with state farms in the Mao era, was never associated with large plantations or estates having hired labor to maximize yield (Etherington and Forster 1993; Sigley 2015).[20] This origin is in stark contrast with tea plantations in the British Empire, which were established from the very beginning on an industrial scale to exploit cheap native labor and use "modern" agricultural techniques (Sharma 2011; Ellis, Coulton, and Mauger 2015). The tendency toward small-scale production also generated an important tradition among Chinese tea producers: valuing quality over quantity. Today, many Chinese producers still deliberately choose to cultivate on small farms using traditional methods to produce quality tea and targeting the high-end niche market within the country. For instance, during my visit in Anhui, a region well known for its high-quality green tea, the manager of a large tea company indicated that on most of their farms, tea leaves are plucked manually and only in spring, even though the company is financially capable of using mechanical harvesting machines to harvest in three seasons.[21] Considering this tradition, we can expect that small-scale production in China implies great attention to farm management rather than an emphasis on minimizing costs. For this reason, many Chinese producers may have a strong willingness to adopt sustainable practices.

Second, over the past two decades, China's tea industry has undergone fundamental changes with respect to the consolidation of producer organizations, which have significantly increased vertical integration in the supply chain. These changes have been driven by the Chinese government's plan for rural development: Since the mid-2000s, the state has provided strong support for farmer professional cooperatives and farmland transfer to increase efficiency in agricultural production (H. Deng et al. 2010; Xinhua 2016; Z. Li 2017). At the same time, rapid urbanization in China has further facilitated the rise of large farms, as farmers (especially young people) who have migrated to cities are motivated to transfer their land use rights (Zhao et al. 2017). As a result, today Chinese farmers rarely grow tea individually as smallholders, but rather participate in professional cooperatives or simply transfer their land use rights to other farmers wanting to build larger farms.[22] These changes have been also conducive to vertical integration, as farmers' professional cooperatives and large farms can more easily secure long-term contracts with processing companies. In many cases, owners of large farms have created their own companies having vertically integrated supply chains that include their own farms, processing factories, and even sales departments.[23] Hence, for many tea companies in China, their capacity for vertical coordination along the supply chain, especially in the cultivation, processing, and refining stages, is no longer weak, and accordingly, they should not face serious technical challenges to establishing traceability systems and promoting new management methods. Additionally, vertically integrated companies having their own brands are likely to have incentives to use eco-certification to build their reputation in the market.

Figure 5.5 illustrates China's tea supply chain, and its structural features suggest a mixed picture of the potential for eco-certification. On one hand, the existence of a large domestic market, rising exports to developing countries, and the lack of leading brands are likely to limit the influence of Northern buyers and investors in China's tea industry and to increase the difficulty of transnational certification programs in engaging with domestic stakeholders. On the other hand, the industry's tradition of valuing quality over quantity and recent improvements in vertical coordination along the supply chain can be conducive to the adoption of eco-certification by Chinese companies. In short, the industry structure itself cannot fully explain the very low uptake of sustainable tea certification in China. Therefore, we must examine the agency and strategies of different stakeholders for introducing the relevant certification programs to the Chinese tea industry.

5.3 The Slow Growth of Sustainable Tea Certification without Any Domestic Champion

This section investigates the entry and slow growth of sustainable tea certification in China. I highlight two findings. First, all certification programs on sustainable tea were initially introduced by Northern buyers or investors, which remain major sources of demand for eco-certification in China's tea industry.[24] Second, due to both the lack of their own interest in the Chinese market and the difficulty of finding domestic partners, transnational certification programs have been unable to closely engage with actors in China's state bureaucracy, and the lack of support from state actors has been a key contributor to the low uptake of sustainable tea certification in China. Below I first examine the development of Fairtrade certification

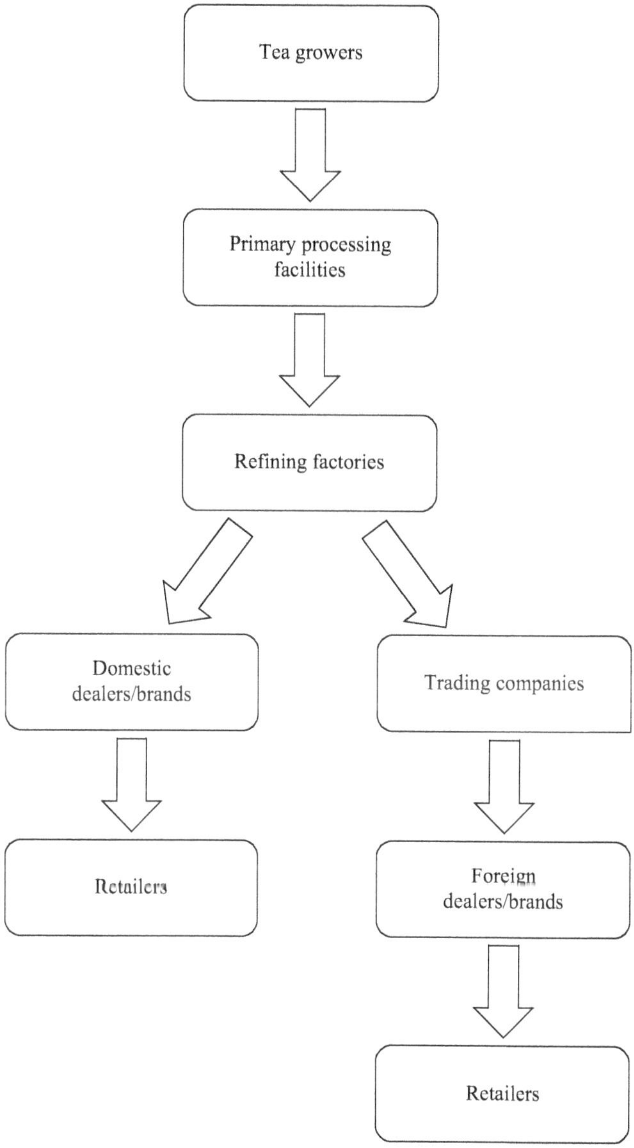

Figure 5.5
Structure of China's tea supply chain.

in China, followed by RA and UTZ, and finally discuss the positions and actions of relevant domestic stakeholders.

5.3.1 Fairtrade

Fairtrade was the first transnational certification program to be introduced to Chinese tea producers by European buyers back in the late 1990s. The first Fairtrade-certified tea producer organization was in Wuyuan, a traditional production county in the Jiangxi province, well known for its high-quality green tea. Fairtrade certification was initially introduced to tea growers in Wuyuan through a local tea manufacturing company—Dazhangshan Organic Food Co., Ltd. (hereafter, "Dazhangshan"). The company was created in the 1990s by the former CEO of the Wuyuan county's state-owned tea company after the government abolished the state's monopoly over distribution and marketing in the tea sector.[25] Due to good ecological conditions and low-input farming practices on tea farms in Wuyuan, Dazhangshan's products were selected by the China Green Food Development Center of the Ministry of Agriculture to be exhibited in organic food fairs in Europe in the mid-1990s. By 1997, the company had gotten the attention of Naturkost Ernst Weber GmbH, a Bavarian organic trading company, which visited tea farms in Wuyuan and helped the company get certified according to the German organic standard.[26]

In 1998, Dazhangshan began to export its certified organic tea to Europe. After the initial establishment of this sourcing relationship, the German buyers found the management system used by the company to organize organic production to be eligible for Fairtrade certification. As a tea manufacturer, Dazhangshan does not own farms but instead contracts with smallholders who grow tea. To ensure the adoption of organic farming practices by farmers, the company established a chain of responsibility system to form many production bases. Each base consists of a primary processing plant with farmers in the same area, and on each base, a farmer is assigned as the general manager to monitor production. This system is in line with Fairtrade standard for small-scale producers, which is used to certify smallholders who run their farm using their own family's labor. Hence, in 2000, Dazhangshan was introduced to Fairtrade International by its German customer. It then formed an organic tea farmer association, uniting its contract suppliers, and applied for Fairtrade certification.

However, the first application was rejected by Fairtrade International. According to the company's chairperson, after the first audit, the lead auditor told him that the company had complied with all standards; but the auditor still anticipated a rejection due to Fairtrade's doubts about the compliance with the criterion on the democratic decision-making process in the farmer association in China's authoritarian context. The subsequent decision was in line with this expectation. In response, Dazhangshan reapplied the following year with the same dossier plus an English copy of the new Organic Law of the Villagers' Committees promulgated by the Chinese government in 1998, which introduced self-government and free elections at the village level.[27] This strategy proved useful: In 2001, the Dazhangshan Organic Tea Farmer Association became the first Fairtrade-certified producer organization in China. Since then, the company has maintained its compliance with both Fairtrade and organic standards.

Farmers in this association have benefited from Fairtrade certification as the relevant price premium has been used to support schools and students in their villages and to purchase organic fertilizers. Moreover, eco-certification has been critical for Dazhangshan to maintain a long-term relationship with its German buyer, securing its position in the European market. According to the company's estimate, as of the mid-2010s, its export volume represented more than half of China's total export of organic tea to the EU, making it the largest Fairtrade-certified producer in the country.[28] Over time, the economic benefits from eco-certification have also strengthened the company's identity as a Fairtrade and organic producer, such that all products it has produced are from Fairtrade-certified organic farms and are only for export to Northern markets.

Despite the early entry of Fairtrade certification in China's tea industry and the success of Dazhangshan, the program has subsequently made little progress in the country. Several factors have contributed to this puzzling outcome. First, as shown by the experience of Dazhangshan, Fairtrade International has been skeptical about the implementation of its standards in China because of the country's political system. This skepticism has significantly reduced Fairtrade International's interest in engaging with stakeholders in China and introducing its program to Chinese producers. Without collaboration with any state actors, the program has also worked in a gray area in China, as the auditing activities for the Fairtrade standard were not accredited by the Chinese government. Moreover, by definition, Fairtrade aims to promote equitable North-South trade relationships, and therefore had little intention to penetrate Southern markets. As a result, Fairtrade International has never attempted to promote its program in China's domestic market, even if its goals of reducing poverty and promoting sustainability could also be championed by some Chinese tea consumers, especially those in the high-end niche market.[29] In fact, the program's local capacity in China has remained limited. To date, Fairtrade International has not yet created an office in Mainland China with full-time staff.[30] Fairtrade's weak organizational capacity in China has also increased the difficulty and cost for Chinese producers to adopt the relevant standards, as producers cannot receive adequate training and advice and must pay for auditors who are not based in China.

In short, the emergence of Fairtrade tea certification in China has been purely driven by Northern buyers, especially in the niche of organic production. Given the small size of China's export market, transnational market forces have been unable to significantly increase the uptake of Fairtrade certification. In addition, because of Fairtrade's market and political orientations, the program has made little effort to proactively reach out to Chinese stakeholders, who may be interested in sustainable production and consumption. Consequently, no actor in the Chinese state or industry has ever helped the program promote its standards in China.

5.3.2 RA and UTZ

RA was also introduced to Chinese tea producers by a Northern buyer: Unilever. In 2011, the multinational corporation began to introduce RA's sustainable tea certification in China in order to fulfill its commitment of globally sourcing tea in Lipton teabags from certified farms. To identify suppliers and facilitate the certification processes, Unilever partnered with local governments in some tea production regions in China. The first RA certificate in China was awarded in August 2012 to a 1,000-hectare tea farm in Lincang, Yunnan—a southwestern province in China famous for black tea. It was the outcome of collaboration among Unilever, RA, and the Department of Commerce of Yunnan's provincial government. In 2011, through the provincial Department of Commerce, Unilever and the municipal government of Lincang signed a MoU in which the company committed to source 2,000 to 3,000 tons of black tea from local farms, and, in response, the local government agreed to provide support for the adoption of RA tea standards by local farmers and manufacturers (Department of Commerce of the Yunnan Province 2013). Accordingly, the local government assisted RA in reaching out to tea producers suitable for certification and organizing training for farmers, and it even covered part of certification costs.[31] Moreover, Yunnan's Department of Commerce also helped RA obtain permission from the national regulatory agency on certification for conducting audits in China. Since the issue of that first certificate, the local government in Lincang has continued its support for RA to promote sustainable tea certification: By the end of 2015, over 2,700 hectares of tea farms supplying four companies in Lincang were RA-certified (Xie and Li 2017).

In this case, the support of the governments in Yunnan and Lincang for a transnational certification program can be understood as a development strategy to boost exports and promote local industry, particularly as the province has remained relatively underdeveloped compared to China's coastal regions. Thus, local government officials have been "quite enthusiastic" to partner with RA, as the program "has demonstrated its contribution to local economy without touching any sensitive topics in China."[32] After the successful experience of collaborating with the government in Yunnan, Unilever and RA have subsequently pursued a similar strategy in other tea production regions. In July 2016, Unilever reached an agreement to build sustainably managed tea farms with the municipal government of Zunyi, in Guizhou, another southwestern province that has rapidly expanded its tea land area in recent years (China Development Gateway 2016). In this case, Unilever has also played the role of a foreign investor by supporting the establishment of new farms compliant with RA standards. But the ultimate impact of this project on sustainable tea production in China remains to be seen, as it only started in late 2016.

Besides working with local governments, RA has also gained support from Unilever's preexisting suppliers in China, who had to get certified to keep their buyer's orders. In such cases, RA-certified tea produced in China is mainly for export.[33] According to the owner of one of the largest Unilever suppliers in China, his company complied with RA standards without any support of the local government, but he had been compensated for the cost of certification by the higher sourcing prices offered by Unilever.[34] However, other than support from Unilever, RA itself has made little effort to promote its certification in China's tea industry. This is partly because of the limited resources that the program has in the field: Since 2012, it has only hired two part-time project consultants in China for training farmers and for business engagement. The program has accredited a Chinese certification body to conduct all audits in China, but this certifier has been also unable to help RA market its tea certification.[35] Both consultants working for RA in China felt that there was a lack of opportunity to engage with state actors in China, as no specific bureau in the Chinese government oversees the tea industry and the industry also remains too small to gain attention in the Ministry of Agriculture.[36]

Therefore, the spread of RA tea certification in China largely has been driven by a Northern-based multinational company—Unilever—and the strategy of relying on this mechanism has quickly shown its limits. Despite having more certified producers than Fairtrade, the uptake of RA certification in China's tea industry remains insignificant due to the small sourcing volume of Unilever in the country. Of about two dozen RA-certified companies in China as of 2017, only two spontaneously sought certification to differentiate their products in the market instead of being driven by their buyers' sourcing requirements.[37] Additionally, for many producers, the incentive for implementing the relevant standards remains weak, as Unilever does not always purchase all of the tea produced on their certified farms.[38] In such situations, certified farms can no longer benefit from the price premium offered by Unilever and have to sell some of their products in a nondifferentiated way to buyers who do not ask for certified tea.

The case of UTZ is very similar to that for RA, although UTZ has relied on other, smaller Northern buyers to introduce its standards to Chinese producers engaging in the export market.[39] As for its local organizational capacity, the program only entered China in 2013 and has hired two local staff. With limited resources, it has lacked the capacity to engage with local stakeholders and so could not build collaborations with any industry associations or government agencies. Operating in China as a foreign NGO, UTZ's leadership has been cautious about coming to the attention of the Chinese government, and has therefore been hesitant to officially register in the country and has asked its local representatives to "keep a low profile."[40] Hence, as of mid-2017, UTZ has certified a very small number of tea producers in China due to the low demand of Northern buyers as well as the lack of domestic partners.

5.3.3 Positions and Actions of Chinese Stakeholders

The analysis above shows that all three transnational certification programs have largely relied on buyers based in the Global North to introduce their standards to Chinese tea producers. Although in the case of RA, the program has partnered with subnational governments in some production regions, this mechanism for spreading transnational governance has not yet become popular in China's tea industry, and its effect on the uptake of certified products in the market has been very limited. Indeed, beyond the few subnational governments discussed above, these transnational programs have not yet found supporters in China's state bureaucracy. However, some Chinese state or quasi-state actors, such as industrial associations, have interacted with transnational programs; unfortunately, for several reasons, they could neither effectively partner with the relevant programs nor provide strong support to incentivize businesses to get certified. I now discuss these domestic actors' positions on sustainable tea certification.

The most relevant Chinese actor in this respect is the China Tea Marketing Association (CTMA), a national association in the tea industry supervised by the All-China Federation of Supply and Marketing Cooperatives (ACFSMC), a ministry-level agency that used to play a central role in the purchase, processing, and sale of agricultural commodities before China introduced market-oriented reforms (Etherington and Forster 1993). The Association's members include enterprises, institutions, social groups, and individuals involved in different stages of China's tea supply chain.[41] In the late 2010s, the entry of sustainable tea certification in the Chinese industry has come to the attention of CTMA. In 2010, with the support of Solidaridad (a Dutch NGO), CTMA launched a project to develop a code of conduct on sustainable production, and in the following year, published "Guidelines on Sustainable Development of the Chinese Tea Industry," which draws on standards of relevant transnational certification programs (CTMA 2011). At first glance, CTMA's guidelines have shown the embryonic form of a homegrown standard system that could facilitate Chinese producers getting certified according to transnational programs, and practitioners involved in the project have even indicated the aspiration to further develop, based on the "Guidelines," a Chinese certification program.[42] However, since 2011, little progress has been made in promoting and implementing these guidelines, of which most stakeholders in the industry remain unaware. According to an expert participating in the development of the "Guidelines," CTMA did not have a clear follow-up plan but just wanted to use the project as a demonstration to follow the state's general policy goals on sustainable development.[43]

The inability of CTMA to further promote the "Guidelines" throughout the industry and convince producers to adopt relevant practices suggests the lack of influence of this association in the market. In fact, unlike the seafood case discussed in chapter 3, where a national industry association is deemed highly important by businesses to represent their interests and communicate government policies, today, CTMA only plays a marginal role in China's tea industry. As already mentioned, the Chinese government never formed a central agency for tea like India's Tea Board to oversee the whole sector, but it did separate the regulation by three ministries: the Ministry of Agriculture for production, the ACFSMC for domestic business, and the MOFCOM for export.[44] Although the ACFSMC was once the most powerful government agency in China's tea sector, able to determine output and export volumes, it gradually lost its monopoly on the distribution and marketing of tea in China's post-reform era, as farmers no longer had to sell all their harvest to the state. The ACFSMC thus created CTMA in 1992 as a quasi-state agency with the hope of maintaining its influence in the tea industry. However, as a legacy organization from the planned economy era, CTMA has little influence in the market today.[45] Hence, it has not yet effectively implemented its guidelines, although it has been eager to develop a scheme to "localize or even replace" relevant transnational certification programs.[46]

To date, a focal industry association still does not exist in China's tea industry, partly due to the fragmentation of the domestic regulatory architecture in this sector (Ding 2010). Accordingly, several associations sponsored by different state agencies coexist. These include, in addition to CTMA, China Tea Science Society (under the Chinese Association for Science and Technology and supported by the Chinese Academy of Agriculture); Chinese Teaman Friendship Association (supervised by the MOFCOM); and China International Tea Culture Institute (supervised by the Ministry of Agriculture). This regulatory structure has not only weakened the influence of each individual association but also increased the difficulty for transnational certification programs to seek partners in China's state organization. From this perspective, the case of China's tea industry is in line with hypothesis 7 on the conditions shaping the support of domestic state actors.

Moreover, the little interest that the Chinese government has displayed in the tea sector has also contributed to such fragmentation. In the post-reform era, the Ministry of Agriculture has actually been the most important state agency for the regulation of the tea industry. But until recently, the ministry's leadership had paid little attention to the crop because of the relatively small output value of tea compared to other commodities in China's agricultural sector.[47] As a result, the office responsible for tea in the Ministry of Agriculture has remained understaffed and lacks the capacity to coordinate different stakeholders along the supply chain to promote sustainable production and consumption.[48] For this reason, it does not seem too surprising that transnational actors have not engaged with officials in the Ministry of Agriculture, such that even those responsible for tea business in the ministry have little or no knowledge about eco-certification in the global market.[49]

Nonetheless, since the mid-2010s, the Chinese government seems to be paying increasing attention to tea, as the country's leadership has begun to promote China's tea culture on the diplomatic front (Sigley 2015; Xinhua and China Daily 2017). Observing this development, in 2016, the Ministry of Agriculture published an ambitious plan to strengthen China's tea industry, which includes a roadmap to promote sustainable production (Ministry of Agriculture 2016). In 2017, the ministry also took the lead in establishing the China Tea Industry Alliance, uniting 157 large tea companies and 34 research institutes to strengthen the industry and brand Chinese tea in the world market (Xinhua 2017b). While this is likely to create opportunities for the growth of sustainable tea certification, we have not yet seen any interaction between the Alliance and transnational certification programs.

Another noteworthy development in the industry concerns a recent initiative led by Chinese non-state actors to promote sustainable production. Seeing the rise of sustainable tea certification and Chinese producers' challenges in adopting sustainability standards, a group of agronomists, farm service providers, and product quality inspectors launched the "Tea Sustainability Union" in 2017 to help Chinese tea companies improve their farm management and monitor the production process.[50] Several transnational certification programs were also invited to join the Union and showed their interest in collaborating with relevant stakeholders. The initiative indeed shows the increasing awareness of sustainability standards and certification in China's tea industry and may provide opportunities for transnational programs to increase their uptake in the country. But its ultimate impact remains to be seen.

The rapid growth in organic tea production in China may also be helpful to further spread transnational certifications that have a broader sustainability focus. Since the establishment of a national organic certification program in 2003, the area devoted to organic tea farms in China has increased more than ten-fold, making China the world's largest organic tea producer (CNCA 2014). In contrast with sustainable tea certification originating outside China, this movement for organic farming has benefited from various types of government support at different levels—the central government wants to reduce agro-chemical pollution through organic practices, while local governments are eager to use organics to brand products from their regions (CNCA and China Agricultural University 2016).[51] My survey of organic tea producers confirms the importance of such government support: More than 80% of the participants had received some type of support from local governments, including technical training, subsidies, and marketing assistance. While such support aims to promote organic production, it has also raised awareness of Chinese producers about sustainable production and made them familiar with the governance mode of eco-certification. As most producers do not solely engage in organic farming, those who have adopted, or have been trained to adopt, organic standards can more easily adopt other sustainability standards. In this sense, the growing attention to organic production and relevant policy support may have provided a fertile ground for the rise of sustainable tea certification. But the relevant transnational programs have yet to leverage this transformation to proactively promote themselves in China.

Table 5.3 summarizes the development paths of different governance initiatives promoting sustainable tea production in China. For the three transnational programs, Northern buyers have been the key driver of their uptake. In the case of RA, Unilever has also partnered with some local governments. On domestic initiatives, competitor schemes have yet to emerge in China, and the rise of organic certification may even offer opportunities for transnational programs having a broader sustainability focus. Unfortunately, transnational programs have not actively engaged with domestic stakeholders, nor have they gained the support of any influential actor in the Chinese state.

Table 5.3
Initiatives promoting sustainable production in China's tea industry

Initiative	Drivers	Collaborators
Fairtrade International	Northern trading companies	None
Rainforest Alliance	Unilever	Local governments in production regions (e.g., Yunnan, Guizhou)
UTZ	Northern tea brands	None
Guidelines on Sustainable Development of the Chinese Tea Industry	CTMA and Solidaridad	None
Tea Sustainability Union	Chinese agronomists, agricultural service providers, and quality inspectors	None
China Organic Certification	CNCA	Local governments, Ministry of Agriculture, Ministry of Environmental Protection (now Ministry of Ecology and Environment)

5.4 The State as a Potential Driver: Evidence from a Survey Experiment

The analysis above shows that transnational eco-certification has gotten little traction in China's tea sector, although some conditions seem ripe for the rise of sustainable tea in the country. But what could motivate uncertified Chinese producers to adopt sustainability standards required by transnational programs? Can foreign markets or the policies of the Chinese government influence producers' decisions? The answers to these questions will shed light on the potential of sustainable tea certification in China and suggest useful strategies for relevant certification programs to increase their uptake. In the absence of observational data, I used a survey experiment with owners or senior managers of tea companies to identify the factors determining the interest of Chinese producers in sustainable tea certification. This study focuses on the most likely adopters of transnational eco-certification in China's tea industry: those who have engaged in organic farming, because they had prior knowledge of the governance mode of certification, and their existing practices tend to be close to the relevant standards.

The experiment was embedded in the Organic Tea Producer Survey conducted between December 2017 and June 2018, using a sample of 215 tea producing companies in 16 Chinese provinces (see more details on sampling in appendix C). Most companies ($N = 183$) participating in the survey have achieved vertical integration by linking tea farms with manufacturing factories, 24 companies focus only on growing tea, and eight companies focus only on processing and refining. These trends provide evidence of increasing vertical integration in the industry as discussed earlier in the chapter. In terms of ownership, 70.7% of the companies are owned by Chinese private entrepreneurs, 10.2% are state owned, and only 1.4% are owned by foreign investors. This largely reflects the landscape of the industry in the post-reform era. In addition, according to the Chinese government's statistical categorization in 2017, more than half of the companies in the sample are micro or small enterprises (i.e., with annual revenue less than RMB 5 million), and only 5% of companies participating in the survey are large agricultural enterprises (i.e., with annual revenue more than RMB 200 million). Although this generally represents the average size of companies in the industry, I recognize that the sample may be slightly biased toward rich companies that have the financial capacity to adopt organic practices. But this again suggests the sample represents a group of Chinese producers that are likely to adopt transnational certification.

In the survey, participants were asked to indicate their willingness to adopt sustainable tea certification, namely, one of the three transnational programs: Fairtrade, RA, and UTZ. The answer to this question, measured on a five-point Likert scale, was used as the outcome variable (*Interest*). The experimental setting allowed me to introduce an explanatory variable, which is the frame provided to respondents before the question on their interest in getting certified to sustainable agriculture standards (*Frame*). Here, survey participants were randomly assigned to one of the three groups. They were asked to read a text about sustainable agriculture certification proposed by Fairtrade, RA, or UTZ. Respondents in the first treatment group received information indicating synergies between eco-certification and the Chinese government's goals on sustainable development, as well as government support for the adoption of relevant standards. The second group read a different paragraph, which highlighted the demand for certified products in developed countries and the benefits of gaining access to foreign markets from getting certified. The third group was used as a placebo control: They received the text for a general introduction to sustainable agricultural certification. Through this framing experiment, we can assess whether Northern buyers and the Chinese state can drive tea producers to adopt transnational eco-certification, as suggested by hypothesis 1 and hypothesis 5 in chapter 2. To ensure that respondents paid enough attention to the frame and reacted immediately to the following question, I screened out respondents who spent too little (less than 3 minutes) or too much (more than 30 minutes) time on the survey. The final sample includes 51 valid observations in each group.[52]

In addition to the frames, I added some covariates reflecting the structural conditions that may constrain companies' capacities to adopt eco-certification. The ownership of companies (state-owned enterprises were used as the baseline) was included in the statistical model to test whether foreign-invested companies are more willing to use eco-certification (which was expected by hypothesis 2). Moreover, to take into account the strategy of certification programs (hypothesis 3) and the influence of industry associations (hypothesis 6), I asked every participant to indicate the frequency of their interactions with industry associations they belong to (*Interaction association*) and environmental NGOs (including certification programs) (*Interaction ENGOs*). This variable allows me to assess whether frequent interactions with these stakeholders increase companies' interest in eco-certification. Following hypothesis 4, I considered companies' financial capacity (*Revenue*) and scale of production (*Production area*). Another variable in this respect is the current practices adopted by producers, as those whose practices are close to new standards are more likely to become certified. I used the number of years for which companies have been certified to organic standards as a proxy to measure this variable (*Years*), as practices of producers who have engaged in organic farming for a long time are likely to be closer to relevant sustainability standards. Finally, as additional controls, I considered companies' prior experiences with organic production. Two variables are used in this respect. The first one is the proportion of organic tea to the total production volume (*Organic proportion*), as companies who have decided to focus on organic production may find it unnecessary to be certified to additional programs. The second one is the impact of organic production on companies' benefits (*Benefit change*), as those receiving economic benefits from organic certification may have a good impression of eco-certification in general and support other programs.

Turning to the results, sustainable tea certification seems attractive for most companies participating in the survey. The mean score of *Interest* is 4.2, implying that Chinese tea producers—at least those who have knowledge about the governance mode of eco-certification and have adopted relatively high standards—are not antagonistic to transnational programs having a broader sustainability focus. Table 5.4 shows the statistical results on the factors shaping companies' interest in sustainable tea certification, from the

Table 5.4

Determinants of Chinese companies' interest in joining sustainable tea certification

	(1)	(2)	(3)	(4)	(5)	(6)
	OLS	OLS	OLS	Ordinal logit	Ordinal logit	Ordinal logit
1. Frame	0.472* (2.45)	0.470* (2.55)	0.502** (2.67)	0.910* (2.31)	0.934* (2.27)	1.049* (2.46)
2. Frame	0.335 (1.76)	0.355 (1.91)	0.392* (2.07)	0.613 (1.59)	0.683 (1.65)	0.779 (1.84)
Revenue	0.0933 (1.38)	–0.0141 (–0.20)	–0.0317 (–0.44)	0.149 (1.07)	–0.00360 (–0.02)	–0.0431 (–0.28)
Production area	–0.0313 (–0.83)	–0.0363 (–0.99)	–0.0326 (–0.88)	–0.0831 (–1.10)	–0.132 (–1.60)	–0.123 (–1.48)
Years	–0.0524*** (–3.71)	0.0539*** (–3.69)	–0.0514*** (–3.47)	–0.117*** (–3.92)	–0.133*** (–3.90)	–0.129*** (–3.75)
2. Ownership (township/ village)		–0.317 (–0.73)	–0.292 (–0.67)		–0.692 (–0.75)	–0.654 (–0.70)
3. Ownership (joint-stock)		–0.321 (–1.00)	–0.256 (–0.78)		–0.485 (–0.67)	–0.323 (–0.44)
4. Ownership (foreign-invested)		0.275 (0.39)	0.254 (0.36)		15.31 (0.01)	15.34 (0.01)
5. Ownership (individuals)		–0.490 (–1.77)	–0.458 (–1.63)		–1.022 (–1.76)	–0.980 (–1.67)
Interaction association		0.0787 (0.95)	0.0740 (0.88)		0.167 (0.92)	0.142 (0.77)
Interaction ENGOs		0.223*** (3.45)	0.215** (3.29)		0.484*** (3.40)	0.472*** (3.29)
Organic proportion			–0.0356 (–0.71)			–0.0539 (–0.49)
Benefit change			0.0961 (0.83)			0.274 (1.05)
N	153	153	153	153	153	153

Note: *t* statistics in parentheses; OLS, ordinary least squares. * $p<0.05$, ** $p<0.01$, *** $p<0.001$.

models of ordinary least squares and ordinal logistic regression.[53] The two models yield very similar results. For the framing experiment, the first frame, which aligns eco-certification with the Chinese government's policy goals, always has statistically significant and substantively strong positive effects. According to the coefficient in column 3 in table 5.4, this frame can increase companies' intention to adopt eco-certification by 0.5 on a 5-point scale (i.e., moving companies from being just "somewhat interested" to almost "very interested"). Likewise, the marginal effect in the ordinal logistic regression (column 6) suggests that companies receiving this treatment are 25% more likely to be "very interested" (*Interest*=5) in joining sustainable tea certification than those in the control group, and 7% more likely than those reading the second frame. In contrast, in all models except that in column 3, the frame emphasizing the benefits of expanding international business cannot motivate Chinese tea companies to become certified. This result provides further evidence of the limited influence of foreign markets on China's tea industry, showing that many producers have little or no interest in export, probably because of the low prices offered by foreign buyers. Therefore, the experimental results suggest that in China's tea sector, highlighting the benefit of eco-certification for the achievement of domestic policy goals on sustainable development and gaining government support should be an effective strategy to increase the uptake of transnational governance.

The analysis also finds no influence of foreign investment, as companies' ownership has insignificant impact on their intention to adopt certification. This result might be caused by the existence of only a few foreign-invested companies in the sample. But this scarcity indeed reflects the dominance of domestic companies in the sector. Accordingly, foreign investment can hardly become a key driver of sustainable tea certification in China. When considering businesses' relationships with other stakeholders, in all model specifications, the coefficient of *Interaction ENGOs* remains positive and statistically significant, meaning that companies interacting frequently with environmental NGOs are more interested in transnational eco-certification. As certification programs and their NGO supporters are all labeled as environmental NGOs, this finding lends support to hypothesis 3 by showing that proactive engagement of these actors can incentivize Chinese companies to adopt relevant sustainability standards. In contrast, the variable *Interaction association* has no significant result, confirming the lack of influential industry associations in China's tea sector.

The variable reflecting companies' current practices merits additional attention. The number of years that companies have engaged in organic farming has statistically negative effects on their interest in getting certified to additional transnational programs. This result can be interpreted as the possibility that producers committed to organic production find it unnecessary to use other programs to improve their production, whereas those who are new to organic certification are more interested in trying other standards. For certification programs aiming to increase their influence in China, the implication is therefore to better target producers who have recently improved their practices through organic certification but are still open to other standards having a broader scope of sustainability. Lastly, companies' revenue and production area did not have significant effects, possibly due to little variation in these variables. Given that my sample reflects the dominance of small enterprises in China's tea industry, these findings suggest that small-scale production should not be a barrier to generating incentives for Chinese tea producers to consider eco-certification.

To summarize, my survey of organic tea producing companies shows that the most likely route to increase the uptake of sustainable tea certification in China is to highlight the resonance of transnational programs with domestic policy goals and gain some government support. While my findings are in line with hypothesis 5 on the importance of subnational governments' support in driving the spread of eco-certification, they show no influence of Northern buyers (hypothesis 1), foreign investment (hypothesis 2), and industry associations (hypothesis 6) in the tea sector. However, the proactive communication strategies of transnational programs and their NGO supporters still seem helpful, as companies frequently interacting with these actors show stronger interest in eco-certification.

5.5 Conclusion

While sustainable tea certification holds promise for reducing environmental impacts, protecting labor rights, and improving the livelihoods of farmers and workers, the relevant programs have made little progress in the world's largest tea producing and consuming country—China. This outcome is even more striking when compared to the rapid increase in certified area and production volume around the world. This chapter identifies the factors contributing to the stagnation of sustainable tea certification in China in the past two decades.

Examining the structure of China's tea supply chain, the chapter first shows that the existence of a large domestic market lacking big brands and economies of scale presents challenges for transnational certification programs to gain traction in China. These structural factors provide some evidence supporting hypothesis 4 on the fit between domestic industry structure and transnational governance. Yet they cannot fully explain the unsuccessful experiences of the relevant transnational programs, as the recent rise of branded Chinese producers, with increased vertical integration and their tradition of valuing quality, are conducive to the adoption of eco-certification. Hence, the more important factors are the strategies of these certification programs in China and the position of domestic stakeholders. By investigating the processes through which different programs entered China, I find that sustainable tea certification has only reached out to a few Chinese producers supplying Northern brands; in the meantime, the relevant programs have not proactively promoted their standards in the country and have not sought support from actors in China's state bureaucracy. As a result, sustainable tea certification remains unknown to nearly all Chinese producers and consumers. Considering the hypotheses specified in chapter 2, we can conclude that transnational market forces identified by hypothesis 1 and hypothesis 2 have been weak in promoting sustainable tea certification in China, and the proactive engagement of certification programs identified by hypothesis 3 also has been missing. As suggested by hypothesis 5, we have seen cases of support from some subnational governments for transnational certification programs to boost the local economy. But unlike the seafood and palm oil sectors, there was no endorsement by a quasi-state industry association for sustainability certification in the tea sector, partly due to the fragmented regulatory system for the commodity in China and the lack of engagement of transnational actors, as suggested by hypothesis 7.

Despite the lack of progress in the past two decades, sustainable tea certification may still have a promising future in China's growing tea industry. The insights drawn from the Organic Tea Producer Survey suggest that Chinese producers do not lack interest in transnational certification programs, and the way in which the benefits of certification are framed influence their willingness to adopt new standards. Given a large, highly profitable domestic market in China, most producers do not want to use certification to expand exports; instead, they are likely to support certification programs that resonate with domestic policy goals and are endorsed and assisted by the Chinese state. This finding again confirms the importance of support from various levels of the government, especially at the subnational level, in the spread of transnational governance in China—a mechanism implied by hypothesis 5. Moreover, in line with hypothesis 3, the survey also shows that the interest of Chinese producers in sustainable tea certification is associated with the interaction with environmental NGOs, including certification programs.

My mixed-method analysis sheds new light on the future of sustainable tea in China. For the relevant certification programs to reach the world's largest market, they need to better show the synergies of their standards with domestic policy goals and engage with state actors to gain support. For instance, China included a plan to achieve "zero growth of fertilizer and pesticide utilization by 2020" in their nationally determined contribution for the Paris Agreement, and sustainable tea certification could help achieve this goal as well as promote further sustainability transitions in the tea industry (National Development and Reform Commission 2015). In addition to state actors, transnational programs could also seek support from non-state actors in China and build linkages between sustainable production and food safety. In fact, the issue of chemical residuals in tea leaves already has been brought to the attention of the Chinese public by environmental NGOs like Greenpeace and has become a major concern of tea consumers in China (Greenpeace 2012, 2016). In this context, more and more producers may want to use eco-certification to gain consumer trust. If certification programs aim to transform the global tea supply chain, they need to proactively promote their standards in China and strategically engage with domestic stakeholders.

6 Conclusion: The Promise and Limits of Transnational Sustainability Governance

In the past three decades, eco-certification has become a popular mode of transnational governance for promoting sustainable production and consumption, first in the Global North and subsequently around the globe. Despite holding promise for leveraging market forces to provide public goods overlooked by the state, this new governance mode always faces challenges to scaling up its impact, especially in large emerging economies. China seems a particularly difficult destination for eco-certification due to the lack of civil society campaigns and political consumerism under its authoritarian regime. Additionally, the role of the state in the economy suggests that the uptake of eco-certification in China may not be fully determined by market dynamics. In this context, does transnational eco-certification still have a role to play? If yes, what can drive Chinese businesses to adopt voluntary standards and practices originating in the Global North? What can the case of China tell us about the future of transnational sustainability governance?

This book addresses these questions by investigating the rise and limits of eco-certification in three of China's commodity chains: seafood, palm oil, and tea. My comparative analyses at the sectoral and firm levels yield three general insights. First, unlike common pessimistic beliefs, it is very possible for eco-certification led by non-state actors to thrive in authoritarian China. This is not only because transnational market agents, such as multinational corporations, can introduce relevant standards to their Chinese suppliers, but more importantly, because actors in China's state bureaucracy can become interested in harnessing transnational governance to pursue development goals for their jurisdictions or industries. As shown in the book's empirical cases, such support by state (or quasi-state) actors has been critical to the rapid growth of transnational certification programs in China's large domestic market, where foreign companies have limited influence.

Second, the striking variation across the three supply chains suggests that the potential for eco-certification in China is highly specific to the political economy context in each sector, especially the interaction between transnational and domestic stakeholders. In other words, to gain traction in China, certification programs and their NGO supporters need to be strategic and proactive in building partnerships with influential stakeholders in the domestic industry. In fact, even in an authoritarian context like that of China, opportunity structures are not always closed to non-state rule makers for finding domestic supporters, if these non-state actors can align their objectives with the interests of the latter.

Third, despite opportunities for the further and faster growth of eco-certification in China, many obstacles remain for transnational eco-certification programs to truly transform the mainstream market. The book shows clear evidence that eco-certification has advantaged large, capital-intensive businesses, leaving most producers and businesses in the relevant sectors unaffected. Without further incentives provided by the state and stronger pressure from civil society and consumers, most Chinese businesses may still lack the willingness or capacity to adopt higher standards. Given the increasingly strong role that the state is playing in Chinese society and the market, there is little doubt that the future of eco-certification and its ultimate impact on the Earth system will be largely determined by the Chinese government's policies on transnational governance. In this respect, different scenarios may occur, depending on the specific strategies used by the state.

To conclude the book, I first summarize the comparison across the three sectors and assess the hypotheses developed in chapter 2. Next, I consider the validity of my findings in large emerging economies beyond China. As the state will likely play an increasingly important role in determining the impacts of transnational governance in emerging economies, I then discuss broader implications for the interaction between public and private governance in three scenarios, as the state might adopt different positions. I finish by proposing a new research agenda on the changing roles of emerging economies in Earth system governance.

6.1 Comparison across the Three Sectors

Chapters 3–5 show that transnational sustainability governance has gained varying degrees of traction in China's different commodity chains. Of the three cases presented, the most prominent rise of eco-certification has occurred in the seafood sector, as demonstrated in chapter 3 by the significant progress of sustainable seafood certification since 2013, driven by an alliance between transnational programs and Chinese state actors. As of 2017, half of the top ten Chinese seafood companies have adopted relevant standards and have begun to sell certified products, not only to Northern buyers but also to domestic consumers. In addition, the major e-retailers in China have set ambitious targets for sourcing MSC- and BAP-certified products. Between the two subsectors of seafood production—wild capture fisheries and aquaculture—certification has been taken up much more readily in China's aquaculture production than in capture fisheries: The MSC has only one certified fishery in China's domestic waters, whereas GAA-BAP and ASC standards have been adopted by hundreds of fish farms across the country. In the industry of tilapia, a farmed species that has been one of the main targets of eco-certification, the proportion of certified products over the total production volume has even been estimated to reach 13%. As more and more Chinese businesses have firmly stated their support for sustainable seafood by producing or sourcing more certified products, the market uptake of certified seafood will likely increase and accelerate in the near future.

In comparison, businesses in China's palm oil supply chain have shown less interest in eco-certification, and the volume of certified palm oil imported to the country remains small. This outcome may not be very surprising, given that China is not a palm oil producer country and consumer awareness of the relevant sustainability issues is low. Nonetheless, the RSPO has still made noteworthy progress in China in the past decade, as an increasing number of companies have joined its membership and adopted its supply chain standard. An important achievement for the RSPO is its successful engagement with all major palm oil traders in the Chinese market, such that these key supply chain actors have shown their willingness to supply the country with more certified commodity. In the downstream part of the supply chain, an increasing number of consumer goods manufacturers have become interested in sustainable palm oil—the result of awareness raising activities organized by the RSPO with support from actors in China's state organization. However, as of mid-2018, certified palm oil represents only 1.5% of China's total consumption by volume. Although this figure shows very weak demand for palm oil certification, one can still expect more rapid increase in the number of certified companies and the uptake of sustainable palm oil in China due to the sourcing commitments made by some influential players in the supply chain.

Lastly, tea is the least successful case in terms of the spread of transnational sustainability governance in China. Although transnational eco-certification, like that of Fairtrade, entered China earlier than did programs in other sectors, to date, all major tea certification programs that exist in Northern markets have remained nearly absent in China—the world's largest tea producer and consumer country. This outcome seems even more striking in comparison with the growth of a domestic organic program run by the Chinese government. To date, most stakeholders in China's tea industry, including businesses and government officials, remain largely unaware of the relevant transnational certification programs. Nonetheless, this lack of progress by transnational programs does not imply that China has an unsuitable environment for the rise of sustainable tea certification. My survey of Chinese tea companies suggests that most producers could have a strong interest in using transnational standards to comply with domestic policy on sustainable development, especially when the Chinese government lends support for the relevant programs.

Taken together, the three sectors show clear differences in the spread of transnational eco-certification measured by the level of business support, ranging from "scant" in the tea sector to "moderately strong" for sustainable seafood, with palm oil located somewhere in between. Table 6.1 gives a cross-sectoral comparison and shows how the factors identified in chapter 2 contributed to this variation. I now discuss each of these factors in turn and evaluate the extent to which the empirical findings are in line with the relevant hypotheses.

6.1.1 Northern Market Agents: Initial Diffusers but with Limited Influence

To begin with, in all three sectors, eco-certification was initially conveyed to China by market agents based in developed countries, after social pressure

Table 6.1
Evidence supporting the hypotheses on the spread of eco-certification

		Seafood	Palm oil	Tea
Business support		Moderately strong	Weak to moderate	Scant
Transnational market forces	Requirements of Northern buyers (hypothesis 1)	Strong before 2013, but decreasing since then	Very weak	Very weak
	Requirements of large multinationals (hypothesis 2)	Absent	Existent, but limited in scale	Existent, but limited in scale
Activities of certification programs	Transnational programs' local capacity and engagement efforts (hypothesis 3)	Strong	Strong	Weak or absent
Fit of industry structure	Market concentration, vertically integrated supply chains, large-scale production (hypothesis 4)	Moderate	Weak	Weak
Endorsement of actors in the Chinese state	Support from local governments (hypothesis 5)	Absent	Absent	Existent, but limited in scale
	Support from national industry associations (hypothesis 6)	Strong	Moderate	Absent
Enabling conditions to win state support	Proactive engagement of transnational actors plus unfragmented domestic regulatory structure (hypothesis 7)	Existent	Existent	Absent

on sustainable production and sourcing had emerged. But the influence of these transnational actors on the penetration of eco-certification in each sector varied, depending on China's role in the relevant global supply chain. For export-oriented Chinese industries that are highly dependent on Northern markets, international trade can be an important channel for the flow of transnational governance, as suggested by hypothesis 1. Evidence supporting this hypothesis exists in China's seafood sector, especially in the initial rise of sustainable seafood certification prior to 2013, when export-oriented processors and farmers became certified in order to gain access to developed markets. For instance, the relatively high adoption rate of eco-certification in China's tilapia industry was mainly driven by American buyers, although the industry has recently begun to expand its sales domestically. My statistical analysis of a national survey of seafood processors also finds that export-oriented companies became more likely to hold MSC or BAP certification in China throughout the early 2010s.

By contrast, in China's palm oil and tea sectors, the fact that most products are consumed domestically has rendered foreign buyers incapable of driving rapid growth in eco-certification, although a few Northern buyers played a central role in introducing the relevant certification programs to China. For example, in the case of tea, only a dozen Chinese companies have adopted Fairtrade standards in their production for export to Europe, whereas most producers in the industry have focused on the domestic market and, therefore, were never under pressure from Northern buyers. The results of my survey experiment provide further evidence of the lack of Northern buyers' influence in this industry, as the prospect of expanding into Northern markets does not trigger companies' interest in getting certified. In fact, even in the case of seafood, I have observed challenges facing transnational certification programs in reaching the traditional domestic market. Hence, given the scale of China and its growing domestic consumption, Northern buyers are unlikely to drive the uptake of eco-certification in China.

With respect to the role of foreign investment or multinational corporations, the three cases show that Northern-based multinational brands can be important disseminators of eco-certification in China, but their influence in the Chinese market remains very limited. For sustainable seafood, multinational retailers like Walmart have even been reluctant to make sourcing commitments for their business in China, so that the uptake of certified seafood in the Chinese market has been driven by Chinese branded producers and e-retailers. In the case of palm oil, while a few multinational brands like Mars, Incorporated, have implemented responsible sourcing policies for their production in China, these actions cannot lead to a noticeable increase in the import volume of certified palm oil to the country due to their insignificant role in the Chinese market. Likewise, Unilever's commitment to sustainable tea has introduced RA certification to a very small number of producers in the large Chinese tea industry. Hence, even if Northern-based multinational corporations fully embrace eco-certification, these market agents alone are unlikely to make significant impact on the sustainability transition in the Chinese market. In short, although Northern buyers and investors are often the actors that initially introduced eco-certification to China, they can hardly constitute the key forces driving the subsequent rise of the relevant programs, not only because of their hesitance to take stronger action, but, more importantly, also because of their limited influence in the large Chinese market.

6.1.2 Agency of Certification Programs: Proactive Engagement on the Ground

When transnational market forces meet their limits, the activities of transnational certification programs and their NGO supporters in the destination country become crucial to generating domestic stakeholders' interest in the relevant rules and standards. The evidence from the three sectors suggests that proactive outreach activities and engagement efforts by these transnational non-market actors in China are necessary for the rapid spread of eco-certification in the country. These activities not only directly raise the awareness of Chinese businesses on the relevant sustainability issues and governance tools but also are helpful in building relationships with domestic regulators and therefore ensuring the legitimacy of their programs.

In the seafood and palm oil sectors, transnational certification programs made noticeable progress in increasing uptake after they had proactively approached some Chinese businesses and industry associations and built strong local teams to engage with domestic stakeholders. In the seafood case, the contrast between the rapid growth of the MSC, ASC, and GAA-BAP on one hand, and the lack of companies certified to FOS on the other hand, further demonstrates the importance of the local activities of transnational programs, as FOS has yet to start outreach activities in China. In the tea sector, all three transnational programs have refrained from devoting resources to expanding their business in China, and this passive strategy has been a key factor in limiting their influence in China's tea industry. In addition, my survey shows that those tea companies frequently interacting with environmental NGOs (including certification programs) are more interested in adopting eco-certification, implying that proactive engagement of certification programs and their NGO partners with local businesses are likely to boost the uptake of the relevant standards. In sum, the three cases together provide support for hypothesis 3 on the importance of proactive engagement efforts and the strong local capacity of transnational programs.

6.1.3 Fit of Domestic Industry Structure with Transnational Rules

In addition to transnational forces, in line with hypothesis 4, my empirical study shows that the structural features of each industry or supply chain in China can limit the spread of transnational governance, and, accordingly, disadvantage some types of businesses. The three cases together provide evidence suggesting that eco-certification is more likely to be adopted by businesses embracing industrial, capital-intensive commodity production. In China's seafood sector, eco-certification has risen in the chains supplying the export and domestic premium markets, where both the degrees of horizontal and of vertical integration are high due to the rise of major brands. My statistical analysis of national surveys of seafood processing companies also shows that large companies with more financial resources are more likely to get certified. Hence, the transformation of China's seafood industry toward horizontal and vertical integration has facilitated the rise of sustainable seafood certification. Nonetheless, the absence of certified companies and products in the chain supplying China's traditional seafood market reminds us that an important part of this industry remains incompatible with the governance mode of eco-certification.

In the cases of palm oil and tea, structural conditions in the supply chains are not always conducive to the adoption of transnational eco-certification. In China's palm oil supply chain, a key barrier to sourcing certified palm oil is the lack of vertical coordination to ensure traceability. This is a particularly salient challenge for Chinese commodity traders that do not own plantations in producing countries. Moreover, the manufacturing stage of the supply chain remains highly fragmented, as palm oil is used in a range of industries where many small companies exist. With respect to tea, the Chinese industry remains highly fragmented and filled with small-scale producers. This has presented a major challenge for transnational certification programs to quickly increase their uptake in the country, although the industry has rapidly increased vertical coordination and maintains a tradition of valuing quality through some good practices. Therefore, the three sectors presented in the book together show that, despite the rapid industrialization in China (including in its agri-food sector), the uptake of eco-certification in the country still suffers from the lack of fit between the governance mode of transnational standards and the structure of domestic industries.

6.1.4 Supporters in the Chinese State: Critical Role in Raising Awareness and Nudging Businesses

The most important factor contributing to the spread of eco-certification in China demonstrated by the three cases is the existence of supporters in the Chinese bureaucracy. As transnational market agents have a limited role in the large Chinese market, and the country's authoritarian context constrains advocacy by certification programs and their NGO supporters, the position of state or quasi-state actors becomes more important in China than anywhere else in determining the fate of transnational governance. Although we have not seen official endorsement by Beijing for any transnational certification programs, the empirics in the three sectors clearly show the rise of support from some national industry associations or subnational governments for transnational eco-certification and the positive effects of such support on businesses' adoption of relevant standards.

Chinese subnational governments have supported transnational governance in the tea sector, especially RA certification. As suggested by hypothesis 5, policy support provided by the local governments in Yunnan, and later Guizhou, facilitated the adoption of the relevant sustainable agriculture standards by tea producers in these regions. Both provinces belong to underdeveloped regions in China, where agriculture remains an important source of economic development. Thus, promoting local tea industries to boost economic growth was the primary motivation for these subnational authorities to endorse transnational governance. To facilitate the adoption of RA standards, these local governments have offered technical training, removed policy barriers for audits, subsidized certification costs, and even helped certified producers reach out to foreign buyers. These measures were critical for the rise of certified farms in these localities. However, such successful experiences have yet to occur in other regions, so that the overall effect of local government support for transnational governance remains very limited in China's tea industry. Moreover, my survey research on organic tea companies also shows that transnational certification programs are more likely to be accepted by Chinese producers when they highlight their benefits for domestic policy on sustainable development and receive support from the Chinese government. This finding confirms the large shadow that the state casts over the uptake of sustainable tea certification in China, implying a promising future for the relevant transnational programs if they can obtain support from local governments across the country.

At the same time, the cases of seafood and palm oil show the critical role that quasi-state industry associations can play in promoting transnational governance in China. In the seafood sector, transnational certification programs for both capture fisheries and aquaculture have built strong partnerships with CAPPMA, the national association of the seafood industry supervised by the Ministry of Agriculture. Such partnerships have been based on the willingness of CAPPMA's leadership to use eco-certification to upgrade China's seafood industry, build reputation of Chinese producers both domestically and internationally, and raise the association's profile in the Chinese government. As a result, CAPPMA took the lead in promoting sustainable seafood certification in China by organizing stakeholder forums and market campaigns and also recommending transnational programs to Chinese producers and retailers. Although CAPPMA could not directly offer financial rewards, the information and advice it provided was taken seriously by businesses, given its authority and expertise in the industry. It also helped transnational programs obtain the consent of state regulators and thus enabled a favorable policy environment for the former's outreach activities in China. Hence, with the endorsement of CAPPMA, China's uptake of sustainable seafood certification has taken off since 2013, as illustrated by an increasing number of certified producers (especially those focusing on the domestic premium market) and also by the strong sourcing commitments of Chinese e-commerce giants. We can hardly imagine such progress without the efforts of CAPPMA.

Likewise, CFNA, a leading trade association comprising major palm oil importers and users in China, has helped the RSPO raise awareness of and engage with influential players in China's palm oil supply chain since the early 2010s, especially state-owned agribusinesses. CFNA also organized stakeholder meetings to introduce the notion of sustainable palm oil to the whole industry, and it produced guidelines on sustainable investment for Chinese companies. CFNA decided to collaborate with the RSPO partly due to the program's growing influence in the global palm oil market, but also because of the opportunity for the association to expand its work and increase its profile both domestically and internationally. As a result, the partnership with CFNA has provided the RSPO with opportunities to establish dialogues with key players in the Chinese market and convince them to support its program. Despite the momentum driven by the RSPO-CFNA partnership, the moral or nudge-like support from CFNA has been unable to persuade many businesses to change their sourcing practices due to the lack of financial incentives. In addition, as palm oil is far from the dominant vegetable oil in China, CFNA itself has been also reluctant to lobby for government regulations supporting the sourcing of certified palm oil.

In sum, the three sectors show that even in China's authoritarian context, subnational governments and quasi-state industry associations can still find that supporting transnational governance is in their interests, and their support, in various forms, can make important contributions to the spread of relevant private standards. More specifically, as part of the Chinese state, their endorsement or nudges can help transnational programs reach out to more local businesses, ensure good relationships with domestic regulators, and increase the credibility and legitimacy of transnational rules in China. Nonetheless, other policy tools (e.g., training and financial rewards) might be able to more strongly incentivize businesses to adopt transnational rules, although such supportive measures are less likely to be used by Chinese state actors, especially industry associations. Therefore, given the limited influence of foreign actors, support from domestic state actors is necessary for the rise in prominence of transnational eco-certification in China. But whether sustainable commodities will become mainstream in the Chinese market depends on the willingness of the relevant state actors to take stronger action.

6.1.5 Conditions for Winning the Support of State Actors

Given the critical role played by state actors in determining the fate of transnational governance in China, more attention should be paid to the conditions shaping their positions. In fact, the three cases studied in this book shed light on two enabling conditions, as suggested by hypothesis 7, for transnational governance programs to win support of state actors in China, especially at the national level. As mentioned earlier, a comparison across the three sectors, and even within the seafood sector, shows that to get support from actors in the Chinese state, certification programs and the NGOs supporting them need to proactively approach the relevant domestic stakeholders. In the seafood sector, frequent interaction between CAPPMA's leadership and transnational certification programs, such as the MSC, the ASC, and GAA-BAP, was crucial for making CAPPMA aware of the potential benefits of eco-certification for industrial upgrading and willing to promote transnational standards. In contrast, without establishing contact with CAPPMA or other public agencies, FOS could not find supporters in the Chinese state. The RSPO case also demonstrates the importance of proactive engagement, as the program was only able to develop a partnership with CFNA after having invited officials from the MOFCOM and CFNA to its annual conferences and its study tours in producing countries. As a result, despite the lack of market pressure for sustainable palm oil in China, CFNA still decided to collaborate with the RSPO on awareness-raising activities. The strategies used by transnational certification programs took a different direction in China's tea sector, as none of the major programs in the Northern markets had a strong interest in expanding their Chinese market. Consequently, these programs on sustainable tea have been very reluctant to reach out to state actors in China and seek their support.

In addition to the actions of certification programs, the domestic regulatory structure in each sector also matters. Among these three commodity sectors, seafood has the most concentrated structure, as the Ministry of Agriculture, which supervises CAPPMA, is the only state agency regulating seafood production, processing, and marketing. In contrast, tea has the most fragmented structure as a legacy of China's planned economy. In the case of palm oil, the MOFCOM is the only agency regulating China's import of the commodity and therefore plays a central role in the regulation of this supply chain. Nonetheless, the MOFCOM has no direct regulatory power over the producers of consumer goods in the food and chemical industries. Therefore, when transnational certification programs were eager to engage with actors in the Chinese state, the concentrated regulatory structure in the seafood sector facilitated their efforts and ultimately contributed to the emergence of CAPPMA's strong support for eco-certification. In comparison, despite the RSPO's proactive engagement, CFNA has been hesitant to provide further support for promoting sustainable palm oil, partly because of the association's perceived inability to influence downstream industries in the supply chain. In the tea sector, it is not surprising that a fragmented regulatory structure and limited engagement efforts made by transnational actors have together resulted in the absence of strong support from any Chinese state actors.

Table 6.2 schematically maps the three empirical cases to reflect how the combination of the two conditions shapes the positions of Chinese state actors on transnational governance. It is worth noting that the cases covered by the book cannot reflect the situation in the lower-left entry in the table, where we expect ambiguity and even resistance by some state actors to transnational governance. Hence, future research needs to consider cases where transnational actors do not actively engage with Chinese state actors, but the domestic regulatory structure is concentrated, and tests whether the combination of these two conditions can cause the resistance of Chinese state actors to transnational governance.[1]

To summarize, the findings across the three sectors generally confirm the validity of the analytical framework developed in chapter 2. The empirical evidence shows that both transnational and domestic stakeholders played a role in driving the rise of eco-certification in China, but it is clear that the influence of Northern buyers and investors remains limited in this large emerging market, especially compared to interventions by actors in China's state bureaucracy, who support transnational governance for their own goals. Hence, to rapidly spread their standards in China, transnational

Table 6.2
Chinese state actors' responses to transnational eco-certification in the three sectors studied

		Domestic regulatory structure in the sector	
		Concentrated	Fragmented
Level of engagement of transnational programs with state actors	High	Seafood: Strong support	Palm oil: Moderate support
	Low	Cases to be discovered: Ambiguous position with possibility of resistance	Tea: Almost no support

certification programs need to proactively engage with potential supporters in the Chinese state. The variation across the three sectors shows the importance of such strategic action in promoting transnational sustainability governance in the world's largest emerging economy.

6.2 Beyond China: Similar Challenges, Different Contexts in Other Emerging Economies

After summarizing the factors shaping the rise of transnational governance in China, we can ask whether similar dynamics exist in other emerging economies, especially rising powers in the global economy, such as the other BRICS countries (i.e., Brazil, Russia, India, and South Africa). To answer this question, I now consider the extent to which the inferences drawn from this study can be applied to other emerging markets. Overall, three broad patterns on the uptake of transnational governance observed in China are likely to also occur in other emerging economies.

First, the rapid growth of domestic markets and South-South trade are reducing the influence of Northern-based market agents on the adoption of eco-certification. As suggested by global value chain scholars, emerging economies—not limited to China—have driven a shift in global trade in the past decade or so to become major end markets (Gereffi 2014; Horner and Nadvi 2018). Hence, commodities having significant sustainability impacts are increasingly produced to meet the demand in these Southern markets, where transnational governance mainly developed by Northern actors remains unpopular. For instance, most of the palm oil produced in Indonesia is consumed either domestically or in India and China, and the Brazilian soy industry keeps growing to support meat consumption in China and in its own market (FAO 2018b). These structural changes mean that producers and retailers in emerging economies have received less and less pressure from Northern businesses to adopt eco-certification standards—a situation similar to the case of China's tea industry, where businesses have little interest in Northern markets. This trend is likely to continue, and even increase, given the growing importance of Southern end markets in global value chains.

Second and related, without a strong influence by Northern market agents, domestic stakeholders, and especially state actors, who support the "on-the-ground" activities of transnational governance programs should be key drivers of eco-certification and sustainability standards in emerging economies. While the precise role of the state governing the market varies across emerging economies, the comparative political economy literature generally agrees that state-led development interventions have been a key commonality between large emerging markets, especially the BRICS countries (Ban and Blyth 2013). Accordingly, state actors in these countries should have the capacity to offer businesses incentives to accept transnational sustainability governance. In other words, nudge-like interventions, such as information sharing or technical advice, and financial rewards of host governments are likely to also work in other emerging markets (Loconto and Dankers 2014). For this reason, it is crucial to assess the relationships between domestic policy and transnational governance to understand the uptake of new standards and practices in emerging economies.

Third, the way in which transnational actors engage with domestic stakeholders has important implications for the fate of the relevant governance programs. As shown by my study on China, most domestic actors were initially unaware of Northern-developed certification programs, and, accordingly, lacked interest in the relevant standards. The same problem might also exist in other emerging economies, as Southern stakeholders have been largely absent in the standard-setting and decision-making processes of many transnational certification programs (E. Bennett 2017; Schleifer, Fiorini, and Fransen 2019). This is highly problematic, given the importance of emerging economies in today's global value chains and the different priorities for sustainability that Southern stakeholders may have. Therefore, to scale up their global impact, transnational eco-certification programs need to invest more resources and energy in emerging economies and proactively approach domestic stakeholders. In other words, to attract more supporters in emerging economies, certification programs must make themselves more inclusive and let Southern stakeholders' voices be heard.

Bearing in mind these broad trends, we must also recognize variations in different country contexts. Drawing on the existing literature, I now use the cases of soy certification in Brazil, fisheries certification in Russia, and tea certification in India to illustrate the applicability of my findings on China in other emerging economies before suggesting directions for future cross-country comparative research.

6.2.1 Brazil

As the world's largest soybean producer country, one of the most serious sustainability issues in Brazil is deforestation caused by soy and livestock production. As a commodity attracting global attention due to its significant environmental impact, soy became a target for certification in the mid-2000s. However, the relevant transnational programs have yet to make a significant impact in Brazil. To date, Brazil has the largest certified soybean area in the world, but the adoption rate of eco-certification in the whole sector of the country remains low: In 2016, the Roundtable on Responsible Soy (RTRS)—a leading soy certification program—only certified 2.1% of the soybean area in the country (Lernoud et al. 2018). As a result, eco-certification remains unable to bring discernible changes in the land-use patterns in Brazil's soy sector (van der Ven, Rothacker, and Cashore 2018).

This limited uptake of soy certification in Brazil can be explained by a combination of two factors. The first is the changing market orientation that has limited the influence of Northern buyers, who have been keen advocates of transnational governance in the form of eco-certification. Today, most soybeans produced in Brazil are sold to Southern markets, especially China and in Brazil's domestic market, which consumed, respectively, 47.2% and 26.7% of Brazilian soybeans in 2017. In comparison, the largest importer of Brazilian soybeans in the Global North—the EU—only consumed 11.3% of the country's production.[2] However, until now, the uptake of certified soy has been mainly driven by European buyers, and most Chinese buyers and supply chain actors remain unaware of both the concept of eco-certification and the relevant programs (Schleifer 2017; Solidaridad 2017).[3] Hence, the rise of Southern end markets and the lack of engagement of certification programs with Southern buyers together have constrained the growth of soy certification in Brazil.

The second factor explaining the low uptake of soy certification in Brazil is the failure of transnational certification programs to collaborate with key domestic stakeholders in the country, including both state and industry actors. As a result, little additional support from domestic actors has been provided to producers for the adoption of relevant standards. In the case of RTRS, a major industry association of Brazilian soy producers— the Brazilian Association of Soybean Growers (Aprosoja Brasil)—was involved in the early stages of the program's creation but later withdrew its support when the program could not establish a compensation mechanism for covering the cost of standard adoption and auditing (Hospes 2014; Schouten and Bitzer 2015). Moreover, although experts have indicated that conservation-minded, responsible producers do exist in Brazil, these actors have rarely been recognized and rewarded by transnational governance initiatives (Nepstad and Shimada 2018). Eco-certification programs have also had little interaction with Brazilian governments, although public regulations in tropical forest regions have made critical contributions to decelerating deforestation in the Brazilian Amazon since 2005 (Nepstad et al. 2014).

In sum, the case of sustainable soy certification in Brazil shows a similar pattern to sustainable tea certification in China, where the rise of Southern markets proves the limits of the influence of Northern buyers and investors in driving the rise of eco-certification in emerging economies. In this market context, support from domestic industry associations and regulators should be a critical driver of the adoption of transnational governance. Without such support, eco-certification has little chance to thrive. Looking ahead, to increase their impact, certification programs such as RTRS should devote more efforts to building alliances with regional governments and industry associations in Brazil.

6.2.2 Russia

The Russian Federation is a major seafood producer, especially for marine capture production. In 2018, the wild capture in marine waters accounted for 92% of the country's total seafood production volume, making Russia the world's fourth largest marine capture producing country.[4] While domestic consumption has been nontrivial, with a per capita fish supply higher than the global average, Russia is also a leading exporter in the global seafood market. By volume, more than 40% of the fish produced in Russia is sold abroad, making the country the world's third largest fish exporter after China and Norway in 2017. Accordingly, sustainable fisheries certification can play an important role in improving the management of fishery resources in Russia. In fact, programs like the MSC were introduced to Russian producers in the late 2000s and have experienced rapid growth in the country since then: As of 2015, the country has become the fifth largest supplier of certified wild-caught seafood in the world (Potts et al. 2016).

A closer look at the uptake of the MSC in Russia reveals the key forces driving the adoption of eco-certification by Russian fisheries, as well as several challenges to the further growth of sustainable seafood in the country.

Like the initial rise of seafood certification in China in the late 2000s, the rise of seafood certification in Russia has been entirely driven by the demand of foreign buyers, especially European ones. A recent study based on interviews with relevant stakeholders finds that, because of the absence of a domestic market for sustainable seafood, "the only motivation for fisheries to obtain certification is to export their products" (Lajus, Stogova, and Keskitalo 2018: 113). However, given that most fish products captured in Russian waters are consumed domestically, many Russian fisheries have lacked incentives to adopt the sustainable practices required by the MSC. Additionally, Russia's export has increasingly shifted toward emerging markets, especially China. According to the calculation of Rabobank (2019), more than half of Russia's seafood export volume was sent to China in 2017. Therefore, the demand for certified seafood in the Chinese market is likely to have more influence on the future growth of eco-certification in Russia.

Moreover, in line with hypothesis 3, the local activities of transnational certification programs and their NGO supporters are helpful for the adoption of relevant standards in Russian fisheries. As in China, transnational environmental NGOs, such as WWF and Ocean Outcome, played a key role in introducing the MSC to Russia's fisheries sector, and these civil society actors have provided important support for facilitating the communication between transnational and local stakeholders in the processes of standard adoption and audits (Pristupa, Lamers, and Amelung 2016; Lajus, Stogova, and Keskitalo 2018). Yet apart from these transnational actors, local civil society groups and research institutions have had little involvement in the adoption of sustainable fisheries certification in the country (Gulbrandsen and Hønneland, 2014; Lajus, Stogova, and Keskitalo 2018).

A more critical barrier to the spread of sustainable fisheries certification in Russia is the lack of support from domestic state actors. According to certified fisheries in the country, the local fisheries authorities neither provided support for nor created any obstacles to the adoption of transnational standards. However, interviews with relevant practitioners suggest that state authorities have had a negative attitude toward the introduction of sustainable seafood into the domestic market due to a fear that Northern-based certification programs would disadvantage local producers and distort the market balance (Pristupa, Lamers, and Amelung 2016; Lajus, Stogova, and Keskitalo 2018). This situation makes for a sharp contrast to the position of CAPPMA in China, where state actors strategically promote eco-certification in the domestic market. As state authorities in Russia also likely have the capacity to create domestic demand for sustainable seafood and improve communication between transnational programs and domestic stakeholders for standard adoption, the future of sustainable seafood in Russia depends on whether transnational programs can build trust and cooperation with the relevant state actors. Without support from such influential domestic stakeholders, fisheries certification is unlikely to make significant progress in the country.

Lastly, as suggested by hypothesis 4 on the importance of domestic industry structure, in Russia, the MSC has favored companies having vertically integrated supply chains while disadvantaging small-scale fisheries (Gulbrandsen and Hønneland 2014; Lajus, Stogova, and Keskitalo 2018). This adds another caveat to the positive sustainability impacts of eco-certification in emerging economies. In short, the rise of sustainable fisheries certification in Russia confirms the influence of Northern market agents on the rise of transnational governance in emerging economies, but the absence of a domestic market of sustainable seafood shows the limits of this mechanism without support of state actors.

6.2.3 India

With a large population and a growing economy, India has emerged in the past two decades as a major producer and consumer in global agricultural and manufacturing supply chains. While the spread of transnational eco-certification in India varies across sectors and products, according to a study commissioned by the United Nations Conference on Trade and Development and conducted by the Indian government, in both the agri-food and textile sectors, the adoption of such private standards has been primarily driven by the demand in developed markets, while domestic consumers and buyers have little knowledge about the relevant programs (Pande 2017).

A typical case is the rise of sustainable tea certification in the country. India is the world's second largest tea producer and exporter after China. But unlike China, it is a major supplier of certified tea in the global tea market: It has the second largest tea areas certified by Fairtrade and RA and the largest tea area certified by UTZ (Lernoud et al. 2018). But most Indian tea producers got certified to enter Northern markets or supply multinational companies having sustainable sourcing requirements, such as Unilever (Pande 2017; Langford 2019). In this sense, the gap between China and India in the uptake of sustainable tea certification should be mainly caused by higher demand for Indian tea in Northern markets and the stronger role of multinational brands in India's tea industry. However, relying on this mechanism to promote eco-certification has limitations due to the existence of a large domestic market in India and growing exports to Southern end markets. For instance, in 2017 less than 20% by volume of the tea produced in India was exported, and more than a third of India's tea export went to Russia and Iran, which are the top two consumers of Indian tea before the UK.[5] Hence, without demand for sustainable tea in the domestic market and other emerging markets, sustainable tea certification is unlikely to make further progress in India.

Another challenge to the growth of eco-certification in India, including its tea industry, is the position of domestic regulators. In general, the Indian state tends to underscore competition between private governance and the national institutions when defining standards on product quality and production processes. Therefore, it has often seen transnational certification programs as trade barriers that add extra costs to Indian producers, especially smallholders (Pande 2017; Schleifer and Sun 2018).[6] This official position means that transnational programs are unlikely to get support from most actors in India's state bureaucracy if they do not open their rule-making processes to domestic authorities. Even though state actors do not adopt policies against any particular program, without the former's support, transnational eco-certification would have a very difficult time gaining traction in the domestic market and spreading its standards more widely in the relevant industries.

Seeing this challenge, one response by transnational advocates of sustainability governance has been to develop homegrown multi-stakeholder initiatives with strong involvement from Indian state actors. A noteworthy example is the creation of the India Sustainable Tea Program (so-called "Trustea") in 2013, an initiative involving multinational buyers (e.g., Hindustan Unilever and Tata Global Beverages), transnational NGOs (e.g., the Sustainable Trade Initiative [IDH] and Solidaridad), certification programs, the Tea Board under India's Ministry of Commerce and Industry, and producer groups aiming to develop and implement a local sustainability code fitting the Indian tea industry's characteristics.[7] Through a partnership between transnational NGOs, businesses, and domestic state actors, the program seeks to provide a cost-effective and practical solution for improving the practices of farmers and factories that have faced challenges in adopting existing transnational standards (Langford 2019). While this program's effectiveness remains to be seen, it has the potential to serve as an alternative model of market-based governance in emerging economies.

In sum, the rise of sustainable tea certification in India has been driven so far by Northern buyers and investors, but as for the case of China, this mechanism to introduce transnational rules has left India's large domestic market untouched. Moreover, the position of the Indian government on transnational governance in general has further limited the growth of tea certification in the country. Nonetheless, a new model to engage with domestic state actors in the form of homegrown standards has emerged in India and might provide an alternative way to achieve the transition to sustainability in India's tea industry.

By briefly considering the spread of eco-certification in three other country cases, I find that the governance mode of eco-certification is far from mainstream in the emerging market context, and, in many cases, the sustainability problems being prioritized and the preferred governance instruments of Northern and Southern stakeholders cannot easily be made to converge. Today, emerging economies have become major players in global value chains, but in most transnational sustainability governance programs, the involvement of actors from these countries remains limited. The rapid expansion of domestic consumption in emerging economies further reminds us that Northern buyers and investors alone can no longer drive significant increases in the uptake of sustainable products in Southern end markets. This mismatch seems to suggest that the existing transnational governance initiatives led by Northern stakeholders need important changes if they are to become viable tools in emerging economies and that this governance mode cannot be the only way to trigger sustainability transitions in these new markets.

A major takeaway from the past experiences of different certification programs is the need to gain support from domestic stakeholders in Southern end markets in order to scale up their global impact. In this respect, one of the most important common phenomena across major emerging economies is the critical role that domestic state actors can play in promoting new standards and practices. Although transnational governance assumes that public regulations are not adequate to reduce the negative environmental and social impacts of economic activities, the evidence in China and other emerging economies shows that the state has maintained a strong influence on businesses' decisions. Without the support of such domestic stakeholders, transnational rules made by non-state actors have little chance of gaining traction in fast-growing emerging markets. While scholars of transnational governance have recently begun to pay increasing attention to the interactions between public and private governance (e.g., Grabs 2020; Renckens 2020; Tzankova 2020), more studies are needed to focus on such interactions and their effects in the context of emerging economies.

At the same time, domestic NGOs have been missing so far in the politics of transnational governance in emerging economies. Whether this is caused by their disinterest in or even opposition to market-based governance or by constraints on exogenous institutions, like the case in China, warrants further consideration. From a business perspective, multinational companies from emerging economies, like COFCO, have risen to prominence and will continue to expand their global operations. As a result, the sustainability policies and governance arrangements chosen by these companies will have huge implications for our world's development pathways and the Earth's biophysical systems. More attention should therefore be given to these Southern-based multinationals, including to their decision-making processes concerning sustainability strategies. Given the growing economic interdependence among emerging economies, future research should also investigate initiatives governing South-South trade and investment, and it should identify the types of governance that can effectively steward economic activities in the Global South for environmental sustainability and social justice.

6.3 Back to the Future: Transnational Sustainability Governance under the Shadow of the State

This book examines the spread of eco-certification in China and finds that despite a lack of strong NGO pressure and consumer activism, transnational governance led by non-state actors can still germinate and grow in this emerging economy under authoritarian rule. A notable insight offered by the study is that actors in China's state bureaucracy may be willing to endorse transnational governance to pursue their own economic and political goals. This result challenges the conventional view that the Chinese state remains hostile to private regulators in order to maintain its rule-making authority (Drezner and Lu 2009; Buckingham and Jepson 2013). However, when state actors have no intention of leveraging transnational rules, the relevant programs will have a difficult time attracting supporters in China because of the limited influence of Northern-based transnational actors in the country. Additionally, a quick scan of other countries in this chapter suggests that the lack of support from domestic state actors is a common challenge for transnational sustainability governance getting traction in emerging markets. Therefore, another discussion on possible actions by the state is warranted here to consider the future of transnational sustainability governance.

As we enter the third decade of the twenty-first century, the Chinese state and the governments of other emerging economies are likely to exert stronger influences on their jurisdictions. This expectation is partly based on a trend of tightened state control in these countries in the past decade. In China, since Xi Jinping came to power in 2012, he has steadily centralized the power of the party-state and increasingly expanded the state's influence in every aspect of Chinese society (Economy 2018; Nathan 2018). A major change in the Xi era has been intensified state interventions in the economy through top-down command and control measures, including regulations and industrial policies (Schubert and Alpermann 2019). Many signs also suggest that the Xi administration has further reduced the space of civil society in China, and accordingly, the Chinese government has become less responsive to citizens and societal actors (Qiaoan and Teets 2020). A noteworthy example in this respect is the enaction of a new Law on the Management of the Activities of Overseas NGOs, which requires every foreign NGO to be supervised by a Chinese state agency at the ministry or provincial government levels.[8] Yet China does not seem to be a unique case of authoritarian entrenchment in the world of emerging economies: Civil society activists in other countries, including India, Brazil, and Russia, also have found their actions increasingly constrained by their respective governments (Mohan 2017; Sauer et al. 2019; Stuvøy 2020).

Furthermore, the outbreak of COVID-19 in the first half of 2020 and the unprecedented government responses around the globe have led everyone to rethink the role of the state in the provision of public goods (Hale et al.

2020; van der Ven and Sun 2021). In nearly all countries, the state has played or is expected to play a dominant role in coping with the pandemic, as well as the subsequent economic downturn. Therefore, it is reasonable to expect the revival of the state in the upcoming decade in global and domestic governance regarding many critical issues, including the environment and sustainable development. This changing role of the state should be especially salient in emerging economies as reflected by the aforementioned trend. Indeed, in China's environmental governance, the Xi administration has emphasized the use of "goal-based governance strategies" through top-down central planning and campaigns (Zhao et al. 2020).[9]

Looking ahead, in this broader context, transnational governance programs have little chance to avoid the state, especially in emerging markets; instead, they will need to more frequently interact with different state actors. And state actors in emerging economies will have to become more reactive to transnational governance, due to the global expansion of Southern multinational companies and the growing influence of relevant programs in the global market. Hence, the ways in which Southern states will react determines the future of transnational sustainability governance and the contributions that this governance mode can make to sustainability of our Earth system. In this section, I lay out three scenarios of states' reactions with very different implications.

6.3.1 Scenario One: Undifferentiated Support by the State

In the first scenario, state actors in emerging markets lend more and more support to transnational sustainability governance but do not differentiate among initiatives varying in stringency of standards and procedural credibility. The position that has been taken so far by CAPPMA on sustainable seafood certification is similar to this approach of undifferentiated support. From the perspective of the host government, this approach seems impartial, and given the state's influence on the market, it holds the promise to quickly raise awareness among Southern businesses and consumers and to change some of their practices. However, this policy may limit the ultimate effectiveness of transnational governance by overlooking the specific features and standards of each program. In this case, transnational governance programs that do not have credible or stringent rules are still championed, and consequently, they may prevail over competing programs that have better governance systems and more rigorous rules to promote sustainable production and consumption.

The main concern of this scenario is the large variation across different eco-certification programs in their credibility and rigor, such that many of them have been criticized as greenwashing (Bullock 2017; Darnall, Ji, and Potoski 2017; van der Ven 2019). For processes of rule-setting and rule implementation, programs that do not adhere to key principles of procedural credibility—including transparency, relevance, engagement, impartiality, and accessibility—are unlikely to achieve their environmental or sustainability objectives (van der Ven 2019). Moreover, the strength of rules promoting environmental or sustainability improvements also varies significantly across programs. For instance, empirical evidence has suggested that industry-backed programs tend to have less stringent rules compared to NGO-backed programs for environmental performance (Darnall, Ji, and Potoski 2017; Judge-Lord, McDermott, and Cashore 2020). However, most consumers are not aware of such variations and may blindly trust eco-certification. To save costs, businesses may also prefer to adopt less stringent rules while still protecting their reputation through certification. All these dynamics provide opportunities for the success of programs that only have weak rules.

In addition, given the rise of many programs in the same issue areas, there is the danger of a race to the bottom when programs water down their rules to increase market uptake (Fransen 2011). In this respect, scholars suggest that over time, some prominent eco-certification programs have gradually shifted their focus on environmental performance toward balancing different sustainability outcomes and promoting producers' economic benefits. Such changes reduce the chances of the relevant certification programs from making significant contributions to Earth system governance (Cashore and Bernstein 2021). Therefore, if state actors provide indiscriminate support to eco-certification without filtering out programs promoting biased, arbitrary, and weak rules, emerging markets risk becoming grounds for greenwashing.

6.3.2 Scenario Two: Careful Steering by the State

To avoid the risks in the first scenario, state actors in emerging economies could adopt a more careful strategy when supporting transnational sustainability governance while not eroding the rule-making authority of relevant programs. To unlock the full potential of this new governance mode, the state should only endorse or award those programs having credible and rigorous rules. This approach requires Southern state actors to have a thorough understanding of the politics of transnational governance, the governance structures, and the content of different programs. Once states are capable of identifying credible and rigorous governance programs, they can use suitable policy tools, such as subsidies and procurement policies, to incentivize Southern businesses and consumers to support the relevant programs. In this situation, transnational sustainability governance is likely to help emerging economies make significant contributions to global sustainable development.

In addition to differentiating good programs from greenwashing, state actors in emerging economies could further provide targeted support to businesses or producers that have been disadvantaged by the existing governance mode of eco-certification, such as smallholders and artisanal producers, helping them build capacity for the adoption of sustainable practices (Glasbergen 2018). By giving additional support to less powerful actors in the supply chain, the state will correct the distributional consequences of private governance and promote a more just pathway for the transition to sustainability. Furthermore, to address the absence of concern for Southern stakeholders in Northern-developed sustainability standards, states in emerging economies need to assist actors based in their countries to more actively participate in the decision-making processes of transnational governance programs. The involvement of stakeholders from emerging economies is urgently needed to address the geographic imbalance in today's global sustainability governance system and to make transnational rules more inclusive and legitimate (Chan et al. 2018; Schleifer, Fiorini, and Fransen 2019).

All in all, this scenario seems to be an ideal situation for state actors fully leveraging rigorous transnational rules to promote sustainable production and consumption in emerging markets. A precondition for achieving this synergy between public and private governance is for relevant state actors to learn about good operating principles for transnational governance and specific rules for sustainability improvements. The challenge, therefore, lies in establishing mutual trust and good communication between transnational governance programs and Southern states.

6.3.3 Scenario Three: Takeover by the State

Alternatively, states in emerging markets may turn their backs on transnational governance by substituting the relevant programs with their own rules and therefore take over the rule-making authority of non-state actors. This approach has been already reflected by the emergence of several homegrown initiatives led by Southern states (Schouten and Bitzer 2015; Sun and van der Ven 2020). Some scholars find it very worrisome, as the state restricts and sometimes even completely removes space for transnational governance in emerging markets (Buckingham and Jepson 2013; Bartley 2014). However, Southern states take this position partly due to a feeling of disadvantage and exclusion caused by Northern-developed transnational rules, and Southern states' interventions may imply a willingness to improve domestic regulations on environmental and social issues (Wijaya and Glasbergen 2016). Hence, this scenario would not necessarily lead to bad sustainability outcomes if state actors can effectively enforce stringent sustainability governance. In that case, transnational governance, as tools that emerged to bridge the regulatory gaps left by states, may no longer be needed.

Moreover, as shown by this book as well as many other studies, transnational governance programs may set very high bars in terms of performance standards and leave the "bottom of the market" unaffected (Marx and Cuypers 2010; Steering Committee of the State-of-Knowledge Assessment of Standards and Certification 2012). As a result, businesses whose preexisting behaviors were far from certification standards remain uncertified, and this uptake pattern limits the additionality of certification impacts on the environment and social justice. This issue can be especially salient in emerging economies, where the bottom of the market is crowded. In this context, the takeover of transnational governance by domestic state actors holds the promise of significantly improving environmental and social performance if the minimum standards are continuously raised. To reach this positive outcome, the state needs to provide additional support to the businesses remaining at the bottom of the market to strengthen their capacity or give them compensation if they decide to leave the market. Otherwise, stronger state regulations for sustainability may cause even more negative impacts than private rules by putting more burdens on small businesses. In this respect, a more constructive perspective is that state regulations and transnational governance can be complementary, rather than rivalrous, so that their dynamic interactions can lead to continuous improvements of both the lowest standards set by the state and the highest standards set by non-state actors in emerging markets.

In sum, the three scenarios discussed here represent only some architypes of Southern states' responses to transnational rules. Therefore, these scenarios do not cover the full spectrum of complex interaction between state and non-state actors in making and enforcing sustainability governance. As state actors in emerging economies increasingly encounter transnational governance initiatives and improve their understanding of this new governance mode, the debate on the interplay between public and private rules will not end. But instead of focusing on arguing about who is in a better position to make and implement rules, researchers and practitioners of sustainable development should pay more attention to the pathways toward synergies between state and non-state initiatives in complex systems of governance at different levels of society.

6.4 Toward a New Research Agenda on Emerging Economies in Earth System Governance

In addition to illustrating the importance of interactions between public and private governance, this book demonstrates the urgent need to understand the roles played by China—and more broadly emerging economies—in the changing global governance system for sustainable development. My analysis sheds light on the extent to which China has been involved in transnational commodity governance and identifies pathways to better engaging actors in emerging economies for sustainability transitions. Given the growing influence of emerging economies in global sustainability governance, the book's findings point to three key research areas to be further explored by future studies.

First, to understand the promises and challenges of sustainability governance in emerging economies, we should better understand the politics of sustainability transitions in these countries. As climate change and other sustainability challenges have become increasingly existential for many people and groups, political contestation on sustainability governance is likely to intensify in emerging economies from the subnational to the national and transnational levels, and ultimately, it will greatly influence the future of the Earth (Colgan, Green, and Hale 2020). But studying these political dynamics is a highly challenging task due to rapid economic and societal transformations in emerging economies. It thus requires researchers to unpack governance processes in these countries by carefully identifying different stakeholders and examining how their interactions among one another and with the rest of the world may shape different transition pathways.

Second, sustainability governance research needs to pay more attention to governance innovations led by emerging economies and to identify conditions capable of triggering such innovations by both state and non-state actors. To date, the dominant paradigms on sustainable development tend to take a Western-centric perspective, assuming that innovations and experiments mainly, if not only, stem from the developed world. However, many global challenges that we have witnessed, including climate change and the COVID-19 pandemic, seem to disprove the idea that the Global North has all the expertise and solutions to effectively govern these challenges (Oldekop et al. 2020). For this reason, it is crucial to examine how effective governance can be homegrown from emerging economies and possible processes to promote multidimensional learning for tackling global sustainability challenges.

Third, and related to the first two research areas, as emerging economies like China continuously expand their global economic and political influences through trade and investment, more effort should be given to assessing the sustainability impacts of overseas engagement of these rising powers as well as the governance arrangements for steering the relevant activities. For instance, in the past decade, China has provided more development finance in the energy sector around the globe than the World Bank and reginal development banks, and therefore is in a position to fundamentally influence global energy transitions (Gallagher 2018). Hence, emerging economies are in the process of moving from being rule takers to rule makers in Earth system governance, and for this reason, their choices in sustainability governance are likely to shape future trajectories of sustainable development around the world. The issue is particularly salient in the case of China's Belt and Road Initiative, for which the effectiveness of environmental governance has large implications for the achievement of global sustainability goals (Ascensão et al. 2018). This area of inquiry needs to examine not only commitments and policies of China and other emerging investors but also their interaction with different stakeholders in recipient countries (Coenen et al. 2020; Hale, Liu, and Urpelainen 2020; K. Gallagher and Qi 2021). In summary, there is little doubt that emerging economies will play a central role in the future of global sustainability governance. To understand their influence and trigger positive changes toward sustainability transitions, it is imperative to provide fine-grained analysis on governance processes in these countries as well as their dynamic interactions with the rest of the world.

* * *

Focusing on eco-certification, a promising private tool governing global commodity chains, this book examines the agency of different types of actors on multiple scales in driving the rise of transnational sustainability governance in China—the world's largest emerging market. My study shows that, under certain conditions, Chinese state actors are willing to engage with Northern-based non-state rule makers in governing sustainable development; yet whether such engagement is durable and strong enough to trigger significant environmental and social impacts remains to be seen. Therefore, the book's findings shed light on both the promise and limits of transnational sustainability governance to lead sustainability transitions in emerging economies—the new center of the global economy in the twenty-first century.

The book, therefore, stimulates further consideration on the role of transnational governance and its interaction with the state in sustainability transformations that are required by the Anthropocene, the current human-dominated geological epoch threatening the Earth system's resilience (Biermann 2014; Young 2017). Two sets of broad issues warrant special attention by future research on transnational sustainability governance and its role in Earth system governance. First, we must more carefully assess to what extent new governance tools, such as private standards and certification, can effectively trigger and steer a transformation process (especially in fast-growing Southern markets) to ensure sustainability of the global environment as well as an equitable share of development benefits. In the field of eco-certification, a focus on impacts has recently emerged in the literature, but this "impacts literature" still suffers from poor data quality, narrow conceptions of impacts, and research design challenges (van der Ven and Cashore 2018). Future studies need to take a more holistic view when conceptualizing the transformational impacts of governance and to adopt mixed-method designs to assess the impacts of relevant initiatives against key governance principles, including credibility, stability, adaptiveness, and inclusiveness (Biermann 2007). Second, more research is needed to study the possible transformations of transnational governance programs themselves as they expand to new places and grow over time. As shown by the case of China in this book, to thrive in a new market, eco-certification programs need to adapt to local contexts and changing market dynamics, and the way in which they do so is likely to determine the scale of contributions they can make to the effective stewardship of the Earth system. Hence, we need to devote more attention to the adaptiveness and reflexivity of transnational governance systems, especially in the context of increasingly intensive interactions between state and non-state actors (Burch et al. 2019).

Our existing development model has brought pressing challenges to the Earth system, which have led to several governance innovations in the past three decades. Transnational governance in the form of eco-certification is one of them. My book adds to the existing literature on Earth system governance by showing that this new governance mode has the potential to transform production and consumption in large emerging economies like China, but this mode also faces many challenges in scaling up its influence in these new markets. This study again reminds us about the complexity of the existing global governance system and the need to encourage collaboration between state and non-state actors to enable the sustainability transformations that our world urgently needs. As the global economy and politics are constantly changing, and China, as an emerging power, begins to take leadership positions on many fronts, anyone who cares about the future of the Earth and human society should make more of an effort to engage with actors there and help China make good contributions to the development of future generations, not only within the country but also beyond.

Appendix A: Field Research and Interviews

To identify the factors that have influenced the rise of transnational eco-certification in China, I mainly draw on original data collected during intensive fieldwork in the country plus a few interviews in Europe. The field research in China was carried out from 2015 to 2017 during four series of trips to more than a dozen sites. During my fieldwork, I conducted a total of 106 semi-structured interviews with practitioners who have worked in China and who represent different stakeholders in the field of eco-certification or voluntary sustainability standards. These stakeholders include but are not limited to: certification programs (i.e., private standard-setting organizations), transnational and domestic NGOs, Chinese and other government agencies, industry associations, certification bodies, research institutes, and businesses. To arrange interviews, I first contacted transnational certification programs working on the chosen commodities. Once an initial contact was established, I followed up with organizations collaborating on the relevant programs in China and with major certified companies. The list of interviewees was further developed based on a snowballing strategy. Additionally, to get opinions on eco-certifications from a wider group of Chinese stakeholders, I also interviewed major companies that have not adopted relevant transnational standards as well as leading experts in each industry, including researchers and auditors. The insights provided by uncertified companies were helpful in establishing counterfactuals to understand what incentives were lacking to support eco-certification.

The average length of these interviews is around 70 minutes.[1] Interviews with stakeholders usually started with a question about the growth of eco-certification in China, then moved on to the major opportunities for and challenges to increasing uptake, and finally asked about the role of the

Chinese government and industry associations in the relevant processes. Interviews with firm representatives were conducted either with companies' general managers and chief executives, or with managers responsible for eco-certification or corporate social responsibility. In the interviews, I began with each firms' history and core business, then moved on to their sustainability strategy and experiences with certification, and finally finished with challenges in implementing transnational standards (for uncertified firms, I tested their knowledge about different certification programs and asked about their willingness to get certified). Through these questions, I tried to probe firms' incentives for joining a given certification program and to discover the key agents driving their participation. In addition to stakeholders in China, I also conducted, in person and by Skype, interviews with senior officials at the headquarters of most certification programs covered by this study to learn about their strategies in China and the challenges to increasing uptake. I sometimes asked them to compare China with other emerging markets.[2] To maintain anonymity and confidentiality, all interviews were codified for references, and I list below the date, location, and description of interviewees without disclosing their affiliations.

Moreover, for each of the three cases studied in this book, I attended at least one stakeholder meeting in China to observe discussions on the key issues in the relevant sectors and establish contacts with practitioners. These meetings enabled me to collect key information about each sector, as well as documents from some major firms. I also made several visits to production sites. In April 2017, with the help of a Chinese NGO, I visited several fish farms in Hainan (a major aquaculture production region) and talked to farmers. In July 2017, I visited tea farms in East China (Anhui, Jiangxi, and Shandong provinces) and interviewed their farm managers. Although I did not conduct ethnographic research, these visits helped me understand the relevant production processes and challenges for Chinese producers in adopting eco-certification standards.

Table A.1
List of interviews

No.	Code	Interviewee	Date	Location	Format
1	NBJ01	China representative, a transnational certification program	7/6/2015	Beijing	In person
2	NBJ02	China representative, a transnational certification program	7/7/2015	Beijing	In person
3	GBJ03	Director of International Cooperation Division, a national government agency	7/8/2015	Beijing	In person
4	NBJ04	Local project manager, a transnational NGO working on sustainability standards	10/16/2015	Beijing	Skype
5	NUK01	Global business director, a certification program	4/12/2016	London	In person
6	NUK02	Global communication official, a transnational NGO working on sustainability standards	6/2/2016	London	In person
7	NNL01	Project manager, a certification program	6/22/2016	Amsterdam	In person
8	NNL02	Official on China affairs, a certification program	6/22/2016	Amsterdam	In person
9	NNL03	Project manager on palm oil, a transnational development NGO	6/28/2016	Utrecht	In person
10	RBJ05	Researcher on oil crops, a Chinese research institute	7/5/2016	Beijing	In person
11	RBJ06	Researcher on sustainable consumption, a Chinese university	7/11/2016	Beijing	In person
12	RBJ07	Expert on sustainability governance, a think tank affiliated with a Chinese ministry	7/12/2016	Beijing	In person
13	NBJ08	Director on market transformation, a transnational environmental NGO	7/18/2016	Beijing	In person
14	BBJ09	Senior manager, a consultancy company specialized in corporate sustainability	7/19/2016	Beijing	In person
15	GBJ10	Director, Cereals and Oils Department, a Chinese trade association	7/20/2016	Beijing	In person

(continued)

Table A.1
(continued)

No.	Code	Interviewee	Date	Location	Format
16	BBJ11	Manager, Department of oils and oilseeds, a Chinese commodity trading company	7/22/2016	Beijing	In person
17	NBJ12	China representative, a certification program	7/22/2016	Beijing	In person
18	ABJ13	National strategic account manager in China, a global auditing company	7/26/2016	Beijing	In person
19	ABJ14	Marketing executive in China, a global auditing company	7/26/2016	Beijing	In person
20	NBJ15	Project consultant in China, a transnational NGO working on sustainability standards	7/26/2016	Beijing	In person
21	IBJ16	Country office manager on sustainable consumption, a United Nations program	7/27/2016	Beijing	In person
22	IBJ17	Deputy head of the Economic and Commercial section, first secretary, embassy of a European country in China	7/27/2016	Beijing	In person
23	RBJ18	Director of the Centre for Forestry Policy on Climate Change, a research institute affiliated with a Chinese ministry	8/10/2016	Beijing	In person
24	NBJ19	Project manager on market transformation, a transnational environmental NGO	8/11/2016	Beijing	In person
25	GBJ19	Official on sustainability standards, a think tank affiliated with a Chinese ministry	8/12/2016	Beijing	In person
26	AQD01	Business manager in China, a global auditing company	8/14/2016	Qingdao, Shandong	In person
27	NBJ20	Project leader, an international development project funded by a European country	8/17/2016	Beijing	In person
28	NBJ21	China Representative, a certification program	8/17/2016	Beijing	In person
29	BBJ22	Sustainable sourcing manager, a multinational food company	8/18/2016	Beijing	Phone

Table A.1
(continued)

No.	Code	Interviewee	Date	Location	Format
30	NBJ23	Project consultant in China, a certification program	8/18/2016	Beijing	In person
31	AQD02	Food department manager and lead auditor in China, a global auditing company	8/20/2016	Qingdao, Shandong	In person
32	RBJ24	Researcher on forest certification, a research institute affiliated with a Chinese ministry	9/5/2016	Beijing	Phone
33	IBJ25	Project manager on sustainable development, embassy of a European country in China	9/8/2016	Beijing	Skype
34	IBJ26	Head of the Political Section, embassy of a European country in China	9/8/2016	Beijing	Skype
35	NMA01	Global communication director, a certification program	10/12/2016	Kuala Lumpur	Skype
36	ICH01	Program manager on trade promotion, a European government	11/2/2016	Bern	In person
37	GCH02	Chinese diplomat experienced in affairs in international trade and sustainability standards	12/7/2016	Geneva	In person
38	NMA02	Former secretary general, a certification program	2/15/2017	Kuala Lumpur	Skype
39	GCH03	Independent consultant and former official of a Chinese ministry	3/1/2017	Geneva	In person
40	BBJ27	Business manager, a seafood trading company	3/10/2017	Beijing	In person
41	RSH01	Researcher on sustainable seafood, a Chinese university	3/13/2017	Shanghai	In person
42	NSH02	Founder and director, a Chinese environmental NGO	3/13/2017	Shanghai	In person
43	NSH03	China representative, a certification program	3/14/2017	Shanghai	In person
44	NSH04	Asian business development director, a certification program	3/14/2017	Shanghai	In person
45	RBJ28	Senior researcher, a research institute affiliated with a Chinese ministry	3/16/2017	Beijing	In person

(continued)

Table A.1
(continued)

No.	Code	Interviewee	Date	Location	Format
46	NBJ29	Project official on climate change and fisheries, a transnational environmental NGO	3/17/2017	Beijing	In person
47	NBJ30	Project official in China, a transnational NGO working on sustainability standards	3/20/2017	Beijing	In person
48	GBJ31	Deputy chief economist, a Chinese industry association	3/20/2017	Beijing	In person
49	GBJ32	Program manager in the International Cooperation Department, a Chinese industry association	3/21/2017	Beijing	In person
50	NQD03	Food safety expert, independent consultant	3/22/2017	Qingdao, Shandong	Phone
51	GBJ33	General manager, a Chinese auditing company	3/23/2017	Beijing	In person
52	GBJ34	Director of the Quality and Standard Research Center, a research institute affiliated to a Chinese ministry	3/27/2017	Beijing	In person
53	NBJ35	Project consultant on sustainable food	3/28/2017	Beijing	In person
54	NBJ36	Expert on sustainability standards	3/29/2017	Beijing	In person
55	NBJ37	Project official on seafood certification	3/29/2017	Beijing	In person
56	ANJ01	Auditor, research fellow, a Chinese auditing company and research institute on organic standards	3/31/2017	Nanjing, Jiangsu	In person
57	BZJ01	General manager, a fishing company	4/5/2017	Yuhuan, Zhejiang	In person
58	GZJ02	Director of fisheries, a county government	4/5/2017	Yuhuan, Zhejiang	In person
59	GZJ03	Director of the Agricultural Technology Extension Centre, a county government	4/6/2017	Yuhuan, Zhejiang	In person
60	GZJ04	Party secretary, a fishing town in East China	4/6/2017	Yuhuan, Zhejiang	In person
61	NHN01	General secretary, a local Chinese business association	4/10/2017	Haikou, Hainan	In person

Table A.1
(continued)

No.	Code	Interviewee	Date	Location	Format
62	NHN02	Program manager, a Chinese environmental NGO	4/10/2017	Haikou, Hainan	In person
63	NHN03	Founder and director, a Chinese environmental NGO	4/10/2017	Haikou, Hainan	In person
64	FHN04	Fish farmer (smallholder)	4/11/2017	Baoluo, Hainan	In person
65	FHN05	Fish farmer (smallholder)	4/11/2017	Baoluo, Hainan	In person
66	FHN06	Fish farmer (smallholder)	4/11/2017	Baoluo, Hainan	In person
67	FHN07	Fish farmer (smallholder)	4/11/2017	Baoluo, Hainan	In person
68	FHN08	Fish farmer (smallholder)	4/11/2017	Baoluo, Hainan	In person
69	BHN09	Deputy general manager, a Chinese seafood company	4/12/2017	Wenchang, Hainan	In person
70	NSH05	Project consultant in China, a certification program	4/13/2017	Shanghai	In person
71	NNJ02	Project manager of the tea program in China, a transnational development NGO	4/13/2017	Nanjing, Jiangsu	In person
72	NQD04	China program manager, a transnational conservation NGO	4/14/2017	Qingdao, Shandong	In person
73	NQD05	China business manager, a certification program	4/14/2017	Qingdao, Shandong	In person
74	ABJ38	General manager, a Chinese auditing company	4/16/2017	Beijing	In person
75	NBJ39	Project consultant in China, a certification program	4/18/2017	Beijing	In person
76	BNJ03	Owner of a tea farm	6/14/2017	Nanjing, Jiangsu	In person
77	GNJ04	Chief engineer, a research institute on aquatic products affiliated with a provincial government	6/19/2017	Nanjing, Jiangsu	In person
78	NNJ05	Program manager, a transnational development NGO	6/19/2017	Nanjing, Jiangsu	In person

(continued)

Table A.1
(continued)

No.	Code	Interviewee	Date	Location	Format
79	RHZ01	Director of the center on plant protection, a research institute affiliated with the Chinese Academy of Agricultural Sciences	6/20/2017	Hangzhou, Zhajiang	In person
80	RHZ02	Director of the Organic Tea R&D Center, a research institute affiliated with the Chinese Academy of Agricultural Sciences	6/22/2017	Hangzhou, Zhejiang	in person
81	RHZ03	Researcher, Organic Tea R&D Center, a research institute affiliated to the Chinese Academy of Agricultural Sciences	6/22/2017	Hangzhou, Zhejiang	In person
82	NBJ40	Project manager on oil crops in China, a transnational development NGO	6/26/2017	Beijing	In person
83	BBJ41	Chairperson, a Chinese agricultural service company	6/26/2017	Beijing	In person
84	GBJ42	Deputy secretary-general, a Chinese industry association	6/27/2017	Beijing	In person
85	NFZ01	Project manager, a Chinese environmental NGO promoting sustainable seafood	6/30/2017	Fuzhou, Fujian	In person
86	BAH01	Chairperson, a large Chinese tea company	7/3/2017	Huangshan, Anhui	In person
87	BAH02	Manager on quality control, a large Chinese tea company	7/3/2017	Huangshan, Anhui	In person
88	BAH03	Factory manager, a large Chinese tea company	7/3/2017	Huangshan, Anhui	In person
89	BAH04	Investor in tea farms	7/3/2017	Huangshan, Anhui	In person
90	GAH05	Director of the Agricultural Commission, a county-level government agency	7/4/2017	Huangshan, Anhui	In person
91	GAH06	Official on tea affairs, a county-level government agency	7/4/2017	Huangshan, Anhui	In person
92	BAH05	Chairperson, a Chinese tea company	7/4/2017	Huangshan, Anhui	In person
93	BAH06	General manager, a Chinese tea company	7/5/2017	Xiuning, Anhui	In person
94	BWY01	Founder and chairperson, a Chinese tea company	7/6/2017	Wuyuan, Jiangxi	In person

Table A.1
(continued)

No.	Code	Interviewee	Date	Location	Format
95	FWY02	Farm manager, a Chinese tea company	7/6/2017	Wuyuan, Jiangxi	In person
96	BWY03	Factory manager, a Chinese tea company	7/6/2017	Wuyuan, Jiangxi	In person
97	BWY04	Director of the Export Department, a Chinese tea company	7/6/2017	Wuyuan	In person
98	BWY05	Vice-general manager, a Chinese tea company	7/6/2017	Wuyuan	In person
99	BWY06	Founder and chairperson, a Chinese tea company	7/7/2017	Wuyuan	In person
100	BRZ01	Production manager, a Chinese tea company	7/10/2017	Rizhao	In person
101	BRZ02	General manager, a Chinese tea company	7/11/2017	Rizhao	In person
102	ICH04	Project consultant, a United Nations agency	8/2/2017	Geneva	In person
103	NIT01	Chief executive official and founder, a certification program	8/22/2017	Milan	Skype
104	NUK03	Chief executive official, a certification program	9/20/2017	London	Skype
105	NNL04	Project manager, a certification program	11/2/2017	Utrecht	Skype
106	NUK04	Project manager, a transnational NGO	3/16/2018	Sterling	Skype

Appendix B: Data on Seafood Processing Companies

The dataset used in chapter 3 was constructed using a sample of seafood processing firms in the Chinese Industrial Enterprises Database, which is accessible through the institutions that subscribe to it.[1] To form my dataset, I extracted data on the aquatic product processing firms between 2005 and 2009 from the original database. The period was chosen for two reasons. First, since the 2010s, the Bureau of Statistics revised their sampling strategy for this database. More importantly, before 2010, certification programs had not yet started to work in China, nor had any Chinese stakeholder supported sustainable seafood certification. Focusing on this period thus allowed me to concentrate on the effects of transnational market agents while excluding the potential influences of support from domestic stakeholders and promotional activities of transnational certification programs. I focus on the processing firms not only due to data availability, but also because the number of certified fisheries and fish farms in China was very low (even none for the MSC) during this period, and most certified farms in China were also owned by large processing firms.

As the MSC and the GAA-BAP were the only two seafood certification programs introduced to China before 2010, the outcome of interest in my quantitative study here is firms' adoption of one of these standards. Accordingly, in the new dataset, I coded firms' certification status for a given year, using open access data on the certified facilities in China until 2011 from the two certification programs. I included the data until 2011 to take into consideration the time needed for assessment and audits after firms decide to apply for certification. The newly constructed binary variable is used as the dependent variable in my regression analysis. Of the certified firms in the focus period, more than 60% exist in the Chinese Industrial Enterprises

Database sample. Among those that cannot be merged, most are traders or contractors without actual processing capacity. Thus, excluding them would not introduce systematic bias to the analysis.

Additionally, according to experts in the industry, once Chinese processors have joined a transnational program, they rarely withdraw, as holding a certificate can help them maintain access to export markets.[2] Indeed, for the firms that can be merged in my dataset, none of them withdrew until 2013. In other words, at least in China's seafood processing industry, certification status is path dependent and rarely changes after firms' initial participation. Therefore, to reduce potential noise in the data caused by market fluctuations after firms' adoption of eco-certification, I exclude the observations of certified firms in the years immediately following their initial certification. In terms of the key explanatory variables in the analysis, I drew data from the original database on firms' trade and ownership, which reflect their exposure to transnational market influences. Moreover, several indicators of corporate performance, such as sales, size, and revenues, are also used to assess the effects of businesses' capacity. Tables B.1–B.4 show the correlation matrix and the results of various robustness checks.

Table B.1
Correlation matrix

	Export ratio	Export value	Foreign invested	Foreign owned	Assets	Employees	Sales
Export ratio	1						
Export value	0.851	1					
Foreign invested	0.236	0.229	1				
Foreign owned	0.121	0.0977	0.521	1			
Assets	0.0977	0.231	0.0828	−0.0111	1		
Employees	0.122	0.264	0.0981	−0.00363	0.447	1	
Sales	0.159	0.377	0.0902	0.000237	0.543	0.472	1
N	6,883						

Table B.2
Random-effects logistic regression (baseline model, 2-year lagged dependent variable)

	(1)	(2)	(3)	(4)	(5)	(6)
	Cert2	Cert2	Cert2	Cert2	Cert2	Cert2
Export ratio	0.973** (3.06)	1.022** (3.00)	0.971** (2.95)			
Export value				0.0695* (2.39)	0.0859** (2.83)	0.0442 (1.52)
Foreign invested	0.784** (2.92)	0.911** (2.92)	0.874** (2.98)	0.840** (2.93)	0.923** (2.97)	0.980** (3.23)
Foreign owned Assets	0.477*** (5.45)			0.421*** (4.05)		
Employees		0.000551*** (3.39)			0.000464** (2.80)	
Sales			0.654*** (5.30)			0.610*** (4.55)
2006.year	0.157 (0.37)	0.227 (0.51)	0.147 (0.34)	0.172 (0.40)	0.223 (0.51)	0.172 (0.40)
2007.year	−0.580 (−1.16)	−0.448 (−0.86)	−0.574 (−1.14)	−0.572 (−1.14)	−0.465 (−0.90)	−0.570 (−1.12)
2008.year	0.273 (0.68)	0.500 (1.13)	0.270 (0.65)	0.302 (0.73)	0.488 (1.11)	0.302 (0.72)
2009.year	−0.0703 (−0.16)	0.213 (0.44)	−0.121 (−0.27)	−0.0385 (−0.09)	0.191 (0.40)	−0.0983 (−0.22)
_cons	−9.857*** (−10.67)	−6.600*** (−6.88)	−13.04*** (−6.64)	−9.587*** (−6.29)	−6.658*** (−6.94)	−12.65*** (−6.18)
lnsig2u_cons	−11.22 (−0.01)	0.542 (0.59)	−0.597 (−0.24)	−0.907 (−0.26)	0.506 (0.53)	−0.00869 (−0.01)
N	6,731	6,776	6,776	6,739	6,786	6,776

Note: $^{*}p<0.05$, $^{**}p<0.01$, $^{***}p<0.001$.

Table B.3

Mixed-effects logistic regression (columns 1–4: one year lagged dependent variable; columns 5–8 two-year lagged dependent variable)

	(1)	(2)	(3)	(4)	(5)	(6)	(7)	(8)
	Cert1	Cert1	Cert1	Cert1	Cert2	Cert2	Cert2	Cert2
Export ratio	1.615***	1.675***			0.973**	1.021**		
	(4.41)	(4.46)			(3.06)	(3.00)		
Export value			0.126***	0.150***			0.0695*	0.0859**
			(3.62)	(4.23)			(2.39)	(2.83)
Foreign invested	0.826**	0.900**	0.890**	0.892**	0.784**	0.908**	0.840**	0.921**
	(2.68)	(2.86)	(2.87)	(2.94)	(2.92)	(2.92)	(2.93)	(2.98)
Assets	0.484***		0.385***		0.477***		0.421***	
	(4.43)		(3.36)		(5.45)		(4.05)	
Employees		0.000416**		0.000256		0.000549***		0.000462**
		(2.81)		(1.74)		(3.42)		(2.83)
2006.year	−0.124	−0.292	−0.143	−0.212	0.157	0.226	0.172	0.222
	(−0.31)	(−0.71)	(−0.36)	(−0.54)	(0.37)	(0.51)	(0.40)	(0.51)
2007.year	−0.175	−0.268	−0.202	−0.239	−0.580	−0.450	−0.572	−0.467
	(−0.47)	(−0.71)	(−0.54)	(−0.64)	(−1.16)	(−0.87)	(−1.14)	(−0.91)
2008.year	−0.608	−0.681	−0.617	−0.629	0.273	0.497	0.302	0.486
	(−1.50)	(−1.64)	(−1.52)	(−1.54)	(0.68)	(1.12)	(0.73)	(1.11)
2009.year	0	0	0	0	−0.0702	0.210	−0.0385	0.187
	(.)	(.)	(.)	(.)	(−0.16)	(0.44)	(−0.09)	(0.40)
_cons	−10.19***	−6.113***	−9.576***	−6.185***	−9.857***	−6.584***	−9.588***	−6.642***
	(−6.04)	(−6.80)	(−6.06)	(−7.12)	(−10.67)	(−7.03)	(−6.29)	(−7.10)
var(_cons [coid]) _cons	0.285	1.069	0.734	0.659	5.32e−31	1.689	0.404	1.631
	(0.16)	(0.60)	(0.48)	(0.39)	(0.00)	(1.11)	(0.29)	(1.06)
N	5,630	5,670	5,637	5,677	6,731	6,776	6,739	6,786

Note: $^{*}p<0.05$, $^{**}p<0.01$, $^{***}p<0.001$.

Table B.4

Complementary log-log regression (random-effects) (columns 1–4: 1-year lagged dependent variable; columns 5–8: two-year lagged dependent variable)

	(1)	(2)	(3)	(4)	(5)	(6)	(7)	(8)
	Cert1	Cert1	Cert1	Cert1	Cert2	Cert2	Cert2	Cert2
Export ratio	1.602*** (4.46)	1.636*** (4.59)			0.966** (3.07)	1.006** (3.02)		
Export volume			0.125*** (3.63)	0.151*** (4.26)			0.0686* (2.38)	0.0853** (2.85)
Foreign invested	0.805** (2.70)	0.857** (2.88)	0.866** (2.90)	0.865** (3.00)	0.771** (2.90)	0.889** (2.94)	0.823** (2.93)	0.902** (3.00)
Assets	0.477*** (4.51)		0.375*** (3.42)		0.469*** (5.50)		0.409*** (4.07)	
Employees		0.000358** (2.70)		0.000223 (1.73)		0.000515*** (3.48)		0.000434** (2.88)
2006.year	0 (.)	0 (.)	0 (.)	0 (.)	0.156 (0.37)	0.223 (0.52)	0.173 (0.41)	0.226 (0.53)
2007.year	–0.0580 (–0.15)	–0.000760 (0.00)	–0.0584 (–0.15)	–0.0342 (–0.09)	–0.580 (–1.17)	–0.442 (–0.87)	–0.569 (–1.15)	–0.454 (–0.90)
2008.year	–0.481 (–1.11)	–0.416 (–0.97)	–0.464 (–1.08)	–0.419 (–0.99)	0.263 (0.66)	0.480 (1.11)	0.289 (0.72)	0.475 (1.12)
2009.year	0.116 (0.30)	0.246 (0.62)	0.141 (0.37)	0.193 (0.51)	–0.0735 (–0.17)	0.202 (0.43)	–0.0411 (–0.09)	0.185 (0.40)
_cons	–10.26*** (–5.71)	–6.171*** (–5.49)	–9.637*** (–6.10)	–6.323*** (–6.83)	–9.781*** (–10.82)	–6.560*** (–7.34)	–9.449*** (–6.35)	–6.641*** (–7.46)
lnsig2u _cons	–1.088 (–0.20)	–0.360 (–0.13)	–0.268 (–0.15)	–0.637 (–0.22)	–8.238 (–0.54)	0.508 (0.60)	–1.014 (–0.26)	0.488 (0.56)
N	5,630	5,670	5,637	5,677	6,731	6,776	6,739	6,786

Note: $*p<0.05$, $**p<0.01$, $***p<0.001$.

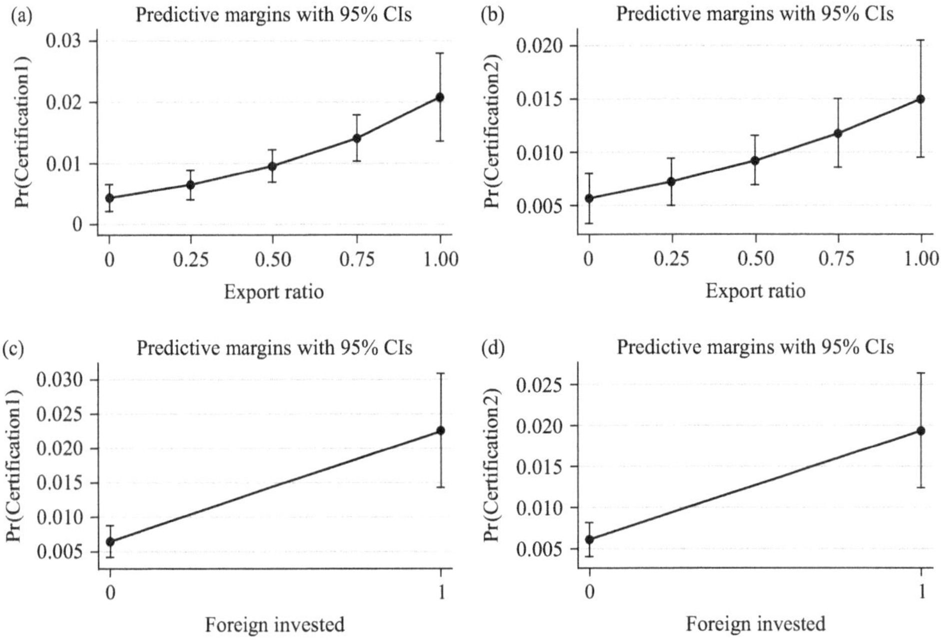

Figure B.1
Marginal effects of foreign market influences on the uptake of seafood certification in China.

Using the marginal effects, figure B.1 further demonstrates the influence of export and foreign investment on firms' adoption of eco-certification. According to the graph (a), holding other variables at their mean value, switching from the domestic market to the export market would increase the probability of certification from .004 to 0.02. This is a quite strong effect given the very small proportion of the positive outcome in our sample. Similarly, the graph (c) shows the clear differences between firms having foreign investors and those which do not.

Appendix C: Data on Organic Tea Producer Companies

The statistical analysis in chapter 5 is based on data drawn from the Organic Tea Producer Survey (OTPS) that I conducted with support from researchers at the Tea Research Institute of the Chinese Academy of Agricultural Sciences from December 2017 to June 2018. The survey focuses on a subgroup of producers who are the most likely adopters of transnational eco-certification but have not yet complied with the relevant standards, namely, those who have knowledge of the Chinese organic certification scheme. The rationale for this sampling strategy is that most Chinese producers who have no experience of eco-certification lack the capacity to adopt transnational rules originating in the Global North; accordingly, to explore the potential of sustainable tea certification in China in the near future, we first studied those companies that have the capacity to pursue certification. I therefore constructed a sample of tea producing companies that have been certified to the Chinese organic scheme across different production regions. Today, most Chinese tea companies have integrated their production chains from farms to processing factories. Thus, it makes more sense to survey these companies rather than the farmers to understand the potential for sustainable tea certification in China, as the former play a central role in organizing production and, in most cases, are the agents making the decision on certification.

The survey questionnaire was edited on an online survey platform (www.wjx.cn) and then sent via Chinese social media applications by local collaborators to owners or senior managers of more than 300 tea producing companies.[1] In total, 215 tea producing companies of different sizes and ownership, located in 18 provinces, participated in the survey. To protect anonymity, respondents did not reveal their company's name. To build a representative sample of producers in each production region, I implemented a quota on company location. The geographical distribution of the participating companies (by number) shows that the sample covers producers in all major tea producing provinces except Hunan, and the sample generally represents the production size of each province (see the sample representativeness in table C.1). In the survey, respondents were asked around 30 questions on various sorts of company information, including data on production, sales, interaction with other stakeholders (such as environmental NGOs), experience with organic certification, certification programs they have joined, and the challenges and expectations of sustainable production. The median completion time for the survey was 10 minutes. Companies that had not been certified to any transnational standards were asked to indicate their interest in joining the relevant programs on a five-point Likert scale from "very uninterested" to "very interested." The answer to this question was used as the outcome variable in my quantitative analysis.

Table C.1
Geographic distribution of companies participating in the OTPS

Province	Production volume as a share of the national total in 2016 (%)	Share of companies in each province participating in the OTPS (%)
Fujian	17.75	12.56
Yunan	15.99	3.72
Hubei	12.31	22.79
Sichuan	11.13	11.63
Hunan	7.73	0.00
Zhejiang	7.16	23.72
Guizhou	5.88	1.40
Anhui	4.66	4.65
Guangdong	3.61	3.26
Henan	2.85	1.40
Guangxi	2.83	2.79
Shaanxi	2.58	1.40
Jiangxi	2.39	2.79
Chongqing	1.54	0.47
Shandong	0.90	1.40
Jiangsu	0.58	4.65
Gansu	0.05	0.00
Hainan	0.04	0.47

As discussed in chapter 5, to better disentangle the effects of the potential demand of foreign markets and support from state actors on firms' incentives to support transnational private governance, I conducted a framing experiment in the survey. In the experiment, respondents were randomly assigned to one of three groups and asked to read a text before they indicated their interest in joining sustainable tea certification. The texts vary across groups to provide different interpretations of sustainable tea certification. In the first group, respondents received a frame that indicates government support for certification and advocates the adoption of relevant standards to help the Chinese state achieve its policy goal on sustainable development. In the second group, the frame emphasizes demand for sustainable agriculture in the global tea market and suggests that joining the relevant programs can help companies expand their international markets. The third group was a placebo control group, where respondents only read a simple introduction of sustainable agriculture (see the framing texts below).

C.1 Frames Used in the Survey Experiment

Boxes C.1–C.3 are English translations of the frames; the words shown in bold in these boxes were also bold in the original text of the survey.

Box C.1
Frame on benefits for the state's policy goals on sustainable development

Sustainable agriculture aims to reasonably use and protect natural resources, reduce pollution from the production process, and protect farmers and workers' rights and improve their livelihood. It has a broader definition than organic agriculture.

In the past decade or so, sustainable agriculture certifications like Rainforest Alliance, UTZ, and Fairtrade have continuously grown. Their standards are **in line with the Chinese state's development goal**. Accordingly, governments at different levels have adopted supportive policies. Adopting these standards can **react to the government's call for sustainable development** and show companies' social responsibility.

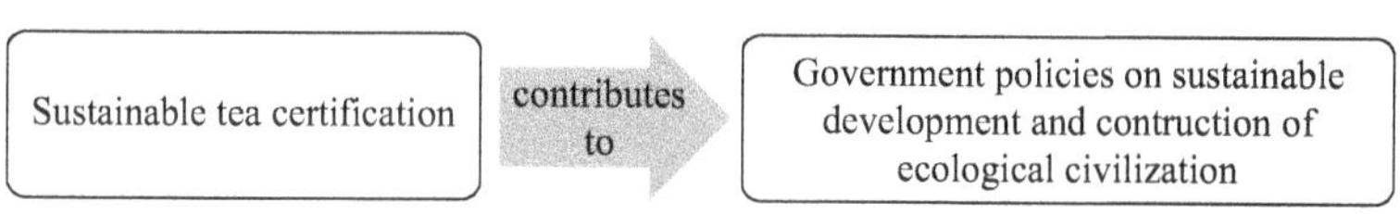

Box C.2

Frame on benefits for foreign market expansion

Sustainable agriculture aims to reasonably use and protect natural resources, reduce pollution from the production process, and protect farmers and workers' rights and improve their livelihoods. It has a broader definition than organic agriculture.

In the past decade or so, sustainable agriculture certifications like Rainforest Alliance, UTZ, and Fairtrade have continuously grown. Their standards have been **recognized and required in the global market, especially Europe and North America.** Adopting these standards can effectively **expand foreign markets** of Chinese tea companies.

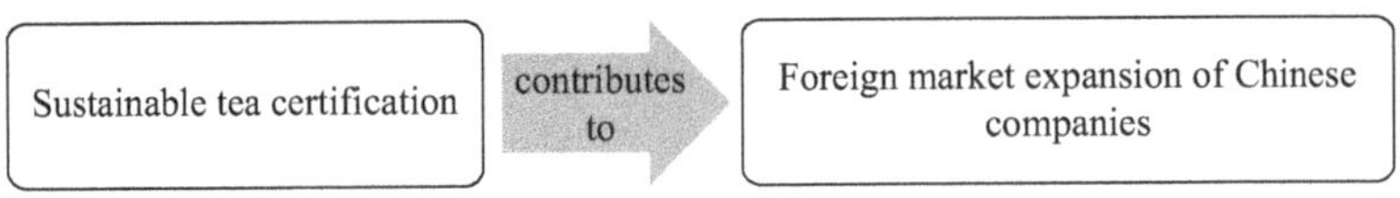

Box C.3

Placebo control frame

Sustainable agriculture aims to reasonably use and protect natural resources, reduce pollution from the production process, and protect farmers' and workers' rights and improve their livelihood. It has a broader definition than organic agriculture.

Your company has yet to adopt **sustainable agriculture certification** such as Rainforest Alliance, UTZ, and Fairtrade.

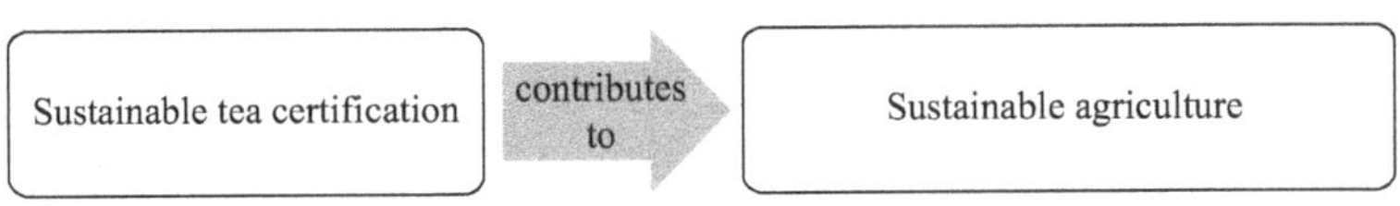

C.2 Data Description

The experiment was fully implemented after a pretest with two dozen respondents. In the pretest, respondents were asked to give their feedback on the frames. I then revised the framing text and officially started the randomization process. As tea certification focuses on agricultural practices, only companies having their own production bases were included in the experiment. To ensure that respondents read their text, they were forced to stay on the page for at least 10 seconds before moving to the next question. After having excluded a few invalid observations in the pretest, I ensured that each group had more than 50 respondents. Tables C.2–C.4 show summary statistics, correlation matrix, and randomization checks of the data used in statistical analysis in chapter 5.

Table C.2
Summary statistics of the Organic Tea Producer Survey

Variable	Mean	Standard deviation	Minimum	Maximum	Coding rules
Interest	4.21	1.01	1	5	1: "very uninterested"; 2: "somewhat uninterested"; 3: "indifferent"; 4: "somewhat interested"; 5: "very interested"
Revenue	2.85	1.29	1	6	1: less than RMB 500,000; 2: RMB 500,000–5 million; 3: RMB 5–10 million; 4: RMB 10–50 million; 5: RMB 50–100 million; 6: more than RMB 100 million
Production area	2.79	2.21	1	8	1: less than 300 mu; 2: 301–600 mu; 3: 601–900 mu; 4: 901–1200 mu; 5: 1200–1500 mu; 6: 1501–2000 mu; 7: 2001–3000 mu; 8: more than 3,000 mu
Years	7.63	5.77	0	20	Years since the first certification to organic standards until 2018.
Ownership	4.13	1.40	1	5	1: state-owned; 2: collective-owned by township/village; 3: joint-stock; 4: foreign-invested; 5: private owned by individuals
Interaction association	4.10	1.07	1	5	1: never; 2: very rarely; 3: occasionally; 4: sometimes; 5: frequently

(continued)

Table C.2
(continued)

Variable	Mean	Standard deviation	Minimum	Maximum	Coding rules
Interaction ENGOs	3.20	1.37	1	5	1: never; 2: very rarely; 3: occasionally; 4: sometimes; 5: frequently
Organic proportion	3.20	1.61	1	5	1: less than 20%; 2: 21–40%; 3: 41–60%; 4: 61–80%; 5: 81–100%.
Benefit change	2.48	0.67	1	3	1: decrease in benefits; 2: no discernable change; 3: increase in benefits

Note: $N = 153$; 1 hectare = 15 mu.

Table C.3
Correlation matrix

Variable	Revenue	Production area	Year	Interaction ENGOs	Interaction association	Organic proportion	Benefit change
Revenue	1						
Production area	0.345	1					
Year	0.260	0.00531	1				
Interaction ENGOs	0.241	0.0615	−0.0534	1			
Interaction association	0.158	0.00315	0.139	0.497	1		
Organic Proportion	−0.268	−0.0453	−0.000463	−0.129	0.00365	1	
Benefit change	0.0685	−0.0255	−0.0618	0.141	0.191	0.00737	1

Note: $N = 153$.

Table C.4
Randomization checks

Variable		Frame = 0 (control group)	Frame = 1 (treatment = supporting the state policy)	Frame = 2 (treatment = expanding foreign markets)
Revenue	Mean	2.69	3.06	2.78
	P-value (two-sample *t*-test)		0.14	0.70
Production area	Mean	2.80	2.90	2.67
	P-value (two-sample *t*-test)		0.82	0.76
Year	Mean	7.31	8.11	7.24
	P-value (two-sample *t*-test)		0.49	0.94
Interaction ENGOs	Mean	3.17	3.43	3.05
	P-value (two-sample *t*-test)		0.35	0.67
Organic proportion	Mean	2.92	3.31	3.35
	P-value (two-sample *t*-test)		0.23	0.18

Note: The *t*-tests show no statistically significant difference in the key covariates across different groups.

Notes

1 Introduction

1. By "eco-certification," I refer to the governance systems that create standards and award labels to compliant firms to guide environmentally and socially responsible production practices. The prefix of "eco-" does not imply that these programs focus solely on environmental issues but reflects that environmental sustainability is an important component of their standards. Researchers have used different terms to describe such systems including "ecolabeling," "(voluntary) sustainability standards," and "non-state market-driven governance."

2. The term "governance" has multiple meanings. Fukuyama (2016) identifies three broad definitions: international cooperation through nonsovereign bodies, effective implementation of state policy, and the regulation of social behavior through networks and other nonhierarchical mechanisms. When describing certification as a mode of governance, the third definition is used.

3. "A shared, public goal" refers to the provision of some global public goods. For instance, in the case of sustainable seafood consumption, this goal can be the reduction of environmental impacts of fisheries on marine ecosystems.

4. The focus of this study is on the adoption (or uptake) of certification standards instead of their sustainability impact. A large market share of certified products may not imply significant improvement of environmental and social conditions, which would be also affected by the stringency of standards and their quality of implementation. That said, adoption is a necessary condition for impact, especially when standards are carefully designed and strictly enforced. I leave the impact question for future research but discuss some scenarios in chapter 6.

5. I am not suggesting that the support of emerging economies is a sufficient condition for the effectiveness of eco-certification in solving any sustainability issues. But the lack of such support will prevent relevant programs from maintaining the stability of the Earth system.

6. Data on aquaculture and tea are drawn from the Food and Agriculture Organization of United Nations (FAO).

7. Some scholars have adopted a broader definition of "transnational governance" that includes governance systems that engage only in information sharing or capacity building and implementation (Andonova, Betsill, and Bulkeley 2009). But my study follows Roger and Dauvergne (2016) to use a narrow definition of transnational governance, which emphasizes the processes in which non-state actors set and enforce rules.

8. A few exceptions include research on forest certification (e.g., Buckingham and Jepson 2013; Bartley 2018), climate change (Hale and Roger 2018), and palm oil certification (Schleifer and Sun 2018).

9. On why some programs are more credible than others, see van der Ven (2019).

10. For territorial plants, another way to measure this variable is by the proportion of the certified land over the total farming area. For the three commodities covered by this study, this measurement can only be applied to tea.

11. The same approach could be also applied to other sectors if it is possible to conduct surveys with relevant firms.

2 Between Markets and States

1. On the 2030 Agenda for Sustainable Development and the Sustainable Development Goals, see https://sustainabledevelopment.un.org/?menu=1300, last accessed on July 4, 2020.

2. This does not mean that intra-firm dynamics are irrelevant to the diffusion of transnational governance. In fact, corporate managers could strategically use transnational governance to seek other benefits (Prakash 2000). But to trigger such processes, some external stakeholders need to first provide information and put pressure on firms. Therefore, my study focuses primarily on the interactions among different organizations.

3. Broadly speaking, actors follow two logics when deciding to accept new institutions or rules: the logic of consequences in pursuit of material benefits and the logic of appropriateness in order to fulfill some moral obligations (March and Olsen 1996).

4. Vedung's conceptualization builds on the classification of coercive, utilitarian, and normative power originally proposed by Amitai Etzioni (1975).

5. We should not exclude the possibility that some states may use transnational governance as a tool to show compliance with public regulations. On such occasions, transnational governance, which is by nature voluntary, would become de facto mandatory.

6. To clarify, economic incentives are not necessarily part of nudging, which can rely on the ways in which information is provided and framed to shape actors' behaviors.

7. For example, for the Chinese market, IKEA had set a target of sourcing 100% FSC certified or recycled timber by 2017; see https://ic.fsc.org/en/news-updates/id/1558, last accessed August 12, 2018.

8. This does not mean that NGO campaigns are always meaningless or have no effect at all in China for promoting sustainability. In the past decade, campaigns launched by civil society groups—including both domestic and foreign organizations—have triggered important policy changes in China on salient issues, including air pollution and food safety (Yasuda 2015; Fedorenko and Sun 2016). With the rise of a highly educated urban middle class willing to support ethical consumption, there is reason to believe that consumer campaigns will play a more important role in the future of China's environmental governance (Li, Zhang, and Jin 2017; Fesenfeld et al. 2020).

9. Lee, Gereffi, and Bauvai (2012) also indicate that different types of value chains are likely to vary in the type of standards that they prefer (i.e., safety vs. quality standards). But this variation is not relevant to my study on eco-certification, because to date, most transnational programs aim to address a range of sustainability issues.

10. On the debates over whether China has developed a unique political economy model for development, see the summary and discussion of Ferchen (2013).

11. On the importance of local governments' discretion in China's economic reform since 1978, see Montinola, Qian, and Weingast (1995); Y. Huang (1999); and Oi (1999).

12. The wide use of mixed signals also implies that the chance that national regulators provide direct policy support for transnational governance is low, because even if they want to support certain rules or programs, they may prefer to leave the implementation of specific policies to subnational governments.

13. The state's supervision of the industry associations in China was slightly loosened in 2013, when the State Council issued an institutional restructuring plan that required the detachment of some industry associations from government agencies. The reform was launched by the Ministry of Civil Affairs in 2015 and is still ongoing.

14. For focal institutions, Green (2014) argues that their strength determines the form of private authority at the transnational level. The rationale I use here is similar to that of Green but focuses instead on the domestic level.

15. I am by no means suggesting these are the only two (necessary) conditions for the emergence of state support. For example, research has suggested that the openness of governance processes is a key condition of transnational actors' influence on domestic policies (Bernstein and Cashore 2012). But openness is often socially constructed and could be changed by actors' strategic engagement.

3 Seafood

1. The term "seafood" refers to the fish and fishery products from seawater as well as freshwater. While this definition covers both aquatic animals and plants, fish predominates in today's seafood market.

2. Although the MSC originally focused on ocean fisheries, as reflected by the program's name, its standards apply to all wild capture fisheries, including freshwater ones. As of 2021, the program has nine certified freshwater fisheries.

3. Interview NIT01.

4. Data as of December 2017, from the GAA-BAP's website, https://www.bapcertification.org/blog/wp-content/uploads/2017/01/BAP-Fact-Sheet-Final.pdf, last accessed on December 26, 2017.

5. Data as of December 2017, downloaded from the GAA-BAP's website https://bapcertification.org/CertifiedFacilities, last accessed on December 5, 2017.

6. Data as of 2017, drawn from the ASC's website, https://www.asc-aqua.org/what-you-can-do/take-action/, last accessed on December 26, 2017.

7. The growth of organic production in China is a noticeable trend and has also appeared in the tea sector, as discussed in chapter 5. In the aquaculture sector, more than 60% of certified organic products are aquatic plants, and this is different from the types of certified organic seafood in Northern markets.

8. Interview ANJ01.

9. Marine capture concerns only the wild capture in China's domestic marine fisheries and excludes China's distant-water fisheries. Although some research suggests that China underreported its distant-water fishing volume, its production in distant-water fisheries remains less than 30% of its total capture production (see Pauly et al. 2014).

10. The directive is the No. 5 Central Document, "Instructions on policy liberalization to accelerate the development of the fishing industry," jointly issued by the Central Committee of the Chinese Communist Party and the State Council.

11. Until recently, China's processing industry remained export oriented, but official data on the volume of imported materials that are reexported remain unavailable (Clarke 2009; Interview NBJ01).

12. Interview NBJ21.

13. As a comparison, the world's second largest consumer—the US—only represents about 5% of global fish consumption by volume (FAO 2016).

14. Interview NSH03. The concern over food safety also has been reported by surveys of Chinese middle-class consumers; see Fabinyi et al. (2016).

15. Interview GBJ34.

16. Interviews BBJ27, BZJ01, GZJ02, and GZJ03.

17. According to the estimation of CAPPMA, around 60% of seafood in China's domestic market goes through traditional wholesale markets (Cui 2017).

18. Interview NUK01.

19. Interview AQD02.

20. Interview NBJ01.

21. Interview NUK01.

22. This view was expressed by practitioners working for both NGOs and government agencies in China (Interviews NBJ21 and GBJ32).

23. Interview AQD02.

24. Quoted from the company's website, https://www.zhangzidao.cn/about?lang=en, accessed June 2021.

25. Interviews NQD04 and NDQ05.

26. The EU lifted the ban on scallops produced in China in 2016, but as of mid-2017, Zhangzidao had not exported any products to the European market (Harkell 2017b).

27. Interview NSH04.

28. Interview NSH04. The data of GAA-BAP as of 2017 still show that over 90% of certified facilities in China are in the tilapia or shrimp industries; see https://www.bapcertification.org/CertifiedFacilities, last accessed on May 6, 2019.

29. See the project's grant application, downloadable at http://www.cappma.org/gtsoct/images/Attachment%20A%20Grant%20application.pdf, last accessed on January 21, 2018.

30. Interview NQD02.

31. Hypotheses 3 and 5–7 are not tested here, because in this initial stage, no transnational certification program has started to work in China, and no domestic stakeholders have provided support for the relevant programs.

32. Before 2012, only the MSC and the GAA-BAP had been introduced in China. Therefore, the dependent variable was constructed according to Chinese firms' certification status for these two programs.

33. Two measures using, respectively, a 1-year lag and 2-year lag were tested, and the results are robust; see more details in appendix B.

34. Interview NUK01.

35. See the introduction on the association's webpage: http://www.cappma.org.cn/elist.php?pid=264&ty=265. Interview GBJ32.

36. This diplomatic role of CAPPMA is also highlighted in Interview NUK03.

37. Interviews NHN02 and HHN03.

38. Interviews NBJ21 and NSH04.

39. Interview GBJ32.

40. Interviews NHN03 and NFZ01.

41. Interview NQD03. For more on the programs of the Sustainable Seafood Forum in 2009 and 2010, see http://www.seafarechina.com/coevent/covents-history/24-2010coevent, last accessed on August 12, 2018.

42. Interview NUK03.

43. Interview NQD05.

44. In China, third-party audits for each new standard must be approved by CNCA. For the ASC certification in this project, the process was streamlined thanks to CAPPMA's support (Interview NQD04).

45. The first period of public comments for the ASC flatfish standard was in June and July 2017, during which a consultation workshop was organized in China with the support of CAPPMA (Interviews NQD04 and NQD05).

46. Interview NFZ01.

47. Interview NSH04.

48. Interview NUK03.

49. Interview NIT01.

50. Interviews NBJ21 and NSH04.

51. The GAA-BAP has a multi-star system: The highest level is the four-star certification, which requires the adoption of standards along the whole supply chain, including hatcheries, feed mills, farms, and processors; the two-star certification applies to farms and processors.

52. Interview GBJ32.

4 Palm Oil

1. Data reported by the European Palm Oil Alliance, http://www.palmoilandfood.eu/en/downloads, last accessed on August 14, 2018.

2. This has been highlighted by the RSPO as the organization's vision and mission, see its website: https://rspo.org/about.

3. A well-known case is IOI Group, a Malaysian plantation giant, which cleared peatlands without required permits. To respond to the NGOs' complaints, the RSPO temporarily suspended the company's certificate in 2016. See Gartl (2016) for more details.

4. See an introduction to these systems on the program's website, http://www.rspo.org/certification/supply-chains, last accessed on June 14, 2020.

5. Data reported by the US Department of Agriculture's reports, "Oilseeds: World Markets and Trade," downloadable at https://usda.library.cornell.edu/concern/publications/tx31qh68h?locale=en, last accessed on May 24, 2020.

6. See the meeting minutes of the RSPO's ninth General Assembly in 2012, https://rspo.org/library/lib_files/preview/291, last accessed on June 22, 2021.

7. An RSPO official acknowledged that these targets were set by a consulting company based on initial assessments of policy and economic environments in relevant countries (Interview NMA01).

8. This reporting period is from July 1, 2017, to June 30, 2018.

9. Data are for the year of 2015, gathered from Interview GBJ10.

10. While soybean oil is by far the most popular vegetable oil in China, its import volume is less than half that of palm oil, as most soybean oil is produced domestically in China using soybean oilseeds imported from other countries.

11. China remains the second largest importer after India. The combined import volume of all EU member states has surpassed that of China in recent years, but no single EU country has imported more than China does.

12. For the official announcement of this policy change, see the website of China's Ministry of Commerce http://www.mofcom.gov.cn/aarticle/b/e/200512/20051201000816.html, last accessed October 31, 2017.

13. Interview NMA02; also see Teoh (2011).

14. Interviews NBJ19 and NBJ20.

15. Potts et al. (2014) estimate that these companies accounted for over 50% by volume of the palm oil imports in China.

16. Interviews RBJ05 and BBJ11.

17. See Cargill's policy on sustainable palm oil at https://www.cargill.com/doc/1432076149492/palm-oil-policy-statement-pdf.pdf, and Wilmar's engagement in the RSPO at https://www.wilmar-international.com/sustainability/certification, last

accessed on July 5, 2020. Such information is in line with the author's observation at the China-RSPO Forum in Chengdu, in July 2016.

18. Interview BBJ11.

19. Interview NBJ12.

20. Interview BBJ11.

21. Interviews NNL02 and NMA02.

22. See the company's website, http://www.beltek.com.cn/list-12-1.html, accessed on November 10, 2017.

23. Beltek's Annual Communication of Progress 2013–2014, downloadable at https://www.rspo.org/file/acop2014/submissions/beltek-huizhou-foods-co-ltd-ACOP2014.pdf, last accessed on November 12, 2017.

24. Interview NMA02.

25. According to the company's website; see http://www.wilmar-international.com/who-we-are/corporate-profile/, last accessed on August 12, 2018.

26. The company never disclosed data on the exact volume of certified palm oil it has imported to China. But in interviews, several practitioners suggested that the company has been one of the largest suppliers of certified palm oil in the Chinese market (Interviews GBJ10 and BBJ11).

27. According to a presentation by the company's representative at the China-RSPO Forum, Chengdu, July 2016, documents collected by the author.

28. Interview BBJ22.

29. Interview NMA01.

30. See the communication of progress in 2016 submitted by the two retailers on the RSPO's website, downloadable at https://rspo.org/file/acop2016/submissions/wal-mart%20stores%20inc-ACOP2016.pdf, and https://rspo.org/file/acop2016/submissions/carrefour-ACOP2016.pdf, last accessed on August 12, 2018.

31. This marginal influence could be explained by the fact that private brand products have been only a small part of these retailers' business in China. In this case, to increase uptake of sustainable palm oil, retailers need to expand their sourcing requirements for all suppliers.

32. Interview NMA02.

33. Interview GBJ10.

34. Interviews BBJ09 and NBJ19.

35. Interviews NNL03 and IBJ17.

36. Interview NBJ08.

37. Interviews BBJ09 and GBJ10.

38. Interview NBJ40.

39. See the association's website, http://en.cccfna.org.cn/read.php?id=1, last accessed on August 12, 2018.

40. Interview GBJ10 and the presentation made by a CFNA official at the China-RSPO Forum, Chengdu, July 2016.

41. The activities discussed in this paragraph were described by a CFNA official and the association's internal documents shared with the author (Interview GBJ10).

42. Interview NBJ40.

43. The DFID has closed in September 2020 and been replaced by the Foreign, Commonwealth & Development Office.

44. Interview NBJ20.

45. According to a speech given by the president of CFNA, cited in RSPO (2013). This MoU had aduration of 5 years, and in March 2018, the two organizations signed a new MoU to further strengthen their partnership.

46. Interview NBJ12.

47. The author's personal communications with representatives of several companies during the first RSPO-China forum, Chengdu, July 2017.

48. On the physical uptake of certified palm oil in China, see the case of COFCO discussed in section 4.3.3 and RSPO (2018a).

49. Interview NBJ19 and RSPO (2017a).

50. Interview GCH03.

51. Interview BBJ11.

52. Interviews NMA02 and NBJ20.

53. Interviews RBJ05, RBJ07, and NBJ40.

54. Interviews NBJ20 and IBJ17.

55. Interview NNL03.

56. Interview BBJ11.

57. Interview NBJ19.

58. Cited by Niu (2015).

59. According to the author's study of all the Annual Communications of Progress submitted by RSPO members based in China. The reports submitted by all companies can be accessed on the RSPO's website https://rspo.org/members/acop.

60. Interview BBJ11.

61. Interviews NBJ19 and NBJ40.

5 Tea

1. The definition of "sustainable tea" is broader than that of "organic," and the latter is subject to public regulations in most countries in the world. While the Chinese organic tea certification can be considered as a type of sustainable tea certification, without additional explanation, the term "sustainable tea certification" in this chapter refers to the transnational eco-certification programs.

2. The data refer to the combined area certified by one of the three major transnational certification schemes (i.e., Fairtrade, Rainforest Alliance, and UTZ) or domestic organic certification schemes.

3. In late 2017, UTZ and Rainforest Alliance announced a merger, but its effect on market uptake remains to be seen. See more details at https://utz.org/merger/, last accessed on August 12, 2018.

4. On the principles of Fairtrade standards, see Fairtrade's website https://www.fairtrade.net/standards/aims-of-fairtrade-standards.html, last accessed on August 12, 2018.

5. Interview BWY01.

6. The program's goals include conserving biodiversity; safeguarding natural resources; increasing farm productivity and profitability; and improving the well-being of farmers, workers, and their families. See more details on the program's website at https://www.rainforest-alliance.org/business/sas/how-certification-works/farm-certification/, last accessed on August 12, 2018.

7. Interview NBJ23.

8. The data on certified area in China were provided by the relevant auditing company at my request (Interview ABJ38). The figures are in line with the data reported in Lernoud et al. (2018).

9. Interviews NNL01 and NNL02.

10. To export organic tea, Chinese producers must be certified according to the relevant schemes of importing countries. The export of Chinese organic tea represents only a small proportion of China's total organic tea production: Blackmore et al. (2012) estimated that as of 2010, only one-sixth of the organic tea produced in China was exported, but this fraction is likely to have decreased in the past decade, given the rapid growth of the Chinese organic tea certification.

11. In the academic literature, little research has focused on the role of tea in international relations and politics in the nineteenth century. For a general introduction on the history of tea, see Griffiths (2011) and Moxham (2009).

12. According to more recent data (CTMA 2017), the amount of tea consumed domestically increased to 1.8 million in 2016.

13. Interview NNJ02.

14. Interviews BAH01 and BWY01. Also see Wu's (2009) discussion of the export-oriented tea supply chain in China.

15. Interview BWY06.

16. This view was expressed by the owners or managers of several Chinese tea companies in a major production region (Interviews BAH01, BAH05, and BAH06).

17. Interview RHZ01.

18. Interview NNJ05.

19. This account of market reforms in China's tea industry is drawn from an interview with the then-CEO of a large state-owned tea company in Jiangxi in the pre-reform era (Interview BWY06).

20. This view was also highlighted by several Chinese experts on tea farming (Interviews RHZ01, RHZ02, and BBJ41).

21. Interview BAH03.

22. Interviews with officials at the Bureau of Agriculture in a tea producing county (Interview GAH05 and GAH06).

23. Interviews with owners or managers of companies adopting this supply chain model (Interviews BNJ03, BAH04, BAH05, and BAH06).

24. Even organic agriculture and certification was originally introduced to Chinese tea producers by European buyers and certifiers, but the later development of a domestic certification scheme by the Chinese government has led organic tea producers in China to focus on the domestic market.

25. Unless otherwise specified, the information presented here on Dazhangshan is drawn from the author's extensive interviews with the company's founder and senior managers (Interviews BWY01–BWY06).

26. In a sense, Dazhangshan's organic certification is a low-hanging fruit, thanks to environmental conditions and low-input farming practices in its tea farms such that the relevant producers have been organic by default.

27. For the full text of this law, see http://www.npc.gov.cn/englishnpc/Law/2007-12/11/content_1383542.htm, last accessed on August 12, 2018.

28. But the export of organic tea is an extremely small niche compared to the total size of China's tea industry (Interview BWY01).

29. On Chinese tea consumers' preferences for sustainability standards, see Iweala and Sun (2021).

30. Interview BWY06.

31. Interviews NBJ23 and NBJ39.

32. Interview NBJ23 with a consultant involved in RA's work in Yunnan.

33. Interview ABJ38.

34. Interview BAH01.

35. Interview ABJ38.

36. Interviews NBJ23 and NBJ39.

37. Interview NBJ23.

38. Interviews NNJ02 and NBJ39.

39. Interviews NNL01 and NNL02.

40. Interview NSH05.

41. See more information on the association's website: http://www.ctma.com.cn/about/jj/, last accessed on August 12, 2018.

42. Interviews NNJ05 and GBJ42.

43. Interview GBJ31.

44. At different times, ACFSMC was part of the former Ministry of Commerce responsible for domestic marketing of all products in a centrally planned economy. For more details on the fragmented regulatory system in China's tea industry until the late 1980s, see Etherington and Forster (1993: 52–69).

45. Interview BBJ41.

46. Interview GBJ42.

47. Personal communication with an official of the Ministry of Agriculture during a stakeholder meeting in Hangzhou, June 21, 2017.

48. Interview RHZ01.

49. Personal communication with the director of the relevant bureau in the Ministry of Agriculture during a stakeholder meeting in Hangzhou, June 21, 2017.

50. In June 2017, I attended the inaugural meeting of this initiative in Hangzhou and conducted both formal and informal interviews with its initiators.

51. Interview ANJ01.

52. Given resource constraints, I could not invite more companies to participate in the survey. Recognizing the limitations of this small sample size, I only interpret the results as illustrative.

53. I used a *t*-test to do balance checking, and the results confirm the randomization (see appendix C).

6 Conclusion

1. Past research on the FSC has shown the opposition of Chinese state actors to transnational governance (Buckingham and Jepson 2013; Bartley 2014, 2018). Accordingly, future research should examine the interaction between Chinese regulators and the FSC to assess whether the case of forest certification fits in the lower-left entry in table 6.2.

2. These data were drawn from the Trese project, downloadable at https://trase.earth/explore, last accessed on June 17, 2020.

3. All buyers of physical RTRS-certified soybeans are listed on the program's website, and no Chinese companies have been listed there; see the full list at http://www.responsiblesoy.org/mercado/compradores-de-soja/?lang=en. The lack of awareness in China's soybean supply chain was also confirmed by an NGO official promoting sustainable soy in China (Interview NBJ40).

4. Data on the seafood production and trade in the Russian Federation are from FAO FishStat, accessible at http://www.fao.org/fishery/statistics/software/fishstatj/en.

5. These numbers were calculated using data from FAOStat (http://www.fao.org/faostat/en/#data) and the UN Comtrade Database (https://comtrade.un.org/data/).

6. This position of the Indian government on voluntary standards in the World Trade Organization was indicated in Interview GCH02.

7. See more details on the program's website at http://www.trustea.org/faq.php, last accessed on August 12, 2018.

8. See the original text of this law on the website of China's National People's Congress at http://www.npc.gov.cn/zgrdw/npc/xinwen/2017-11/28/content_2032719.htm, last accessed on June 24, 2020.

9. On the conceptualization of "goal-based governance," see Kanie and Biermann (2017).

Appendix A

1. Due to the norms and political context in China, I did not record all interviews.

2. These interviews were recorded.

Appendix B

1. My access to this dataset is courtesy of researchers at a Chinese university.

2. Interviews AQD01 and AQD02.

Appendix C

1. Social media applications, especially those on mobile phones, have become very popular in China, even for people living in rural areas. Thus an internet-based survey did not lead us to draw a biased sample of tea companies, as almost all of them can be reached by Chinese social media applications such as WeChat.

References

Abbott, Kenneth W., and Duncan Snidal. 2009. "The Governance Triangle: Regulatory Standards Institutions and the Shadow of the State." In *The Politics of Global Regulation*, edited by Walter Mattli and Ngaire Woods, 44–88. Princeton, NJ: Princeton University Press.

Adolph, Christopher, Vanessa Quince, and Aseem Prakash. 2017. "The Shanghai Effect: Do Exports to China Affect Labor Practices in Africa?" *World Development* 89 (1): 1–18.

Allen, Katie. 2012. "China Overtakes US as World's Biggest Grocery Market | World News | The Guardian." 2012. https://www.theguardian.com/world/2012/apr/04/china-biggest-grocery-market-world.

Amnesty International. 2016. "The Great Palm Oil Scandal: Labour Abuses behind Big Brand Names." London: Amnesty International.

Anderson, James L., Diego Valderrama, and Darryl Jory. 2016. "Shrimp Production Review." Presented at the GAA GOAL Conference, Guangzhou, September 20.

Andonova, Liliana B. 2004. *Transnational Politics of the Environment: The European Union and Environmental Policy in Central and Eastern Europe*. Global Environmental Accord: Strategies for Sustainability and Institutional Innovation. Cambridge, MA: MIT Press.

Andonova, Liliana B. 2014. "Boomerangs to Partnerships? Explaining State Participation in Transnational Partnerships for Sustainability." *Comparative Political Studies* 47 (3): 481–515.

Andonova, Liliana B., Michele M. Betsill, and Harriet Bulkeley. 2009. "Transnational Climate Governance." Global Environmental Politics 9 (2): 52–73. https://doi.org/10.1162/glep.2009.9.2.52.

Andonova, Liliana B., Thomas N. Hale, and Charles B. Roger. 2017. "National Policy and Transnational Governance of Climate Change: Substitutes or Complements?" *International Studies Quarterly* 61 (2): 253–268.

Andonova, Liliana B., and Ronald B. Mitchell. 2010. "The Rescaling of Global Environmental Politics." *Annual Review of Environment and Resources* 35 (1): 255–282.

Andonova, Liliana B., and Yixian Sun. 2019. "Private Governance in Developing Countries: Drivers of Voluntary Carbon Offset Programs." *Global Environmental Politics* 19 (1): 99–122.

Ang, Yuen Yuen. 2009. "State, Market, and Bureau-Contracting in Reform China." PhD dissertation, Stanford University, Stanford, CA.

Ang, Yuen Yuen. 2012. "Counting Cadres: A Comparative View of the Size of China's Public Employment." *China Quarterly* 211 (September): 676–696.

Ascensão, Fernando, Lenore Fahrig, Anthony P. Clevenger, Richard T. Corlett, Jochen A. G. Jaeger, William F. Laurance, and Henrique M. Pereira. 2018. "Environmental Challenges for the Belt and Road Initiative." *Nature Sustainability* 1 (5): 206–209.

Auld, Graeme. 2014. *Constructing Private Governance: The Rise and Evolution of Forest, Coffee, and Fisheries Certification*. New Haven, CT: Yale University Press.

Auld, Graeme, Steven Bernstein, and Benjamin Cashore. 2008. "The New Corporate Social Responsibility." *Annual Review of Environment and Resources* 33 (1): 413–435.

Auld, Graeme, Stefan Renckens, and Benjamin Cashore. 2015. "Transnational Private Governance between the Logics of Empowerment and Control." *Regulation and Governance* 9 (2): 108–124.

Bailey, Megan, Helen Packer, Laurenne Schiller, Michael Tlusty, and Wilf Swartz. 2018. "The Role of Corporate Social Responsibility in Creating a Seussian World of Seafood Sustainability." *Fish and Fisheries* 19 (5): 782–790. https://doi.org/10.1111/faf.12289.

Balaton-Chrimes, Samantha, and Kate Macdonald. 2016. "Wilmar and Palm Oil Grievances: The Promise and Pitfalls of Problem Solving." 8. Non-Judicial Redress Mechanisms Report. Melbourne: Corporate Accountability Research.

Ban, Cornel, and Mark Blyth. 2013. "The BRICs and the Washington Consensus: An Introduction." *Review of International Political Economy* 20 (2): 241–255.

BAP. 2017. "GAA, BAP Make Splash at China Seafood and Fisheries Expo." Best Aquaculture Practices—Best Aquaculture Practices Certification. 2017. https://bapcertification.org/blog/gaa-bap-china-expo/.

BAP. 2018. "China's Largest Retailer Commits to BAP for More Responsible Seafood." Best Aquaculture Practices—Best Aquaculture Practices Certification. 2018. https://bapcertification.org/blog/jdcom-new-commitment/.

Barkin, J. Samuel, and Elizabeth R. DeSombre. 2013. *Saving Global Fisheries: Reducing Fishing Capacity to Promote Sustainability*. Cambridge, MA: MIT Press.

Barnett, Clive, Paul Cloke, Nick Clarke, and Alice Malpass. 2011. *Globalizing Responsibility: The Political Rationalities of Ethical Consumption*. RGS-IBG Book Series. Malden, MA: Wiley-Blackwell.

Bartley, Tim. 2003. "Certifying Forests and Factories: States, Social Movements, and the Rise of Private Regulation in the Apparel and Forest Products Fields." *Politics and Society* 31 (3): 433–464.

Bartley, Tim. 2007. "Institutional Emergence in an Era of Globalization: The Rise of Transnational Private Regulation of Labor and Environmental Conditions." *American Journal of Sociology* 113 (2): 297–351.

Bartley, Tim. 2010. "Transnational Private Regulation in Practice: The Limits of Forest and Labor Standards Certification in Indonesia." *Business and Politics* 12 (03): 1–34.

Bartley, Tim. 2014. "Transnational Governance and the Re-Centered State: Sustainability or Legality?: Re-Centered State." Regulation & Governance 8 (1): 93–109. https://doi.org/10.1111/rego.12051.

Bartley, Tim. 2018. *Rules without Rights: Land, Labor, and Private Authority in the Global Economy*. Transformations in Governance. New York: Oxford University Press.

Bartley, Tim, Sebastian Koos, Hiram Samel, Gustavo Setrini, and Nik Summers. 2015. *Looking behind the Label: Global Industries and the Conscientious Consumer*. Global Research Studies. Bloomington: Indiana University Press.

Bates, Robert. 2014. "The New Institutionalism." In *Institutions, Property Rights, and Economic Growth: The Legacy of Douglass North*, edited by Sebastián Galiani and Itai Sened, 51–65. Cambridge: Cambridge University Press.

Baur, Dorothea, and Guido Palazzo. 2011. "The Moral Legitimacy of NGOs as Partners of Corporations." *Business Ethics Quarterly* 21 (4): 579–604.

Belton, Ben, Simon R. Bush, and David C. Little. 2018. "Not Just for the Wealthy: Rethinking Farmed Fish Consumption in the Global South." *Global Food Security* 16 (March): 85–92.

Bennett, Andrew, and Jeffrey Checkel. 2014. "Process Tracing: From Philosophical Roots to Best Practices." In *Process Tracing: From Metaphor to Analytic Tool*, edited by Andrew Bennett and Jeffrey T. Checkel, 1–37. Strategies for Social Inquiry. Cambridge: Cambridge University Press.

Bennett, Elizabeth A. 2017. "Who Governs Socially-Oriented Voluntary Sustainability Standards? Not the Producers of Certified Products." *World Development* 91 (3): 53–69.

Berliner, Daniel, and Aseem Prakash. 2014. "Public Authority and Private Rules: How Domestic Regulatory Institutions Shape the Adoption of Global Private Regimes." *International Studies Quarterly* 58 (4): 793–803.

Bernstein, Steven. 2002. "Liberal Environmentalism and Global Environmental Governance." *Global Environmental Politics* 2 (3): 1–16.

Bernstein, Steven, and Benjamin Cashore. 2007. "Can Non-State Global Governance Be Legitimate? An Analytical Framework." *Regulation and Governance* 1 (4): 347–371.

Bernstein, Steven, and Benjamin Cashore. 2012. "Complex Global Governance and Domestic Policies: Four Pathways of Influence." *International Affairs* 88 (3): 585–604.

Biermann, Frank. 2007. "'Earth System Governance' as a Crosscutting Theme of Global Change Research." *Global Environmental Change* 17 (3): 326–337.

Biermann, Frank. 2014. *Earth System Governance: World Politics in the Anthropocene*. Earth System Governance: A Core Research Project of the International Human Dimensions Programme on Global Environmental Change. Cambridge, MA: MIT Press.

Blackmore, Emma, James Keeley, Rhiannon Pyburn, Ellen Mangus, Chen Lu, and Yuhui Qiao. 2012. *Pro-Poor Certification: Assessing the Benefits of Sustainability Certification for Small-Scale Farmers in Asia*. Natural Resource Issues 25. London: International Institute for Environment and Development (UK).

Bloomfield, Michael John. 2012. "Is Forest Certification a Hegemonic Force? The FSC and Its Challengers." *Journal of Environment and Development* 21 (4): 391–413.

Bloomfield, Michael John. 2014. "Shame Campaigns and Environmental Justice: Corporate Shaming as Activist Strategy." Environmental Politics 23 (2): 263–281.

Bloomfield, Michael John. 2017a. *Dirty Gold: How Activism Transformed the Jewelry Industry*. Earth System Governance. Cambridge, MA: MIT Press.

Bloomfield, Michael John. 2017b. "Global Production Networks and Activism: Can Activists Change Mining Practices by Targeting Brands?" *New Political Economy* 22 (6): 727–742.

Bloomfield, Michael John. 2020. "South-South Trade and Sustainability: The Case of Ceylon Tea." *Ecological Economics* 167 (January): 1–8.

Boström, Magnus, Michele Micheletti, and Peter Oosterveer. 2019. "Studying Political Consumerism." In *The Oxford Handbook of Political Consumerism*, edited by Magnus Boström, Michele Micheletti, and Peter Oosterveer, xvi–24. Oxford: Oxford University Press. https://doi.org/10.1093/oxfordhb/9780190629038.013.44.

Braga, Tania, Aileen Ionescu-Somers, and Ralf Seifert. 2010. "Unilever Sustainable Tea Part1: Leapfrogging to Mainstream." Utrecht: The Dutch Sustainable Trade Initiative (IDH). https://www.idhsustainabletrade.com/uploaded/2016/07/Unilever-Sustainable-Tea-Part-I.pdf.

Brandi, Clara, Tobia Cabani, Christoph Hosang, Sonja Schirmbeck, Lotte Westermann, and Hannah Wiese. 2015. "Sustainability Standards for Palm Oil: Challenges for Smallholder Certification under the RSPO." *Journal of Environment and Development*, July.

BRECC. 2017. "50 Questions on Fairtrade." Beijing: BRECC and NAPP.

Broughton, Edward I., and Damian G. Walker. 2010. "Policies and Practices for Aquaculture Food Safety in China." *Food Policy* 35 (5): 471–478.

Buckingham, Kathleen, and Paul Jepson. 2013. "Forest Certification with Chinese Characteristics: State Engagement with Non-State Market-Driven Governance." *Eurasian Geography and Economics* 54 (3): 280–299.

Bulkeley, Harriet, Liliana B. Andonova, Michele M. Betsill, Daniel Compagnon, Thomas Hale, Matthew Hoffmann, Peter Newell, Matthew Paterson, Charles Roger, and Stacy D. VanDeveer. 2014. *Transnational Climate Change Governance*. New York: Cambridge University Press.

Bullock, Graham. 2017. *Green Grades: Can Information Save the Earth?* Cambridge, MA: MIT Press.

Bullock, Graham, and Hamish van der Ven. 2020. "The Shadow of the Consumer: Analyzing the Importance of Consumers to the Uptake and Sophistication of Ratings, Certifications, and Eco-Labels." *Organization and Environment* 33 (1): 75–95.

Burch, Sarah, Aarti Gupta, Cristina Y. A. Inoue, Agni Kalfagianni, Åsa Persson, Andrea K. Gerlak, Atsushi Ishii, et al. 2019. "New Directions in Earth System Governance Research." *Earth System Governance* 1 (January): 100006. https://doi.org/10.1016/j.esg.2019.100006.

Bureau of Fisheries, ed. 2016. *China Fishery Statistical Yearbook 2016*. Beijing: China Agriculture Press.

Busch, Lawrence. 2014. "Governance in the Age of Global Markets: Challenges, Limits, and Consequences." *Agriculture and Human Values* 31 (3): 513–523.

Bush, S. R., B. Belton, D. Hall, P. Vandergeest, F. J. Murray, S. Ponte, P. Oosterveer, et al. 2013. "Certify Sustainable Aquaculture?" *Science* 341 (6150): 1067–1068.

Bush, Simon R. 2018. "Understanding the Potential of Eco-Certification in Salmon and Shrimp Aquaculture Value Chains." *Aquaculture* 493 (August): 376–383.

Büthe, Tim. 2002. "Taking Temporality Seriously: Modeling History and the Use of Narratives as Evidence." *American Political Science Review* 96 (3): 481–493.

Byerlee, Derek, Walter P. Falcon, and Rosamond Naylor. 2017. *The Tropical Oil Crop Revolution: Food, Feed, Fuel, and Forests*. New York: Oxford University Press.

Cabello, Felipe C. 2006. "Heavy Use of Prophylactic Antibiotics in Aquaculture: A Growing Problem for Human and Animal Health and for the Environment." *Environmental Microbiology* 8 (7): 1137–1144.

Cai, Zhen, and Francisco X. Aguilar. 2013. "Consumer Stated Purchasing Preferences and Corporate Social Responsibility in the Wood Products Industry: A Conjoint Analysis in the U.S. and China." *Ecological Economics* 95 (November): 118–127.

Cai, Zhen, Yi Xie, and Francisco X. Aguilar. 2017. "Eco-Label Credibility and Retailer Effects on Green Product Purchasing Intentions." *Forest Policy and Economics* 80 (July): 200–208.

Cao, L., R. Naylor, P. Henriksson, D. Leadbitter, M. Metian, M. Troell, and W. Zhang. 2015. "China's Aquaculture and the World's Wild Fisheries." *Science* 347 (6218): 133–135.

Cao, Ling, Yong Chen, Shuanglin Dong, Arthur Hanson, Bo Huang, Duncan Leadbitter, David C. Little, et al. 2017. "Opportunity for Marine Fisheries Reform in China." *Proceedings of the National Academy of Sciences* 114 (3): 435–442.

CAPPMA. 2017. "China's Tilapia Industry Development Report." Presented at the 14th China International Tilapia Industry Development Forum, Haikou. November 23.

Carlson, Anna, and Charles Palmer. 2016. "A Qualitative Meta-Synthesis of the Benefits of Eco-Labeling in Developing Countries." *Ecological Economics* 127 (July): 129–145.

Cashore, Benjamin. 2002. "Legitimacy and the Privatization of Environmental Governance: How Non-State Market-Driven (NSMD) Governance Systems Gain Rule-Making Authority." *Governance* 15 (4): 503–529.

Cashore, Benjamin, Graeme Auld, and Deanna Newsom. 2004. *Governing through Markets: Forest Certification and the Emergence of Non-State Authority*. New Haven, CT: Yale University Press.

Cashore, Benjamin, and Steven Bernstein. 2021. "Bringing the Environment Back In: Overcoming the Tragedy of the Diffusion of the Commons Metaphor." Significantly revised version of the paper presented at the Ostrom Workshop at Indiana University, April 23, 2018.

Cashore, Benjamin, Fred Gale, Errol Meidinger, and Deanna Newsom, eds. 2006. *Confronting Sustainability: Forest Certification in Developing and Transitioning Countries*. New Haven, CT: Yale School of Forestry and Environmental Studies.

CCICED (China Council for International Cooperation on Environment and Development). 2016. "China's Role in Greening Global Supply Chains." CCICED Special Policy Study Report. http://www.cciced.net/cciceden/POLICY/rr/prr/2016/201612/P020161214521503400553.pdf.

CFNA. 2010. "Prospects and Challenges of Sustainable Palm Oil for China." Beijing: CFNA, UKaid, and Defra. https://www.china.rspo.org/publications/download/57e1e3d25853ba1.

CFNA. 2015. "Guide for Overseas Investment and Production of Sustainable Palm Oil by Chinese Enterprises: Draft Version 3.0." Beijing: China-UK Collaboration on International Forest Investment and Trade Programme (InFIT).

Chan, Sander, Robert Falkner, Matthew Goldberg, and Harro van Asselt. 2018. "Effective and Geographically Balanced? An Output-Based Assessment of Non-State Climate Actions." *Climate Policy* 18 (1): 24–35.

Chang, Kaison. 2015. "World Tea Production and Trade: Current and Future Development." Rome: FAO. http://www.fao.org/3/a-i4480e.pdf.

Chang, Kaison, and Margarita Brattlof. 2015. "Socio-Economic Implications of Climate Change for Tea Producing Countries." Rome: FAO.

Chen, Juan, John L. Innes, and Robert A. Kozak. 2011. "An Exploratory Assessment of the Attitudes of Chinese Wood Products Manufacturers towards Forest Certification." *Journal of Environmental Management* 92 (11): 2984–2992.

Chen, Lichun, Han Han, and Wang Wenhua. 2017. "Guideline on Responsible Seafood Sourcing for China Retail Industry." The 10-Year Framework of Programmes on Sustainable Consumption and Production. Beijing: CCFA and CAPPMA.

Chen, Zongmao, and Yajun Yang. 2011. *Zhong guo cha jing*. 1. Auflage. Shanghai: Shanghai wen hua chu ban she.

China Development Gateway. 2016. "Unilever and the Government of Zunyi Signed a Letter of Intent for the Project on Sustainable Tea Farm." http://cn.chinagate.cn/news/2016-07/10/content_38848945.htm.

China Economic Net. 2014. "Teabags Sale in China Is Less than 4% of the Total Consumption of Tea." China Economic Net. 2014. http://www.ce.cn/cysc/sp/info/201411/15/t20141115_3911610.shtml.

China Sustainable Retail Roundtable. 2015. "Responsible Seafood Sourcing Guideline." Beijing: China Sustainable Retail Roundtable.

Chiu, Alice, Luping Li, Shujing Guo, Junfei Bai, Chris Fedor, and Rosamond Lee Naylor. 2013. "Feed and Fishmeal Use in the Production of Carp and Tilapia in China." *Aquaculture* 414–415 (November): 127–134. https://doi.org/10.1016/j.aquaculture.2013.07.049.

Christmann, Petra, and Glen Taylor. 2001. "Globalization and the Environment: Determinants of Firm Self-Regulation in China." *Journal of International Business Studies* 32 (3): 439–458.

Chrun, Elizabeth, Nives Dolšak, and Aseem Prakash. 2016. "Corporate Environmentalism: Motivations and Mechanisms." *Annual Review of Environment and Resources* 41 (1): 341–362.

Clapp, Jennifer. 2015. "ABCD and Beyond: From Grain Merchants to Agricultural Value Chain Managers." *Canadian Food Studies / La Revue canadienne des études sur l'alimentation* 2 (2): 126–135.

Clapp, Jennifer, and Doris A. Fuchs, eds. 2009. *Corporate Power in Global Agrifood Governance*. Food, Health, and the Environment. Cambridge, MA: MIT Press.

Clarke, Shelley. 2009. "Understanding China's Fish Trade and Traceability Systems." Hong Kong: TRAFFIC East Asia. http://www.trafficj.org/publication/09_understanding_china_fish.pdf.

Clay, Jason W. 2004. *World Agriculture and the Environment: A Commodity-by-Commodity Guide to Impacts and Practices*. Washington, DC: Island Press.

CNCA. 2014. *Report on the Development of China's Organic Industry (Zhongguo Youji Chanye Fazhan Baogao)*. Beijing: China Zhijian Publishing House.

CNCA, and China Agricultural University. 2016. *China's Organic Product Certification and Development of the Industry (Zhongguo Youji Chanpin Renzheng Yu Changye Fazhan) 2016*. Beijing: China Zhijian Publishing House.

Coenen, Johanna, Simon Bager, Patrick Meyfroidt, Jens Newig, and Edward Challies. 2020. "Environmental Governance of China's Belt and Road Initiative." *Environmental Policy and Governance*, July. https://doi.org/10.1002/eet.1901.

Colchester, Marcus. 2011. "Palm Oil and Indigenous Peoples in South East Asia." International Land Coalition (ILC). http://www.forestpeoples.org/sites/fpp/files/publication/2010/08/palmoilindigenouspeoplesoutheastasiafinalmceng_0.pdf.

Colchester, Marcus, Patrick Anderson, Asep Yunan Firdaus, Fatilda Hasibuan, and Sophie Chao. 2011. "Human Rights Abuses and Land Conflicts in the PT Asiatic Persada Concession in Jambi: Report of an Independent Investigation into Land Disputes and Forced Evictions in a Palm Oil Estate." Forest Peoples Programme, Sawit-Watch, and HuMa. http://www.forestpeoples.org/sites/default/files/publication/2011/11/final-report-pt-ap-nov-2011-low-res-1.pdf.

Colgan, Jeff D., Jessica F. Green, and Thomas N. Hale. 2020. "Asset Revaluation and the Existential Politics of Climate Change." *International Organization* 75 (2): 586–610. https://doi.org/10.1017/S0020818320000296.

Collier, David. 1993. "The Comparative Method." In *Political Science: The State of the Discipline II*, edited by Ada W. Finifter, 105–119. Washington, DC: American Political Science Association.

Conroy, Michael E. 2007. *Branded! How the Certification Revolution Is Transforming Global Corporations*. Gabriola, BC: New Society Publishers.

CTMA. 2011. "Guidelines on Sustainable Development of the Chinese Tea Industry." http://www.ctma.com.cn/uploads/soft/120417/2_1631018671.doc.

CTMA. 2016. "Report on China's Tea Consumption Market." http://www.ctma.com.cn/zhuanyefuwu/zhuanyebaogao/2017/0208/57463.html.

CTMA. 2017. "Analysis of Production and Marketing of Chinese Tea in 2016." http://www.ctma.com.cn/zhuanyefuwu/zhuanyebaogao/2018/0111/58911.html.

Cui, He. 2015. "China's Fisheries in Transition (Zhuang xing zhong de zhong guo yu ye)." *China Fisheries News*, November 23, 2015, B4.

Cui, He. 2017. "New Characteristics of Seafood Consumption in China." Presented at the Global Aquaculture Summit 2017, Fuzhou.

Cutler, A. Claire, Virginia Haufler, and Tony Porter, eds. 1999. *Private Authority and International Affairs*. SUNY Series in Global Politics. Albany: State University of New York Press.

Darnall, Nicole, Hyunjung Ji, and Matthew Potoski. 2017. "Institutional Design of Eco-labels: Sponsorship Signals Rule Strength." *Regulation and Governance* 11 (4): 438–450.

Dauvergne, Peter. 2016. *Environmentalism of the Rich*. Cambridge, MA: MIT Press.

Dauvergne, Peter. 2017. "Is the Power of Brand-Focused Activism Rising? The Case of Tropical Deforestation." *Journal of Environment and Development* 26 (2): 135–155.

Dauvergne, Peter, and Genevieve LeBaron. 2014. *Protest Inc: The Corporatization of Activism*. Malden, MA: Polity Press.

Dauvergne, Peter, and Jane Lister. 2013. *Eco-Business: A Big-Brand Takeover of Sustainability*. Cambridge, MA: MIT Press.

Daviron, Benoit, and Isabelle Vagneron. 2011. "From Commoditisation to De-Commoditisation . . . and Back Again: Discussing the Role of Sustainability Standards for Agricultural Products." *Development Policy Review* 29 (1): 91–113.

DeFries, Ruth S., Jessica Fanzo, Pinki Mondal, Roseline Remans, and Stephen A. Wood. 2017. "Is Voluntary Certification of Tropical Agricultural Commodities Achieving Sustainability Goals for Small-Scale Producers? A Review of the Evidence." *Environmental Research Letters* 12 (3): 033001.

Deloitte China. 2017. "China E-Retail Market Report 2016." https://www2.deloitte.com/cn/en/pages/consumer-industrial-products/articles/cip-china-online-retail-market-report-2016.html.

Deng, Guosheng, and Scott Kennedy. 2010. "Big Business and Industry Association Lobbying in China: The Paradox of Contrasting Styles." *China Journal* 63 (January): 101–125.

Deng, Hengshan, Jikun Huang, Zhigang Xu, and Scott Rozelle. 2010. "Policy Support and Emerging Farmer Professional Cooperatives in Rural China." *China Economic Review* 21 (4): 495–507.

Department of Commerce of the Yunnan Province. 2013. "Breakthrough of Agricultural Exports in the Province." http://www.bofcom.gov.cn/bofcom/433191191798874112/20130124/345290.html.

Ding, Junzhi. 2010. "Records and Trends of the Global Tea Industry: New Thoughts on Strengthening China's Tea Industry." *Guangdong Tea Industry* 1: 2–10.

Dingwerth, Klaus, and Philipp Pattberg. 2009. "World Politics and Organizational Fields: The Case of Transnational Sustainability Governance." *European Journal of International Relations* 15 (4): 707–743.

Distelhorst, Greg, Richard M. Locke, Timea Pal, and Hiram Samel. 2015. "Production Goes Global, Compliance Stays Local: Private Regulation in the Global Electronics Industry." *Regulation and Governance* 9 (3): 224–242.

Djelic, Marie-Laure, and Kerstin Sahlin-Andersson, eds. 2006. *Transnational Governance: Institutional Dynamics of Regulation*. New York: Cambridge University Press.

Drezner, Daniel W., and Mimi Lu. 2009. "How Universal Are Club Standards? Emerging Markets and Volunteerism." In *Voluntary Programs*, edited by Matthew Potoski and Aseem Prakash, 180–206. Cambridge, MA: MIT Press.

Eberlein, Burkard, Kenneth W. Abbott, Julia Black, Errol Meidinger, and Stepan Wood. 2014. "Transnational Business Governance Interactions: Conceptualization and Framework for Analysis: Transnational Business Governance." *Regulation and Governance* 8 (1): 1–21.

Economy, Elizabeth. 2010. *The River Runs Black: The Environmental Challenge to China's Future*. 2nd ed. Ithaca, NY: Cornell University Press.

Economy, Elizabeth C. 2014. "Environmental Governance in China: State Control to Crisis Management." *Daedalus* 143 (2): 184–197.

Economy, Elizabeth C. 2018. *The Third Revolution: Xi Jinping and the New Chinese State*. New York: Oxford University Press.

Economy, Elizabeth, and Michael Levi. 2014. *By All Means Necessary: How China's Resource Quest Is Changing the World*. New York: Oxford University Press.

Elliott, Dorinda. 2017. "The Power of COFCO's Greening Supply Chain—Paulson Institute." Paulson Institute. March 7, 2017. http://www.paulsoninstitute.org/paulson-blog/2017/03/07/the-power-of-cofcos-greening-supply-chain/.

Ellis, Markman, Richard Coulton, and Matthew Mauger. 2015. *Empire of Tea: The Asian Leaf That Conquered the World*. London: Reaktion Books.

Espach, Ralph. 2005. "Private Regulation Amid Public Disarray: An Analysis of Two Private Environmental Regulatory Programs in Argentina." *Business and Politics* 7 (2): 1–36.

Espach, Ralph. 2009. *Private Environmental Regimes in Developing Countries: Globally Sown, Locally Grown*. New York: Palgrave Macmillan.

Esty, Daniel C., and Andrew S. Winston. 2006. *Green to Gold: How Smart Companies Use Environmental Strategy to Innovate, Create Value, and Build Competitive Advantage*. New Haven, CT: Yale University Press.

Etherington, Dan M., and Keith Forster. 1993. *Green Gold: The Political Economy of China's Post-1949 Tea Industry*. New York: Oxford University Press.

Etzioni, Amitai. 1975. *A Comparative Analysis of Complex Organizations: On Power, Involvement, and Their Correlates*. New York: Simon & Schuster.

Fabinyi, Michael, and Neng Liu. 2016. "The Social Context of the Chinese Food System: An Ethnographic Study of the Beijing Seafood Market." *Sustainability* 8 (3): 244.

Fabinyi, Michael, Neng Liu, Qingyu Song, and Ruyi Li. 2016. "Aquatic Product Consumption Patterns and Perceptions among the Chinese Middle Class." *Regional Studies in Marine Science* 7 (September): 1–9.

Falkner, Robert. 2003. "Private Environmental Governance and International Relations: Exploring the Links." *Global Environmental Politics* 3 (2): 72–87.

Fiorini, Matteo, Philip Schleifer, and Regina Taimasova. 2017. "Social and Environmental Standards: From Fragmentation to Coordination." Geneva: International Trade Centre.

FAO, ed. 2016. *The State of World Fisheries and Aquaculture 2016: Contributing to Food Security and Nutrition for All*. The State of World Fisheries and Aquaculture 2016. Rome: FAO.

FAO. 2018a. "FAOSTAT Crop Statistics: Crops." http://www.fao.org/faostat/en/#data/QC.

FAO. 2018b. "FAOSTAT Trade Dataset: Crops and Livestock Products." http://www.fao.org/faostat/en/#data/TP.

FAO, ed. 2018c. *The State of World Fisheries and Aquaculture 2018—Meeting the Sustainable Development Goals*. The State of World Fisheries and Aquaculture 2018. Rome: FAO.

Farrell, Henry, and Abraham Newman. 2015. "The New Politics of Interdependence: Cross-National Layering in Trans-Atlantic Regulatory Disputes." *Comparative Political Studies* 48 (4): 497–526.

Fedorenko, Irina, and Yixian Sun. 2016. "Microblogging-Based Civic Participation on Environment in China: A Case Study of the PM 2.5 Campaign." *VOLUNTAS: International Journal of Voluntary and Nonprofit Organizations* 27 (5): 2077–2105.

Ferchen, Matt. 2013. "Whose China Model Is It Anyway? The Contentious Search for Consensus." *Review of International Political Economy* 20 (2): 390–420.

Fesenfeld, Lukas Paul, Michael Wicki, Yixian Sun, and Thomas Bernauer. 2020. "Policy Packaging Can Make Food System Transformation Feasible." *Nature Food* 1 (3): 173–182.

Fesenfeld, Lukas P., Yixian Sun, Michael Wicki, and Thomas Bernauer. 2021. "The Role and Limits of Strategic Framing for Promoting Sustainable Consumption and Policy." *Global Environmental Change* 68 (May): 102266. https://doi.org/10.1016/j.gloenvcha.2021.102266.

Finamore, Barbara. 2018. *Will China Save the Planet?* Environmental Futures. Medford, MA: Polity Press.

Fransen, Luc. 2011. "Why Do Private Governance Organizations Not Converge? A Political-Institutional Analysis of Transnational Labor Standards Regulation." *Governance* 24 (2): 359–387.

Fransen, Luc, and Thomas Conzelmann. 2015. "Fragmented or Cohesive Transnational Private Regulation of Sustainability Standards? A Comparative Study: Fragmented or Cohesive Private Regulation." *Regulation and Governance* 9 (3): 259–275.

Friend of the Sea. 2018. "Friend of the Sea Annual Report 2017–2018." Friend of the Sea. http://www.friendofthesea.org/public/page/fos-foe_annual_report_2016_web.pdf.

Fuchs, Doris A., and Agni Kalfagianni. 2010. "The Causes and Consequences of Private Food Governance." *Business and Politics* 12 (3): 1–34. https://doi.org/10.2202/1469-3569.1319.

Fuchs, Doris A., Agni Kalfagianni, and Maarren Arentsen. 2009. "Retail Power, Private Standards, and Sustainability in the Global Food System." In *Corporate Power in Global Agrifood Governance*, edited by Jennifer Clapp and Doris A. Fuchs, 29–59. Food, Health, and the Environment. Cambridge, MA: MIT Press.

Fukuyama, Francis. 2016. "Governance: What Do We Know, and How Do We Know It?" *Annual Review of Political Science* 19 (1): 89–105.

GAA. 2014. "Commitment to Excellence: A Young Guolian Sets Sights on Future Global Aquaculture Alliance." *Global Aquaculture Alliance* (blog). https://www.aquaculturealliance.org/blog/commitment-to-excellence-a-young-guolian-sets-sights-on-future/.

GAA. 2015. "GAA Signs MoU with China Aquatic Products Processing and Marketing Alliance Global Aquaculture Alliance." *Global Aquaculture Alliance* (blog). https://www.aquaculturealliance.org/blog/gaa-signs-mou-with-china-aquatic-products-processing-and-marketing-alliance/.

Gale, Fred P., and Marcus Haward. 2011. *Global Commodity Governance: State Responses to Sustainable Forest and Fisheries Certification*. Basingstoke, UK: Palgrave Macmillan.

Gallagher, Kelly Sims. 2014. *The Globalization of Clean Energy Technology: Lessons from China*. Urban and Industrial Environments. Cambridge, MA: MIT Press.

Gallagher, Kelly Sims, and Qi Qi. 2021. "Chinese Overseas Investment Policy: Implications for Climate Change." *Global Policy*. https://doi.org/10.1111/1758-5899.12952.

Gallagher, Kevin P. 2018. "China's Global Energy Finance: Poised to Lead." *Energy Research & Social Science* 35 (January): 15–16.

Garcia-Johnson, Ronie. 2000. *Exporting Environmentalism: U.S. Multinational Chemical Corporations in Brazil and Mexico*. Global Environmental Accord. Cambridge, MA: MIT Press.

Garrett, Rachael D., Kimberly M. Carlson, Ximena Rueda, and Praveen Noojipady. 2016. "Assessing the Potential Additionality of Certification by the Round Table on Responsible Soybeans and the Roundtable on Sustainable Palm Oil." *Environmental Research Letters* 11 (4): 045003.

Gartl, Annette. 2016. "Palm Oil Expansion: Greenpeace Report Reveals Devastating Impact of IOI Environmental Violations." *Changing Times*. https://changingtimes.media/2016/06/16/greenpeace-report-reveals-devastating-impact-of-ioi-environmental-violations/.

George, Alexander L., and Andrew Bennett. 2005. *Case Studies and Theory Development in the Social Sciences*. BCSIA Studies in International Security. Cambridge, MA: MIT Press.

Gereffi, Gary. 2014. "Global Value Chains in a Post-Washington Consensus World." *Review of International Political Economy* 21 (1): 9–37.

Gereffi, Gary, Ronie Garcia-Johnson, and Erika Sasser. 2001. "The NGO-Industrial Complex." *Foreign Policy* 125 (July/August): 56–65.

Gereffi, Gary, John Humphrey, and Timothy Sturgeon. 2005. "The Governance of Global Value Chains." *Review of International Political Economy* 12 (1): 78–104.

Gibbon, Peter, Jennifer Bair, and Stefano Ponte. 2008. "Governing Global Value Chains: An Introduction." *Economy and Society* 37 (3): 315–338.

Glasbergen, Pieter. 2018. "Smallholders Do Not Eat Certificates." *Ecological Economics* 147 (May): 243–252.

Glasbergen, Pieter, and Greetje Schouten. 2015. "Transformative Capacities of Global Private Sustainability Standards: A Reflection on Scenarios in the Field of Agricultural Commodities." *Journal of Corporate Citizenship* 2015 (58): 85–101.

Godfrey, Mark. 2014. "China's 'Dragon Head' Seafood Giants Will Drive Next Generation M&A." 2014. https://www.seafoodsource.com/features/china-s-dragon-head-seafood-giants-will-drive-next-generation-m-a.

Gómez Tovar, Laura, Lauren Martin, Manuel Angel Gómez Cruz, and Tad Mutersbaugh. 2005. "Certified Organic Agriculture in Mexico: Market Connections and Certification Practices in Large and Small Producers." *Journal of Rural Studies, Certifying Rural Spaces: Quality-Certified Products and Rural Governance* 21 (4): 461–474.

Grabs, Janina. 2020. *Selling Sustainability Short? The Private Governance of Labor and the Environment in the Coffee Sector*. New York: Cambridge University Press.

Graz, Jean-Christophe, and Andreas Nölke, eds. 2008. Transnational Private Governance and Its Limits. London: Routledge.

Green, Jessica F. 2014. *Rethinking Private Authority: Agents and Entrepreneurs in Global Environmental Governance*. Princeton, NJ: Princeton University Press.

Greenpeace. 2008. "How Unilever Palm Oil Suppliers Are Burning up Borneo." http://www.forestpeoples.org/sites/fpp/files/publication/2010/08/palmoilindigenouspeoplesoutheastasiafinalmceng_0.pdf.

Greenpeace. 2012. "Tea—Investigation Report of Pesticide Residues in Tea in 2012." Greenpeace China. http://www.greenpeace.org.cn/wp-content/uploads/2012/04/tea-pesticide.pdf.

Greenpeace. 2016. "Tea—Investigation Report of Pesticide Residues in Tea in 2016." Greenpeace China. https://www.greenpeace.org.cn/wp-content/uploads/2016/09/%E4%B8%AD%E5%9B%BD%E8%8C%B6%E5%8F%B6%E5%86%9C%E6%AE%8B%E8%B0%83%E6%9F%A5%E6%8A%A5%E5%91%8A0918.pdf.

Greenpeace India. 2012. "Frying the Forest: How India's Use of Palm Oil Is Having a Devastating Impact on Indonesia's Rainforests, Tigers and the Global Climate." Bengaluru: Greenpeace India. https://wayback.archive-it.org/9650/20200401155004/http://p3-raw.greenpeace.org/india/Global/india/docs/palm_oil_report_2012.pdf.

Greenpeace India. 2014. "Trouble Brewing: Pesticide Residues in Tea Samples from India." Greenpeace India. https://www.greenpeace.org/india/Global/india/image/2014/cocktail/download/TroubleBrewing.pdf.

Griffiths, John Charles. 2011. Tea: A History of the Drink That Changed the World. Paperback ed. London: Andre Deutsch.

Guarín, Alejandro, and Peter Knorringa. 2014. "New Middle-Class Consumers in Rising Powers: Responsible Consumption and Private Standards." *Oxford Development Studies* 42 (2): 151–171.

Gulbrandsen, Lars H. 2009. "The Emergence and Effectiveness of the Marine Stewardship Council." *Marine Policy* 33 (4): 654–660.

Gulbrandsen, Lars H. 2010. *Transnational Environmental Governance: The Emergence and Effects of the Certification of Forests and Fisheries*. Cheltenham, UK: Edward Elgar.

Gulbrandsen, Lars H. 2014. "Dynamic Governance Interactions: Evolutionary Effects of State Responses to Non-State Certification Programs." *Regulation and Governance* 8 (1): 74–92.

Gulbrandsen, Lars H., and Geir Hønneland. 2014. "Fisheries Certification in Russia: The Emergence of Nonstate Authority in a Postcommunist Economy." *Ocean Development and International Law* 45 (4): 341–359.

Gupta, Bishnupriya. 2008. "The History of the International Tea Market, 1850–1945." In *EH.Net Encyclopedia*, edited by Robert Whaples. http://eh.net/encyclopedia/the-history-of-the-international-tea-market-1850-1945/.

Guttman, Dan. 2015. "The Global Vernacular of Governance and Instruments: Translating between the Operating Systems of China and the United States." *Asia Pacific Journal of Public Administration* 37 (4): 253–263. https://doi.org/10.1080/23276665.2015.1119971.

Guttman, Dan, Oran Young, Yijia Jing, Barbara Bramble, Maoliang Bu, Carmen Chen, Kathinka Furst, et al. 2018. "Environmental Governance in China: Interactions between the State and 'Nonstate Actors.'" *Journal of Environmental Management* 220 (August): 126–35. https://doi.org/10.1016/j.jenvman.2018.04.104.

Hale, Thomas. 2020. "Transnational Actors and Transnational Governance in Global Environmental Politics." *Annual Review of Political Science* 23: 1–18. https://doi.org/10.1146/annurev-polisci-050718-032644.

Hale, Thomas, Naam Angrist, Beatriz Kira, Anna Petherick, and Samuel Webster. 2020. "Variation in Government Responses to COVID-19." Version 6.0. Blavatnik School of Government Working Paper. Oxford: Blavatnik School of Government, University of Oxford.

Hale, Thomas, and David Held, eds. 2011. *Handbook of Transnational Governance: Institutions and Innovations*. Malden, MA: Polity Press.

Hale, Thomas, Chuyu Liu, and Johannes Urpelainen. 2020. "Belt and Road Decision-Making in China and Recipient Countries: How and To What Extent Does Sustainability Matter?" ISEP & BSG Report. Washington, DC, and Oxford: ISEP, BSG, and ClimateWorks Foundation.

Hale, Thomas, and Charles Roger. 2014. "Orchestration and Transnational Climate Governance." *Review of International Organizations* 9 (1): 59–82. https://doi.org/10.1007/s11558-013-9174-0.

Hale, Thomas, and Charles Roger. 2018. "Domestic Politics and Chinese Participation in Transnational Climate Governance." In *Global Governance and China: The Dragon's Learning Curve*, edited by Scott Kennedy, 250–271. Global Institutions. London: Routledge.

Hall, Rodney Bruce, and Thomas J. Biersteker, eds. 2002. *The Emergence of Private Authority in Global Governance*. Cambridge Studies in International Relations 85. New York: Cambridge University Press.

Hansen, Mette Halskov, Hongtao Li, and Rune Svarverud. 2018. "Ecological Civilization: Interpreting the Chinese Past, Projecting the Global Future." *Global Environmental Change* 53 (November): 195–203.

Hanson, Arthur, He Cui, Linlin Zou, Shelley Clarke, Geoffrey Muldoon, Jason Potts, and Huihui Zhang. 2011. "Greening China's Fish and Fish Products Market Supply Chains." Winnipeg: International Institute for Sustainable Development (IISD).

Hao, R., R. Zhao, S. Qiu, L. Wang, and H. Song. 2015. "Antibiotics Crisis in China." *Science* 348 (6239): 1100–1101.

Harkell, Louis. 2017a. "ASC Accreditation Not a Game Changer for Chinese Tilapia Companies." Undercurrent News. 2017. https://www.undercurrentnews.com/2017/06/05/asc-sustainability-accreditation-not-a-game-changer-for-chinese-tilapia-companies/.

Harkell, Louis. 2017b. "China's Seafood Giants Bank Double-Digit Sales Growth on Weak Renminbi, Increased Domestic Demand." Undercurrent News. 2017. https://www.undercurrentnews.com/2017/03/01/chinas-seafood-giants-bank-double-digit-sales-growth-on-weak-renminbi-increased-domestic-demand/.

Harkell, Louis. 2017c. "Still No EU Scallop Sales for Zoneco but Firm Sustains Return to Black." Undercurrent News. 2017. https://www.undercurrentnews.com/2017/05/02/still-no-eu-scallop-sales-for-zoneco-but-firm-sustains-return-to-black/.

Harkell, Louis. 2018. "Chinese Shrimp Importers Renege on Orders amid Supply Glut." Undercurrent News. 2018. https://www.undercurrentnews.com/2018/02/06/chinese-shrimp-importers-renege-on-orders-amid-supply-glut/.

Harrison, Kathryn. 1998. "Talking with the Donkey: Cooperative Approaches to Environmental Protection." *Journal of Industrial Ecology* 2 (3): 51–72.

Haufler, Virginia. 2001. *A Public Role for the Private Sector: Industry Self-Regulation in a Global Economy*. Washington, DC: Carnegie Endowment for International Peace.

He, Pan, Giovanni Baiocchi, Klaus Hubacek, Kuishuang Feng, and Yang Yu. 2018. "The Environmental Impacts of Rapidly Changing Diets and Their Nutritional Quality in China." *Nature Sustainability* 1 (3): 122–127.

He, Yini. 2015. "Chinese Tea Aims to Go Global on Belt and Road Initiative." Chinadaily.Com.Cn. 2015. http://www.chinadaily.com.cn/business/2015-07/31/content_21461042.htm.

Henders, Sabine, U. Martin Persson, and Thomas Kastner. 2015. "Trading Forests: Land-Use Change and Carbon Emissions Embodied in Production and Exports of

Forest-Risk Commodities." *Environmental Research Letters* 10 (12): 125012. https://doi.org/10.1088/1748-9326/10/12/125012.

Henderson, Rebecca, and Frederik Nellemann. 2012. "Sustainable Tea at Unilever." Harvard Business School Case 712-438, Boston, MA.

Henson, Spencer, and John Humphrey. 2010. "Understanding the Complexities of Private Standards in Global Agri-Food Chains as They Impact Developing Countries." *Journal of Development Studies* 46 (9): 1628–1646.

Ho, Peter. 2007. "Embedded Activism and Political Change in a Semiauthoritarian Context." *China Information* 21 (2): 187–209.

Hoare, Alison. 2015. "Tracking Illegal Logging and the Related Trade: What Progress and Where Next?" Chatham House Report. London: Royal Institute of International Affairs.

Hofman, Peter S., Jeremy Moon, and Bin Wu. 2017. "Corporate Social Responsibility under Authoritarian Capitalism: Dynamics and Prospects of State-Led and Society-Driven CSR." *Business and Society* 56 (5): 651–671.

Horner, Rory, and Khalid Nadvi. 2018. "Global Value Chains and the Rise of the Global South: Unpacking Twenty-First Century Polycentric Trade." *Global Networks* 18 (2): 207–237.

Hospes, Otto. 2014. "Marking the Success or End of Global Multi-Stakeholder Governance? The Rise of National Sustainability Standards in Indonesia and Brazil for Palm Oil and Soy." *Agriculture and Human Values* 31 (3): 425–437.

Hsueh, Roselyn. 2011. *China's Regulatory State: A New Strategy for Globalization*. Cornell Studies in Political Economy. Ithaca, NY: Cornell University Press.

Hu, Dinghuan, Thomas Reardon, Scott Rozelle, Peter Timmer, and Honglin Wang. 2004. "The Emergence of Supermarkets with Chinese Characteristics: Challenges and Opportunities for China's Agricultural Development." *Development Policy Review* 22 (5): 557–586.

Huang, Philip C. C. 2011. "China's New-Age Small Farms and Their Vertical Integration: Agribusiness or Co-Ops?" *Modern China* 37 (2): 107–134.

Huang, Yasheng. 1999. *Inflation and Investment Controls in China: The Political Economy of Central-Local Relations during the Reform Era*. Cambridge: Cambridge University Press.

Huang, Yasheng. 2008. *Capitalism with Chinese Characteristics: Entrepreneurship and the State*. Cambridge: Cambridge University Press.

IFC. 2011. "The World Bank Group Framework and IFC Strategy for Engagement in the Palm Oil Sector." Washington, DC: International Finance Corporation. https://www.ifc.org/wps/wcm/connect/159dce004ea3bd0fb359f71dc0e8434d/WBG+Framework+and+IFC+Strategy_FINAL_FOR+WEB.pdf?MOD=AJPERES.

iFISH. 2016. "China Sustainable Seafood Database: Tilapia Evaluation Report." http://www.ifishonline.org/ifishimage/pdf/1705905101-1XX-1M-NN_evaluation3y3c0x8l SOURCEPDF.pdf.

ISEAL Alliance. 2015. "Building Demand for Sustainable Commodities: How Brands and Retailers Are Engaging Domestic Markets in Brazil, China and India." London: ISEAL Alliance.

Ivarsson, Inge, and Claes Göran Alvstam. 2010. "Supplier Upgrading in the Home-Furnishing Value Chain: An Empirical Study of IKEA's Sourcing in China and South East Asia." *World Development* 38 (11): 1575–1587.

Iweala, Sarah, and Yixian Sun. 2021. "The Many Aspects of Sustainability Governance: Unpacking Consumers' Support for Tea Standards in China and the UK." Presented at the International Studies Association Annual Convention, April 8.

Jacquet, Jennifer, Daniel Pauly, David Ainley, Sidney Holt, Paul Dayton, and Jeremy Jackson. 2010. "Seafood Stewardship in Crisis." *Nature* 467 (7311): 28–29.

Jaffee, Steven, and Spencer Henson. 2004. "Standards and Agro-Food Exports from Developing Countries: Rebalancing the Debate." WPS3348. Policy Research Working Papers. Washington, DC: World Bank.

Johnson, Thomas. 2010. "Environmentalism and NIMBYism in China: Promoting a Rules-Based Approach to Public Participation." *Environmental Politics* 19 (3): 430–448.

Judge-Lord, Devin, Constance L. McDermott, and Benjamin Cashore. 2020. "Do Private Regulations Ratchet Up? How to Distinguish Types of Regulatory Stringency and Patterns of Change:" *Organization and Environment* 33 (1): 96–125.

Kalfagianni, Agni, and Doris Fuchs. 2015. "Private Agri-Food Governance and the Challenges for Sustainability." In *Handbook on the Globalization of Agriculture*, 274–290. Northampton, MA: Edward Elgar.

Kanie, Norichika, and Frank Biermann, eds. 2017. *Governing through Goals: Sustainable Development Goals as Governance Innovation*. Earth System Governance. Cambridge, MA: MIT Press.

Kaplinsky, Raphael, Anne Terheggen, and Julia Tijaja. 2011. "China as a Final Market: The Gabon Timber and Thai Cassava Value Chains." *World Development* 39 (7): 1177–1190.

Kennedy, Scott. 2005. *The Business of Lobbying in China*. Cambridge, MA: Harvard University Press.

Kennedy, Scott. 2007. "Transnational Political Alliances: An Exploration with Evidence from China." *Business and Society* 46 (2): 174–200.

Kennedy, Scott. 2010. "The Myth of the Beijing Consensus." *Journal of Contemporary China* 19 (65): 461–477.

King, Andrew A., Michael J. Lenox, and Ann Terlaak. 2005. "The Strategic Use of Decentralized Institutions: Exploring Certification with the ISO 14001 Management Standard." *Academy of Management Journal* 48 (6): 1091–1106. https://doi.org/10.5465/amj.2005.19573111.

King, Gary, Robert O. Keohane, and Sidney Verba. 1994. *Designing Social Inquiry: Scientific Inference in Qualitative Research*. Princeton, NJ: Princeton University Press.

Klooster, Dan. 2006. "Environmental Certification of Forests in Mexico: The Political Ecology of a Nongovernmental Market Intervention." *Annals of the Association of American Geographers* 96 (3): 541–565.

Knill, Christoph, and Dirk Lehmkuhl. 2002. "Private Actors and the State: Internationalization and Changing Patterns of Governance." *Governance* 15 (1): 41–63.

Koh, L. P., J. Miettinen, S. C. Liew, and J. Ghazoul. 2011. "Remotely Sensed Evidence of Tropical Peatland Conversion to Oil Palm." *Proceedings of the National Academy of Sciences* 108 (12): 5127–5132.

Koh, Lian Pin, and David S. Wilcove. 2008. "Is Oil Palm Agriculture Really Destroying Tropical Biodiversity?" *Conservation Letters* 1 (2): 60–64.

Kostka, Genia. 2016. "Command without Control: The Case of China's Environmental Target System." *Regulation and Governance* 10 (1): 58–74.

Lajus, D., D. Stogova, and E. C. H. Keskitalo. 2018. "The Implementation of Marine Stewardship Council (MSC) Certification in Russia: Achievements and Considerations." *Marine Policy* 90 (April): 105–114.

Lambin, Eric F., and Tannis Thorlakson. 2018. "Sustainability Standards: Interactions between Private Actors, Civil Society, and Governments." *Annual Review of Environment and Resources* 43 (1): 369–393. https://doi.org/10.1146/annurev-environ-102017-025931.

Langford, Natalie J. 2019. "The Governance of Social Standards in Emerging Markets: An Exploration of Actors and Interests Shaping Trustea as a Southern Multi-Stakeholder Initiative." *Geoforum* 104 (August): 81–91.

LeBaron, Geneviève. 2018. "The Global Business of Forced Labour: Report of Findings." Sheffield, UK: SPERI and Univeristy of Sheffield.

Lee, Joonkoo, Gary Gereffi, and Janet Beauvais. 2012. "Global Value Chains and Agrifood Standards: Challenges and Possibilities for Smallholders in Developing Countries." *Proceedings of the National Academy of Sciences* 109 (31): 12326–12331.

Lei, Zhang, Wenling Liu, and Peter Oosterveer. 2019. "Institutional Changes and Changing Political Consumerism in China." In *The Oxford Handbook of Political*

Consumerism, edited by Magnus Boström, Michele Micheletti, and Peter Oosterveer, 582–602. Oxford: Oxford University Press.

Lernoud, Julia, Jason Potts, Gregory Sampson, Salvador Garibay, Matthew Lynch, Vivek Voora, Helga Willer, and Joseph Wozniak. 2017. "The State of Sustainable Markets: Statistics and Emerging Trends 2017." Geneva: ITC, IISD, FiBL.

Lernoud, Julia, Jason Potts, Gregory Sampson, Bernhard Schlatter, Gabriel Huppe, Vivek Voora, Helga Willer, Joseph Wozniak, and Duc Dang. 2018. *The State of Sustainable Markets 2018—Statistics and Emerging Trends*. Geneva: ITC.

Lewis, Joanna I. 2013. *Green Innovation in China: China's Wind Power Industry and the Global Transition to a Low-Carbon Economy*. Contemporary Asia in the World. New York: Columbia University Press.

Li, Hongmei, Youxin Ma, Wenjie Liu, and Wenjun Liu. 2012. "Soil Changes Induced by Rubber and Tea Plantation Establishment: Comparison with Tropical Rain Forest Soil in Xishuangbanna, SW China." *Environmental Management* 50 (5): 837–848.

Li, Yan, Yi Lu, Xiyue Zhang, Leping Liu, Minghan Wang, and Xiaoqun Jiang. 2016. "Propensity of Green Consumption Behaviors in Representative Cities in China." *Journal of Cleaner Production* 133 (October): 1328–1336.

Li, Yan, Lei Zhang, and Min Jin. 2017. "Report on Consumer Awareness and Behaviour Change in Sustainable Consumption." China Sustainable Consumption Research Program. The 10-Year Framework of Programme on Sustainable Consumption and Production Patterns. Beijing: China Chain Store and Franchise Association.

Li, Zhou. 2017. *Reform and Development of Agriculture in China*. Research Series on the Chinese Dream and China's Development Path. Singapore: Springer.

Lieberthal, Kenneth, and David M. Lampton, eds. 1992. *Bureaucracy, Politics, and Decision Making in Post-Mao China*. Studies on China 14. Berkeley, CA: University of California Press.

Lieberthal, Kenneth, and Michel Oksenberg. 1988. *Policy Making in China: Leaders, Structures, and Processes*. Princeton, NJ: Princeton University Press.

Lijphart, Arend. 1971. "Comparative Politics and the Comparative Method." *American Political Science Review* 65 (3): 682–693.

Lin, Li-Wen. 2009. "Legal Transplants through Private Contracting: Codes of Vendor Conduct in Global Supply Chains as an Example." *American Journal of Comparative Law* 57 (3): 711–744.

Lindkvist, Knut Bjørn, Torbjørn Trondsen, and Jinghua Xie. 2008. "Restructuring the Chinese Seafood Industry, Global Challenges and Policy Implications." *Marine Policy* 32 (3): 432–441.

Lister, Jane. 2011. *Corporate Social Responsibility and the State: International Approaches to Forest Co-Regulation*. Vancouver: UBC Press.

Liu, Jianguo, and Jared Diamond. 2005. "China's Environment in a Globalizing World." *Nature* 435 (June): 1179–1186.

Liu, Jianguo, and Peter H. Raven. 2010. "China's Environmental Challenges and Implications for the World." *Critical Reviews in Environmental Science and Technology* 40 (9–10): 823–851.

Locke, Richard M. 2013. *The Promise and Limits of Private Power: Promoting Labor Standards in a Global Economy*. Cambridge Studies in Comparative Politics. New York: Cambridge University Press.

Loconto, Allison, and Cora Dankers. 2014. *Impact of International Voluntary Standards on Smallholder Market Participation in Developing Countries: A Review of the Literature*. Agribusiness and Food Industries Series 3. Rome: FAO.

Lund-Thomsen, Peter, and Adam Lindgreen. 2014. "Corporate Social Responsibility in Global Value Chains: Where Are We Now and Where Are We Going?" *Journal of Business Ethics* 123 (1): 11–22.

Mahoney, James. 2000. "Path Dependence in Historical Sociology." *Theory and Society* 29 (4): 507–548.

Malesky, Edmund J., and Layna Mosley. 2018. "Chains of Love? Global Production and the Firm-Level Diffusion of Labor Standards." *American Journal of Political Science* 62 (3): 712–728.

Malets, Olga. 2015. "When Transnational Standards Hit the Ground: Domestic Regulations, Compliance Assessment and Forest Certification in Russia." *Journal of Environmental Policy and Planning* 17 (3): 332–359.

Manning, Stephan, Frank Boons, Oliver von Hagen, and Juliane Reinecke. 2012. "National Contexts Matter: The Co-Evolution of Sustainability Standards in Global Value Chains." *Ecological Economics* 83 (November): 197–209.

March, James G., and Johan P. Olsen. 1996. "Institutional Perspectives on Political Institutions." *Governance* 9 (3): 247–264.

Marschke, Melissa, and Ann Wilkings. 2014. "Is Certification a Viable Option for Small Producer Fish Farmers in the Global South? Insights from Vietnam." *Marine Policy* 50 (December): 197–206.

Martin, Will. 2005. "State Trading and China's Agricultural Import Policies." *Canadian Journal of Agricultural Economics/Revue Canadienne d'agroeconomie* 49 (4): 441–457.

Marx, Axel, and Dieter Cuypers. 2010. "Forest Certification as a Global Environmental Governance Tool: What Is the Macro-Effectiveness of the Forest Stewardship Council?" *Regulation and Governance* 4 (4): 408–434.

Mattli, Walter, and Ngaire Woods. 2009. "In Whose Benefit? Explaining Regulatory Change in Global Politics." In *The Politics of Global Regulation*, edited by Walter Mattli and Ngaire Woods, 1–43. Princeton, NJ: Princeton University Press.

Mayer, Frederick, and Gary Gereffi. 2010. "Regulation and Economic Globalization: Prospects and Limits of Private Governance." *Business and Politics* 12 (3): 1–25.

McGuire, William. 2014. "The Effect of ISO 14001 on Environmental Regulatory Compliance in China." *Ecological Economics* 105 (September): 254–264.

Mertha, Andrew. 2009. "'Fragmented Authoritarianism 2.0': Political Pluralization in the Chinese Policy Process." *China Quarterly* 200 (December): 995.

Milder, Jeffrey, and Deanna Newsom. 2015. "2015 SAN/Rainforest Alliance Impacts Report." New York: Rainforest Alliance.

Miller, Tom. 2010. "Why Foreigners Are Beating China's Tea-Makers on Their Home Turf." FT Chinese. 2010. http://www.ftchinese.com/story/001029102.

Ministry of Agriculture. 2006. "National Five-Year Plan for Fisheries Development: 2006–2010 ('Quan guo yu ye fazhan di shi yi ge wu nian gui hua')." http://www.moa.gov.cn/gk/ghjh_1/200611/t20061117_722835.htm.

Ministry of Agriculture. 2016. "Opinions of the Ministry of Agriculture on Seizing Opportunities to Strengthen the Tea Industry." Ministry of Agriculture of the People's of Republic of China. http://www.moa.gov.cn/nybgb/2016/shierqi/201711/t20171125_5919527.htm.

Moeltner, Klaus, and G. Cornelis van Kooten. 2003. "Voluntary Environmental Action and Export Destinations: The Case of Forest Certification." *Journal of Agricultural and Resource Economics* 28 (2): 302–315.

Mohan, Rohini. 2017. "Opinion | Narendra Modi's Crackdown on Civil Society in India." *New York Times*, January 9, 2017, sec. Opinion. https://www.nytimes.com/2017/01/09/opinion/narendra-modis-crackdown-on-civil-society-in-india.html.

Mol, Arthur P. J., and Neil T. Carter. 2006. "China's Environmental Governance in Transition." *Environmental Politics* 15 (2): 149–170.

Montinola, Gabriella, Yingyi Qian, and Barry R. Weingast. 1995. "Federalism, Chinese Style: The Political Basis for Economic Success in China." *World Politics* 48 (01): 50–81.

Mosley, Layna. 2010. *Labor Rights and Multinational Production*. Cambridge Studies in Comparative Politics. New York: Cambridge University Press.

Moxham, Roy. 2009. A Brief History of Tea. London: Robinson. http://catalog.hathitrust.org/api/volumes/oclc/276226128.html.

MSC. 2016. "Chinese Retailers Support MSC Sustainable Seafood Week | Marine Stewardship Council." 2016. https://www.msc.org/media-centre/press-releases/chinese-retailers-support-msc-sustainable-seafood-week.

MSC. 2017a. "MSC and Chinese Partners Including Tmall Announce Commitment to Sustainability." London: Marine Stewardship Council." https://www.msc.org/media-centre/press-releases/msc-and-chinese-partners-including-tmall-announce-commitment-to-sustainability.

MSC. 2017b. "MSC Annual Report 2016–17." London: Marine Stewardship Council. https://www.msc.org/docs/default-source/default-document-library/about-the-msc/msc-annual-report-2016-17-english.pdf?sfvrsn=737f5fab_18.

Nadvi, Khalid. 2014. "'Rising Powers' and Labour and Environmental Standards." *Oxford Development Studies* 42 (2): 137–150.

National Development and Reform Commission. 2015. "Enhanced Actions on Climate Change: China's intended nationally determined contribution." UNFCCC intended nationally determined contributions. Beijing: National Development and Reform Commission, People's Republic of China. http://www4.unfccc.int/ndcregistry/PublishedDocuments/China%20First/China%27s%20First%20NDC%20Submission.pdf.

Nathan, Andrew J. 2018. "China: Back to the Future." ChinaFile. May 10, 2018. https://www.chinafile.com/library/nyrb-china-archive/china-back-future.

Naylor, Rosamond L., Rebecca J. Goldburg, Jurgenne H. Primavera, Nils Kautsky, Malcolm C. M. Beveridge, Jason Clay, Carl Folke, Jane Lubchenco, Harold Mooney, and Max Troell. 2000. "Effect of Aquaculture on World Fish Supplies." *Nature* 405 (6790): 1017.

Nepstad, Daniel, David McGrath, Claudia Stickler, Ane Alencar, Andrea Azevedo, Briana Swette, Tathiana Bezerra, et al. 2014. "Slowing Amazon Deforestation through Public Policy and Interventions in Beef and Soy Supply Chains." *Science* 344 (6188): 1118–1123.

Nepstad, Daniel, and João Shimada. 2018. "Winning Farmer Support to Reduce Deforestation (Commentary)." Mongabay. *Conservation News* (blog). June 24, 2018. https://news.mongabay.com/2018/06/winning-farmer-support-to-reduce-deforestation-commentary/.

Neubauer, Philipp, Olaf P. Jensen, Jeffrey A. Hutchings, and Julia K. Baum. 2013. "Resilience and Recovery of Overexploited Marine Populations." *Science* 340 (6130): 347–349.

Newell, Peter, Philipp Pattberg, and Heike Schroeder. 2012. "Multiactor Governance and the Environment." *Annual Review of Environment and Resources* 37 (1): 365–387.

Newsom, Deanna, and Jeffrey Milder. 2018. "2018 Rainforest Alliance Impacts Report: Partnership, Learning, and Change." New York: Rainforest Alliance.

Ng, Desmond. 2013. "Latest Market Development, Issues, and Challenges Faced by Malaysian Palm Oil Industry in China." Presented at the MPOC Industry Interaction 2013, Kuala Lumpur, November 15. http://www.mpoc.org.my/upload/Latest-Development-Issues-Challenges-Malaysian-Palm-Oil-in-China-Desmond.pdf.

Niu, Rose. 2015. "A Step Forward for China's Agribusiness—and the Fight against Global Climate Change." December 7, 2015. http://www.paulsoninstitute.org/paulson-blog/2015/12/07/a-step-forward-for-chinas-agribusiness-and-the-fight-against-global-climate-change/.

North, Douglass C. 1990. *Institutions, Institutional Change, and Economic Performance.* The Political Economy of Institutions and Decisions. Cambridge: Cambridge University Press.

Oi, Jean Chun. 1999. *Rural China Takes Off: Institutional Foundations of Economic Reform.* Berkeley, CA: University of California Press.

Oldekop, Johan A., Rory Horner, David Hulme, Roshan Adhikari, Bina Agarwal, Matthew Alford, Oliver Bakewell, et al. 2020. "COVID-19 and the Case for Global Development." *World Development* 134 (October): 105044. https://doi.org/10.1016/j.worlddev.2020.105044.

Orden, David, Cheng Fuzhi, Hoa Nguyen, Ulrike Grote, Marcelle Thomas, Kathleen Mullen, and Dongsheng Sun. 2007. *Agricultural Producer Support Estimates for Developing Countries: Measurement Issues and Evidence from India, Indonesia, China, and Vietnam.* IFPRI Research Report 152. Washington, DC: International Food Policy Research Institute.

O'Rourke, Dara. 2006. "Multi-Stakeholder Regulation: Privatizing or Socializing Global Labor Standards?" *World Development* 34 (5): 899–918.

Ostrom, Elinor. 2008. "The Challenge of Common-Pool Resources." *Environment: Science and Policy for Sustainable Development* 50 (4): 8–21.

Owuor, S. O., K. Butterbach-Bahl, A. C. Guzha, S. Jacobs, L. Merbold, M. C. Rufino, D. E. Pelster, E. Díaz-Pinés, and L. Breuer. 2018. "Conversion of Natural Forest Results in a Significant Degradation of Soil Hydraulic Properties in the Highlands of Kenya." *Soil and Tillage Research* 176 (March): 36–44.

Páez-Osuna, Federico. 2001. "The Environmental Impact of Shrimp Aquaculture: Causes, Effects, and Mitigating Alternatives." *Environmental Management* 28 (1): 131–140.

Pan, Ke, and Wen-Xiong Wang. 2012. "Trace Metal Contamination in Estuarine and Coastal Environments in China." *Science of the Total Environment* 421 (April): 3–16.

Pande, Manish. 2017. "The India Story: Impact of Private Sustainability Standards on Market Access and Sustainable Development." UNCTAD/SER.RP/2017/9. UNCTAD Research Paper. Geneva: United Nationals Conference on Trade and Development. http://unctad.org/en/PublicationsLibrary/ser-rp-2017d9_en.pdf.

Parker, Peggy. 2016. "EU Ends 19-Year Ban on Chinese Scallop Imports with Approval of Zhangzidao's Yesso Product." Undercurrent News. 2016. https://www.undercurrent

news.com/2016/03/23/eu-ends-19-year-ban-on-chinese-scallop-imports-with-approval-of-zhangzidaos-yesso-product-2/.

Pattberg, Philipp. 2005. "What Role for Private Rule-Making in Global Environmental Governance? Analysing the Forest Stewardship Council (FSC)." *International Environmental Agreements: Politics, Law and Economics* 5 (2): 175–189.

Pauly, Daniel, Dyhia Belhabib, Roland Blomeyer, William W. W. L. Cheung, Andrés M. Cisneros-Montemayor, Duncan Copeland, Sarah Harper, et al. 2014. "China's Distant-Water Fisheries in the 21st Century." *Fish and Fisheries* 15 (3): 474–488.

Pei, Liang. 2016. "The Role of China Retail Sector for the Development of Sustainable Seafood Supply Chain." Presented at the SeaWeb Seafood Summit, Malta. https://www.seafoodsummit.org/wp-content/uploads/2016/03/Securing%20a%20Sustainable%20Future%20for%20China.pdf.

Pemberton, Marianne. 2011. "Playing Fair[Trade] with Nestlé: The Evolution of an Unlikely Partnership in the Conventional Coffee Market." *Studies in Political Economy* 87 (1): 65–92. https://doi.org/10.1080/19187033.2011.11675020.

Peña, Alejandro M. 2016. *Transnational Governance and South American Politics: The Political Economy of Norms*. International Political Economy Series. Basingstoke, UK: Palgrave Macmillan.

Pérez-Ramírez, Mónica, Bruce Phillips, Daniel Lluch-Belda, and Salvador Lluch-Cota. 2012. "Perspectives for Implementing Fisheries Certification in Developing Countries." *Marine Policy* 36 (1): 297–302.

Perkins, Richard, and Eric Neumayer. 2010. "Geographic Variations in the Early Diffusion of Corporate Voluntary Standards: Comparing ISO 14001 and the Global Compact." *Environment and Planning A* 42 (2): 347–365.

Pichler, Melanie. 2013. "'People, Planet and Profit': Consumer-Oriented Hegemony and Power Relations in Palm Oil and Agrofuel Certification." *Journal of Environment and Development* 22 (4): 370–390.

Pickles, John, Stephanie Barrientos, and Peter Knorringa. 2016. "New End Markets, Supermarket Expansion and Shifting Social Standards." *Environment and Planning A: Economy and Space* 48 (7): 1284–1301.

Pirker, Johannes, Aline Mosnier, Florian Kraxner, Petr Havlík, and Michael Obersteiner. 2016. "What Are the Limits to Oil Palm Expansion?" *Global Environmental Change* 40 (September): 73–81.

Ponte, Stefano. 2014. "'Roundtabling' Sustainability: Lessons from the Biofuel Industry." Geoforum 54 (July): 261–271. Potoski, Matthew, and Aseem Prakash. 2009. "Voluntary Clubs: An Introduction." In *Voluntary Programs: A Club Theory Perspective*, edited by Matthew Potoski and Aseem Prakash, 1–14. Cambridge, MA: MIT Press.

Ponte, Stefano, and Peter Gibbon. 2005. "Quality Standards, Conventions and the Governance of Global Value Chains." *Economy and Society* 34 (1): 1–31.

Potts, Jason, Garbiel A. Huppe, Jason Dion, Vivek Voora, and Maya Forstater. 2014. "Meeting China's Global Resource Needs: Managing Sustainability Impacts to Ensure Security of Supply—Palm Oil Pilot Study." Winnipeg: International Institute for Sustainable Development (IISD).

Potts, Jason, Ann Wilkings, Matthew Lynch, and Scott McFatridge. 2016. *State of Sustainability Initiatives Review: Standards and the Blue Economy*. Winnipeg: International Institute for Sustainable Development. http://public.eblib.com/choice/publicfullrecord.aspx?p=4532673.

Poynton, Scott. 2013. "Wilmar's 'No Deforestation' Commitment Could Revolutionise the Way Food Is Grown." *The Guardian*. https://www.theguardian.com/sustainable-business/wilmar-no-deforestation-commitment-food-production.

Prakash, Aseem. 2000. *Greening the Firm: The Politics of Corporate Environmentalism*. Cambridge and New York: Cambridge University Press.

Prakash, Aseem, and Matthew Potoski. 2006a. *The Voluntary Environmentalists: Green Clubs, ISO 14001, and Voluntary Regulations*. New York: Cambridge University Press.

Prakash, Aseem, and Matthew Potoski. 2006b. "Racing to the Bottom? Trade, Environmental Governance, and ISO 14001." *American Journal of Political Science* 50 (2): 350–364.

Prakash, Aseem, and Matthew Potoski. 2007a. "Investing Up: FDI and the Cross-Country Diffusion of ISO 14001 Management Systems." *International Studies Quarterly* 51 (3): 723–744.

Prakash, Aseem, and Matthew Potoski. 2007b. "Collective Action through Voluntary Environmental Programs: A Club Theory Perspective." *Policy Studies Journal* 35 (4): 773–792.

Pristupa, Alexey O., Machiel Lamers, and Bas Amelung. 2016. "Private Informational Governance in Post-Soviet Waters: Implications of the Marine Stewardship Council Certification in the Russian Barents Sea Region." *Fisheries Research*, Special Issue: Fisheries Certification and Eco-Labeling: Benefits, Challenges and Solutions, 182 (October): 128–135.

Pye, Oliver. 2016. "Deconstrucing the Roundtable on Sustainable Palm Oil." In *The Oil Palm Complex: Smallholders, Agribusiness, and the State in Indonesia and Malaysia*, edited by R. A. Cramb and John F. McCarthy, 409–441. Singapore: NUS Press.

Qi, G. Y., S. X. Zeng, C. M. Tam, H. T. Yin, J. F. Wu, and Z. H. Dai. 2011. "Diffusion of ISO 14001 Environmental Management Systems in China: Rethinking on Stakeholders' Roles." *Journal of Cleaner Production* 19 (11): 1250–1256.

Qi, Ye, Li Ma, Huanbo Zhang, and Huimin Li. 2008. "Translating a Global Issue into Local Priority: China's Local Government Response to Climate Change." *Journal of Environment and Development* 17 (4): 379–400.

Qiaoan, Runya, and Jessica C. Teets. 2020. "Responsive Authoritarianism in China—A Review of Responsiveness in Xi and Hu Administrations." *Journal of Chinese Political Science* 25 (1): 139–153.

Rabobank. 2019. "World Seafood Trade Map 2019." Utrecht: Rabobank. https://research.rabobank.com/far/en/sectors/animal-protein/world-seafood-trade-map.html.

Rainforest Action Network. 2013. "Conflict Palm Oil: How U.S. Snack Food Brands Are Contributing to Orangutan Extinction, Climate Change and Human Rights Violations." San Francisco: Rainforest Action Network.

Raynolds, Laura T. 2000. "Re-Embedding Global Agriculture: The International Organic and Fair Trade Movements." *Agriculture and Human Values* 17 (3): 297–309.

Raynolds, Laura T. 2004. "The Globalization of Organic Agro-Food Networks." *World Development* 32 (5): 725–743.

Raynolds, Laura T. 2009. "Mainstreaming Fair Trade Coffee: From Partnership to Traceability." *World Development* 37 (6): 1083–1093.

Renckens, Stefan. 2020. *Private Governance and Public Authority: Regulating Sustainability in a Global Economy*. Cambridge: Cambridge University Press.

Reuters. 2014. "UPDATE 2-Chinese Palm Oil Imports to Remain Low Despite Resumed Bank Lending." *Reuters*, 2014. https://www.reuters.com/article/china-palm-oil-shandong-changhua/update-1-chinas-2nd-biggest-palm-oil-importer-says-banks-resume-lending-to-it-idUSL3N0QY20920140828.

Richardson, Ben. 2015. "Making a Market for Sustainability: The Commodification of Certified Palm Oil." *New Political Economy* 20 (4): 545–568.

Roger, Charles, and Peter Dauvergne. 2016. "The Rise of Transnational Governance as a Field of Study." *International Studies Review* 18 (3): 415–437.

Rose, Sarah. 2010. *For All the Tea in China: How England Stole the World's Favorite Drink and Changed History*. New York: Viking.

Roth, Aleda V., Andy A. Tsay, Madeleine E. Pullman, and John V. Gray. 2008. "Unraveling the Food Supply Chain: Strategic Insights from China and the 2007 Recalls." *Journal of Supply Chain Management* 44 (1): 22–39.

RSPO. 2013. "RSPO Addresses Key Industry Players at Major Chinese Oil Summit." RSPO—Roundtable on Sustainable Palm Oil. https://www.rspo.org/news-and-events/news/rspo-addresses-key-industry-players-at-major-chinese-oil-summit.

RSPO. 2016. "RSPO Impact Report 2016." Geneva and Kuala Lumpur: Roundtable on Sustainable Palm Oil.

RSPO. 2017a. "China Says Yes to Sustainable Palm Oil | Articles." Roundtable on Sustainable Palm Oil. https://rspo.org/news-and-events/news/china-says-yes-to-sustainable-palm-oil.

RSPO. 2017b. "Impact Update 2017." Roundtable on Sustainable Palm Oil. https://www.rspo.org/toc/RSPO-Impact-Update-Report-2017_221117.pdf.

RSPO. 2018a. "Impact Report 2018." Roundtable on Sustainable Palm Oil. https://www.rspo.org/toc/RSPO-Impact-Update-Report-2017_221117.pdf.

RSPO. 2018b. "RSPO Launches China Sustainable Palm Oil Alliance with CFNA and WWF | Articles." Roundtable on Sustainable Palm Oil. 2018. https://rspo.org/news-and-events/news/rspo-launches-china-sustainable-palm-oil-alliance-with-cfna-and-wwf.

Ru, Jiang, and Leonard Ortolano. 2009. "Development of Citizen-Organized Environmental NGOs in China." *VOLUNTAS: International Journal of Voluntary and Nonprofit Organizations* 20 (2): 141–168.

Rueda, Ximena, Rachael D. Garrett, and Eric F. Lambin. 2017. "Corporate Investments in Supply Chain Sustainability: Selecting Instruments in the Agri-Food Industry." *Journal of Cleaner Production* 142 (January): 2480–2492.

Ruggie, J. G. 2004. "Reconstituting the Global Public Domain—Issues, Actors, and Practices." *European Journal of International Relations* 10 (4): 499–531.

Ruysschaert, Denis, and Denis Salles. 2014. "Towards Global Voluntary Standards: Questioning the Effectiveness in Attaining Conservation Goals." *Ecological Economics* 107 (November): 438–446.

Sasser, Erika N., Aseem Prakash, Benjamin Cashore, and Graeme Auld. 2006. "Direct Targeting as an NGO Political Strategy: Examining Private Authority Regimes in the Forestry Sector." *Business and Politics* 8 (3): 1–32.

Sauer, Sérgio, Acácio Leite, Karla Oliveira, and Alex Shankland. 2019. "The Implications of Closing Civic Space for Sustainable Development in Brazil." mimeo, IDS and ACT Alliance. https://opendocs.ids.ac.uk/opendocs/handle/20.500.12413/14507.

Saxon, Earl, and Sarah Roquemore. 2011. "Palm Oil." In *The Root of the Problem: What's Driving Tropical Deforestation Today?*, edited by Doug Boucher, Pipa Elias, Katherine Lininger, Calen May-Tobin, Sarah Roquemore, and Earl Saxon, 51–60. Cambridge, MA: Union of Concerned Scientists. https://www.ucsusa.org/sites/default/files/legacy/assets/documents/global_warming/UCS_DriversofDeforestation_Chap6_PalmOil.pdf.

Schleifer, Philip. 2016. "Private Governance Undermined: India and the Roundtable on Sustainable Palm Oil." *Global Environmental Politics* 16 (1): 38–58.

Schleifer, Philip. 2017. "Private Regulation and Global Economic Change: The Drivers of Sustainable Agriculture in Brazil." *Governance* 30 (4): 687–703.

Schleifer, Philip, Matteo Fiorini, and Graeme Auld. 2019. "Transparency in Transnational Governance: The Determinants of Information Disclosure of Voluntary Sustainability Programs." *Regulation and Governance* 13 (4): 488–506.

Schleifer, Philip, Matteo Fiorini, and Luc Fransen. 2019. "Missing the Bigger Picture: A Population-Level Analysis of Transnational Private Governance Organizations Active in the Global South." *Ecological Economics* 164 (October): 106362.

Schleifer, Philip, and Yixian Sun. 2018. "Emerging Markets and Private Governance: The Political Economy of Sustainable Palm Oil in China and India." *Review of International Political Economy* 25 (2): 190–214.

Schneider, Mindi. 2017. "Dragon Head Enterprises and the State of Agribusiness in China." *Journal of Agrarian Change* 17 (1): 3–21.

Schouten, Greetje, and Verena Bitzer. 2015. "The Emergence of Southern Standards in Agricultural Value Chains: A New Trend in Sustainability Governance?" *Ecological Economics* 120 (Supplement C): 175–184.

Schouten, Greetje, and Pieter Glasbergen. 2011. "Creating Legitimacy in Global Private Governance: The Case of the Roundtable on Sustainable Palm Oil." *Ecological Economics* 70 (November): 1891–1899.

Schroeder, Miriam. 2011. *Local Climate Governance in China: Hybrid Actors and Market Mechanisms*. Basingstoke, UK: Palgrave Macmillan.

Schubert, Gunter, and Björn Alpermann. 2019. "Studying the Chinese Policy Process in the Era of 'Top-Level Design': The Contribution of 'Political Steering' Theory." *Journal of Chinese Political Science* 24 (2): 199–224.

Sharma, Jayeeta. 2011. *Empire's Garden: Assam and the Making of India*. Radical Perspectives. Durham, NC: Duke University Press.

Shen, Gongming, and Mikko Heino. 2014. "An Overview of Marine Fisheries Management in China." *Marine Policy* 44 (February): 265–272.

Shen, Jiwen. 2017. "Cui He: Things That CAPPMA Should Do in the Transition of Seafood Industry." *Fishery Advance Magazine*, 2017.

Sigley, Gary. 2015. "Tea and China's Rise: Tea, Nationalism and Culture in the 21st Century." *International Communication of Chinese Culture* 2 (3): 319–341.

Smith, M. D., C. A. Roheim, L. B. Crowder, B. S. Halpern, M. Turnipseed, J. L. Anderson, F. Asche, et al. 2010. "Sustainability and Global Seafood." *Science* 327 (5967): 784–786.

Solidaridad. 2017. "China's Soy Crushing Industry Impacts on the Global Sustainability Agenda." Beijing: Sustainable Soy Trade Platform.

Spires, Anthony J. 2011. "Contingent Symbiosis and Civil Society in an Authoritarian State: Understanding the Survival of China's Grassroots NGOs." *American Journal of Sociology* 117 (1): 1–45.

Stalley, Phillip. 2010. *Foreign Firms, Investment, and Environmental Regulation in the People's Republic of China*. Stanford, CA: Stanford University Press.

Starobin, Shana M. 2021. "Credibility beyond Compliance: Uncertified Smallholders in Sustainable Food Systems." *Ecological Economics* 180 (February): 106767.

Steering Committee of the State-of-Knowledge Assessment of Standards and Certification. 2012. "Towards Sustainability: The Roles and Limitations of Certification." Washington, DC: RESOLVE.

Stern, Rachel E., and Kevin J. O'Brien. 2012. "Politics at the Boundary: Mixed Signals and the Chinese State." *Modern China* 38 (2): 174–198.

Stolle, Dietlind, and Michele Micheletti. 2013. *Political Consumerism: Global Responsibility in Action*. New York: Cambridge University Press.

Stuvøy, Kirsti. 2020. "'The Foreign Within': State–Civil Society Relations in Russia." *Europe-Asia Studies* 72 (7): 1103–1024.

Sun, Yixian, and Hamish van der Ven. 2020. "Swimming in Their Own Direction: Explaining Domestic Variation in Homegrown Sustainability Governance for Aquaculture in Asia." *Ecological Economics* 167 (January): 106445.

Sunstein, Cass R. 2014. *Why Nudge?: The Politics of Libertarian Paternalism*. New Haven, CT: Yale University Press.

Tabuchi, Hiroko. 2017. "As U.S. Cedes Leadership on Climate, Others Step Up at Davos." *New York Times*, December 22, 2017, sec. Business Day. https://www.nytimes.com/2017/01/21/business/dealbook/world-economic-forum-davos-climate-energy.html.

Talbot, John M. 2002. "Tropical Commodity Chains, Forward Integration Strategies and International Inequality: Coffee, Cocoa and Tea." *Review of International Political Economy* 9 (4): 701–734.

Tan, Yeling. 2014. "Transparency without Democracy: The Unexpected Effects of China's Environmental Disclosure Policy." *Governance* 27 (1): 37–62.

Taylor, Peter Leigh. 2005. "In the Market but Not of It: Fair Trade Coffee and Forest Stewardship Council Certification as Market-Based Social Change." *World Development* 33 (1): 129–147.

Teets, Jessica C. 2014. *Civil Society under Authoritarianism: The China Model*. New York: Cambridge University Press.

Teets, Jessica C. 2017. "The Power of Policy Networks in Authoritarian Regimes: Changing Environmental Policy in China." *Governance* 31 (1): 125–141.

Teoh, Chenghai. 2011. "Spearheading Development & Promotion of Sustainable Palm Oil in China." Presented at the 9th Annual Roundtable Conference on Sustainable Palm Oil, Sabah Borneo, November 22.

Thaler, Richard H., and Cass R. Sunstein. 2009. *Nudge: Improving Decisions about Health, Wealth and Happiness*. London: Penguin Books.

The Press Association. 2017. "Sustainable Seafood: The First 20 Years—A History of the Marine Stewardship Council." http://20-years.msc.org/.

Tilman, David, Kenneth G. Cassman, Pamela A. Matson, Rosamond Naylor, and Stephen Polasky. 2002. "Agricultural Sustainability and Intensive Production Practices." *Nature* 418 (6898): 671–677.

Tlusty, Michael F., and Heather Tausig. 2015. "Reviewing GAA-BAP Shrimp Farm Data to Determine Whether Certification Lessens Environmental Impacts." *Reviews in Aquaculture* 7 (2): 107–116. https://doi.org/10.1111/raq.12056.

Toffel, Michael W., Jodi L. Short, and Melissa Ouellet. 2015. "Codes in Context: How States, Markets, and Civil Society Shape Adherence to Global Labor Standards." *Regulation and Governance* 9 (3): 205–223.

Tzankova, Zdravka. 2020. "Can Private Governance Boost Public Policy? Insights from Public–Private Governance Interactions in the Fisheries and Electricity Sectors." *Regulation and Governance*. https://doi.org/10.1111/rego.12317.

Undercurrent News. 2012. "China's 'Insatiable Demand' to Dictate Global Seafood Industry." https://www.undercurrentnews.com/2012/10/26/chinas-insatiable-demand-to-dictate-global-seafood-industry/.

Undercurrent News. 2017. "GAA Expands China Presence with CAPPMA Partnership, New Office." https://www.undercurrentnews.com/2017/01/12/gaa-expands-china-presence-with-cappma-partnership-new-office/.

Unger, Jonathan, and Anita Chan. 1995. "China, Corporatism, and the East Asian Model." *Australian Journal of Chinese Affairs* 33 (January): 29–53.

US Department of Agriculture. 2018. "Aquaculture Trade—All Years and All Countries." https://www.ers.usda.gov/webdocs/DataFiles/47759/AquacultureTradeFull.xls?v=43167.

Vandenbergh, Michael P. 2007. "The New Wal-Mart Effect: The Role of Private Contracting in Global Governance." *UCLA Law Review* 54: 913–970.

van der Ven, Hamish. 2015. "Correlates of Rigorous and Credible Transnational Governance: A Cross-Sectoral Analysis of Best Practice Compliance in Eco-Labeling." *Regulation and Governance* 9 (3): 276–293.

van der Ven, Hamish. 2019. *Beyond Greenwash? Explaining Credibility in Transnational Eco-Labeling*. New York: Oxford University Press.

van der Ven, Hamish, and Benjamin Cashore. 2018. "Forest Certification: The Challenge of Measuring Impacts." *Current Opinion in Environmental Sustainability* 32 (June): 104–111.

van der Ven, Hamish, Catherine Rothacker, and Benjamin Cashore. 2018. "Do Eco-Labels Prevent Deforestation? Lessons from Non-State Market Driven Governance in the Soy, Palm Oil, and Cocoa Sectors." *Global Environmental Change* 52 (September): 141–151.

van der Ven, Hamish, and Yixian Sun. 2021. "Varieties of Crises: Comparing the Politics of COVID-19 and Climate Change." *Global Environmental Politics* 22 (1): 13–22. https://doi.org/10.1162/glep_a_00590.

van der Wal, Sanne. 2008. "Sustainability Issues in the Tea Sector: A Comparative Analysis of Six Leading Producing Countries." Amsterdam: Centre for Research on Multinational Corporations (SOMO).

van Rooij, Benjamin, Rachel E. Stern, and Kathinka Fürst. 2016. "The Authoritarian Logic of Regulatory Pluralism: Understanding China's New Environmental Actors." *Regulation and Governance* 10 (1): 3–13.

Vedung, Evert. 1998. "Policy Instruments: Typologies and Theories." In *Carrots, Sticks and Sermons: Policy Instruments and Their Evaluation*, edited by Marie-Louise Bemelmans-Videc, Ray C. Rist, and Evert Vedung, 21–58. Piscataway, NJ: Transaction Publishers.

Veeck, Gregory. 2008. "China's Exports and Imports of Agricultural Products under the WTO." *Eurasian Geography and Economics* 49 (5): 569–585.

Vijay, Varsha, Stuart L. Pimm, Clinton N. Jenkins, and Sharon J. Smith. 2016. "The Impacts of Oil Palm on Recent Deforestation and Biodiversity Loss." Edited by Madhur Anand. *PLOS ONE* 11 (7): e0159668.

Villasante, Sebastián, David Rodríguez-González, Manel Antelo, Susana Rivero-Rodríguez, José A. de Santiago, and Gonzalo Macho. 2013. "All Fish for China?" *AMBIO* 42 (8): 923–936.

Vogel, David. 1995. *Trading Up: Consumer and Environmental Regulation in a Global Economy*. Cambridge, MA: Harvard University Press.

Vogel, David. 2008. "Private Global Business Regulation." *Annual Review of Political Science* 11 (1): 261–282.

Wade, Robert. 2004. *Governing the Market: Economic Theory and the Role of Government in East Asian Industrialization*. Paperback edition. Princeton, NJ: Princeton University Press.

Wade, Robert. 2010. "After the Crisis: Industrial Policy and the Developmental State in Low-Income Countries." *Global Policy* 1 (2): 150–161.

Walmart. 2005. "New Certification for Wal-Mart Shrimp Another Example of Environmental Leadership." November 17, 2005. https://corporate.walmart.com/_news_/news-archive/2005/11/17/new-certification-for-wal-mart-shrimp-another-example-of-environmental-leadership.

Walmart. 2006. "Wal-Mart Takes Lead on Supporting Sustainable Fisheries." February 3, 2006. https://corporate.walmart.com/_news_/news-archive/2006/02/06/wal-mart-takes-lead-on-supporting-sustainable-fisheries.

Wang, Yuhua. 2015. *Tying the Autocrat's Hands: The Rise of the Rule of Law in China*. New York: Cambridge University Press.

Wapner, Paul. 1995. "Politics beyond the State Environmental Activism and World Civic Politics." *World Politics* 47 (3): 311–340.

Wei, Guoxue, Jikun Huang, and Jun Yang. 2012. "The Impacts of Food Safety Standards on China's Tea Exports." *China Economic Review* 23 (2): 253–264.

Weller, Robert P. 2012. "Responsive Authoritarianism and Blind-Eye Governance in China." In *Socialism Vanquished, Socialism Challenged*, edited by Nina Bandelj and Dorothy J. Solinger, 83–100. Oxford: Oxford University Press.

Wheeler, David. 2001. "Racing to the Bottom? Foreign Investment and Air Pollution in Developing Countries." *Journal of Environment and Development* 10 (3): 225–245.

Wijaya, A., and P. Glasbergen. 2016. "Toward a New Scenario in Agricultural Sustainability Certification? The Response of the Indonesian National Government to Private Certification." *Journal of Environment and Development* 25 (2): 219–246.

Willer, Helga, Gregory Sampson, Vivek Voora, Duc Dang, and Julia Lernoud. 2019. *The State of Sustainable Markets 2019: Statistics and Emerging Trends*. http://www.deslibris.ca/ID/10102592.

Wilmar. 2013. "No Deforestation, No Peat, No Exploitation Policy." http://www.wilmar-international.com/sustainability/wp-content/themes/wilmar/sustainability/assets/Wilmar%20Integrated%20Policy%20-%20FINAL%20-%205%20Dec%202013.pdf.

Wong, Christine, and Valerie J. Karplus. 2017. "China's War on Air Pollution: Can Existing Governance Structures Support New Ambitions?" *China Quarterly* 231 (September): 662–684.

World Bank. 2013. "Fish to 2030: Prospects for Fisheries and Aquaculture." 83177-GLB. Washington, DC: World Bank Group.

World Bank, ed. 2017. *The Sunken Billions Revisited: Progress and Challenges in Global Marine Fisheries*. Environment and Sustainable Development. Washington, DC: World Bank Group.

Wu, Chen. 2009. "From Tea Garden to Cup: China's Tea Sustainability Report." Beijing: Social Resources Institute.

Xie, Jin, and Chunlin Li. 2017. "Lincang: Zhi wei cha xiang piao wan li." Ministry of Agriculture of the People's Republic of China. http://www.moa.gov.cn/xw/qg/201711/t20171117_5904043.htm.

Xinhua. 2016. "China Promotes Transfer of Farmland Use Right." http://english.gov.cn/policies/latest_releases/2016/10/31/content_281475479420893.htm.

Xinhua. 2017a. "A Small Leaf Driving a Big Industry: On China's Tea Industry in Transition." Xinuanet. http://www.xinhuanet.com/food/2017-05/19/c_1120999249.htm.

Xinhua. 2017b. "Establishment of China Tea Industry Alliance." http://www.xinhuanet.com/fortune/2017-05/18/c_1120995589.htm.

Xinhua, and China Daily. 2017. "Xi Backs Spread of Nation's Tea Culture." http://www.chinadaily.com.cn/china/2017-05/19/content_29408783.htm.

Xu, Pei, Yinchu Zeng, Quentin Fong, Todd Lone, and Yuanyuan Liu. 2012. "Chinese Consumers' Willingness to Pay for Green- and Eco-Labeled Seafood." *Food Control* 28 (1): 74–82.

Yang, Zhengyong, Sheng Li, Boou Chen, Huiyu Kang, and Minghong Huang. 2016. "China's Aquatic Product Processing Industry: Policy Evolution and Economic Performance." *Trends in Food Science and Technology* 58 (December): 149–154.

Yasuda, John Kojiro. 2015. "Why Food Safety Fails in China: The Politics of Scale." *China Quarterly* 223 (September): 745–769.

Yicai. 2017. "A Teabag of Black Tea with the Sales over 100 Million Euros: Why Lipton Can Run Unhindered across the Whole Country." https://www.yicai.com/news/4723376.html.

Young, Oran R. 2002. *The Institutional Dimensions of Environmental Change: Fit, Interplay, and Scale*. Global Environmental Accord. Cambridge, MA: MIT Press.

Young, Oran R. 2017. *Governing Complex Systems: Social Capital for the Anthropocene*. Earth System Governance. Cambridge, MA: MIT Press.

Young, Oran R., Dan Guttman, Ye Qi, Kris Bachus, David Belis, Hongguang Cheng, Alvin Lin, et al. 2015. "Institutionalized Governance Processes: Comparing Environmental Problem Solving in China and the United States." *Global Environmental Change* 31 (March): 163–173.

Yue, Ning, Hua Kuang, Lin Sun, Linhai Wu, and Chuanlai Xu. 2010. "An Empirical Analysis of the Impact of EU's New Food Safety Standards on China's Tea Export." *International Journal of Food Science and Technology* 45 (4): 745–750.

Zadek, Simon. 2012. "China: The Path to Responsible Business and Sustainable Growth." *The Guardian*, March 23, 2012, sec. Guardian Sustainable Business. http://www.theguardian.com/sustainable-business/blog/china-sustainability-corporate-social-responsibility.

Zeng, Fanxu, Jia Dai, and Jeffrey Javed. 2019. "Frame Alignment and Environmental Advocacy: The Influence of NGO Strategies on Policy Outcomes in China." *Environmental Politics* 28 (4): 747–770.

Zeng, Ka, and Josh Eastin. 2007. "International Economic Integration and Environmental Protection: The Case of China." *International Studies Quarterly* 51 (4): 971–995.

Zhan, Xueyong, and Shui-Yan Tang. 2013. "Political Opportunities, Resource Constraints and Policy Advocacy of Environmental NGOs in China." *Public Administration* 91 (2): 381–399.

Zhang, Lei, Arthur P. J. Mol, and Guizhen He. 2016. "Transparency and Information Disclosure in China's Environmental Governance." *Current Opinion in Environmental Sustainability* 18 (February): 17–24.

Zhao, Xiaofan, Oran R. Young, Ye Qi, and Dan Guttman. 2020. "Back to the Future: Can Chinese Doubling Down and American Muddling Through Fulfill 21st Century Needs for Environmental Governance?" *Environmental Policy and Governance* 30 (2): 59–70.

Zhao, Xiaofeng, Yuqian Zheng, Xianjin Huang, Mei-Po Kwan, and Yuntai Zhao. 2017. "The Effect of Urbanization and Farmland Transfer on the Spatial Patterns of Non-Grain Farmland in China." *Sustainability* 9 (8): 1438.

Zou, Shichun, Weihai Xu, Ruijie Zhang, Jianhui Tang, Yingjun Chen, and Gan Zhang. 2011. "Occurrence and Distribution of Antibiotics in Coastal Water of the Bohai Bay, China: Impacts of River Discharge and Aquaculture Activities." *Environmental Pollution* 159 (10): 2913–2920.

Zou, Xiaoqiang. 2013. "Consumption Status and Trends of Palm Oil in China." Presented at the MPOC Industry Interaction 2013, Kuala Lumpur, November 15. http://www.mpoc.org.my/upload/Consumption-Status-Trends-Palm-Oil-China-Dr-Zou-Xiaoqiang.pdf.

Index